# TREGELLES ON DANIEL

# THE FOUR EMPIRES OF DANIEL (Chapters II, VII, & VI

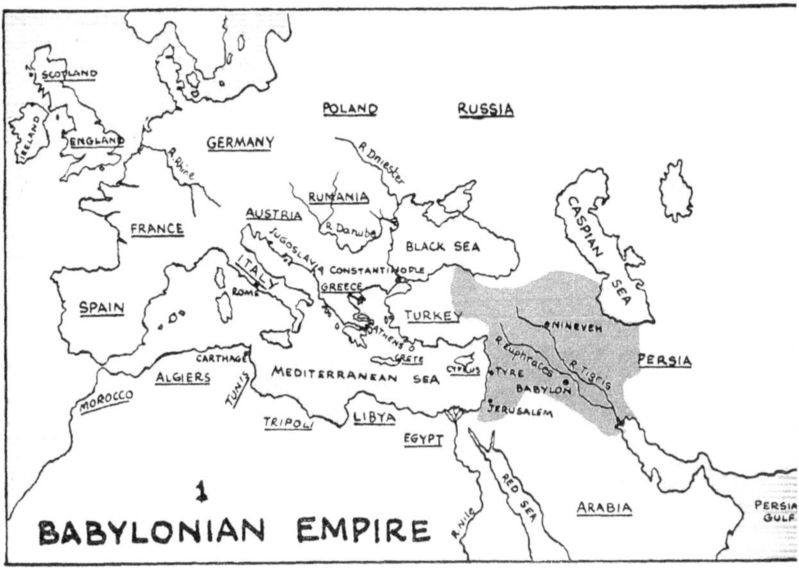

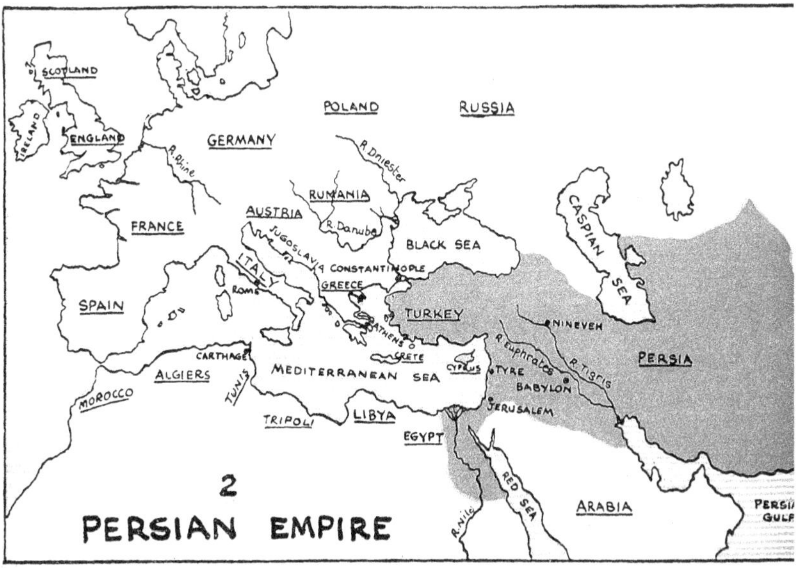

**1
BABYLONIAN EMPIRE**

**2
PERSIAN EMPIRE**

*At one period Thrace was also included in this Empire*

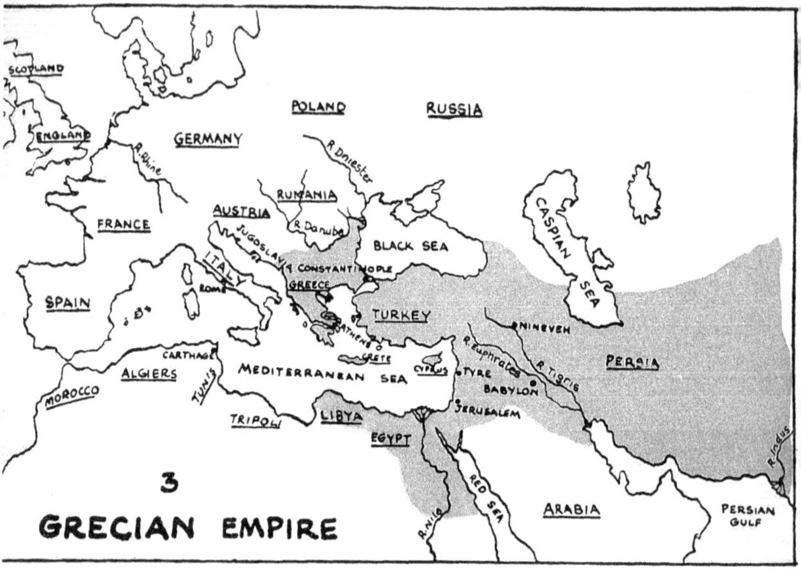

**3**
**GRECIAN EMPIRE**

**4**
**ROMAN EMPIRE**

# TREGELLES ON DANIEL

## Remarks on the Prophetic Visions in the Book of Daniel

### S. P. Tregelles, LL.D.

'Ο 'ΑΝΑΓΙΝΩΣΚΩΝ ΝΟΕΙΤΩ.—Matt. xxiv. 15.

When ye therefore shall see the abomination of desolation, spoken of by Daniel the prophet, stand in the holy place, whoso readeth, let him understand.

Eugene, Oregon

Wipf and Stock Publishers
199 W 8th Ave, Suite 3
Eugene, OR 97401

Tregelles on Daniel
Remarks on the Prophetic Visions in the Book of Daniel
By Tregelles, S. P.
ISBN 13: 978-1-55635-615-5
ISBN 10: 1-55635-615-3
Publication date 9/10/2007
Previously published by The Sovereign Grace Advent Testimony, 1852

# PREFACE

## TO THE FOURTH EDITION

The Remarks on the Prophecies in Daniel, contained in the following pages, originally appeared in separate portions, at different times, from 1845 to 1847. They were then printed and published just as I had time to prepare them from the notes with which I was furnished, which had been carefully and efficiently taken whilst I went through these portions of prophecy orally with some Christian friends. My work of preparation, from the notes which were put into my hands for the purpose, was carried on while I had but little access to books of reference, and thus I could give my "Remarks" no such complete revision as I could have wished.

When the last of the separate parts appeared, the whole was published in one volume, which has *twice* been reprinted, just as it was, to meet an existing demand, without however any revision on my part, or I believe any intentional alteration.

These three impressions having been out of print for some time, I was requested to publish a new edition, but I was unwilling that the book should be again printed without giving to the whole that careful and thorough revision which ought to be bestowed on everything relating to those truths which God has taught in His word. I have, therefore, examined every part with Scripture; and although the alterations in the statements of the "Remarks" are but few, yet here and there various additions have been made, such as appeared to me to be either needful or desirable. It has thus been during more than two years under my hand, at times, for the purpose of this revision.

To the original "Remarks", as first published, I have now *added* so much as almost to make this to be a new book. It contains all that was published before, but with more than an equal quantity in addition of what is new.

The principal material *enlargements* have been in the "Note on the Year-day System" (which has now extended to a whole chapter, in order to consider the subject *fully*), the "Note on the Interpretation of Daniel xi by past History", and the "Note on Prophetic Interpretation in Connection with Popery and the Corruption of Christianity." In this last-mentioned Note I have now endeavoured fully to show how the word of God meets Romish and non-evangelical error, and that the simple application of Scripture, as literally understood, does not in any sense palliate Popery, whether regarded in its doctrines or its practices.

It is not, I believe, needful to specify the minor enlargements and alterations throughout the "Remarks"; they have been introduced without making any change in the general principles as to the explanation of Daniel, or in their application to particular details.

The "Note on the Roman Empire and its Divisions" is entirely an addition.

In "Concluding Remarks" I have stated some particulars relative to the origin of the following pages, and also spoken of some of the dangers against which students of prophecy do well to be on their guard.

The "Map of the Ancient Persian and Roman Empires", and the "Explanatory Notice", are also amongst the additions now made.

The reader will perceive that my "Remarks" are so connected with the portions of Scripture to which they relate, that, for them to be rightly followed, the Bible should be kept open for continual reference.

I believe that these "Remarks" have already been found of use to some, in their endeavours to know what is taught us in the word of God. That they may continue to be blessed to this end is my earnest desire and prayer. Whatever leads us simply to the Scripture, which is the testimony of the Holy Ghost concerning Jesus Christ our Lord, in His sufferings and in His glory, may be known by our souls as replete with establishment in the apprehension of His truth and grace.

If readers, who pass by all *Prefaces*, find themselves on good terms with the books they read, authors perhaps have no right to complain; but as with our friends, so with our books; might not many mistakes be avoided, and after-explanations be rendered needless, if we took care not to overlook the conventional ceremony of an introduction?

S. P. T.

*Plymouth,*
*August* 18, 1852.


In issuing a fresh reprint of this volume no alteration has been made beyond mere verbal corrections and occasionally the addition of a brief note or of a few words; an Alphabetical Index has also been added. I have not judged it best to make allusions to works on the subject which have appeared since 1852: I have not, however, neglected them; though in no case have I seen it needful to change the views previously expressed; indeed, on many points they have been materially confirmed. I had two reasons for not discussing the opinions expressed in more recent works; the one is that such discussions would so add to the bulk of the volume as to change its character, which unless it were needful I did not wish: the other is that it would have been too great a demand on my time and attention, seeing that it is not right for me to do anything which would materially interfere with that work in which I have specially to seek to serve the Church of Christ; I mean the Greek Testament on Ancient Authorities, for which I have collated *every* accessible ancient Greek document, and of which the four Gospels were some time ago completed, before I was compelled by seriously impaired health to lay aside my work for a time.

It is not for those who value the word of God to shut their eyes to the condition of things in the professing Church. On the one side we find the sacrifice of Christ owned as a fact, but its application to us is made to depend on ecclesiastical ordinances and not on the operation of the Holy Ghost in leading the soul of the sinner to the blood of the Cross: on the other hand there are those who would own Christ (and in word perhaps the Holy Ghost) as acting on the soul, and thus they speak of our deliverance by a Redemption in power by a living Saviour, while redemption by price paid, a perfect propitiation wrought out once and for ever by the death of Christ, is utterly ignored and even denied. Thus on either side the truth of God is rejected; but what rejection equals that in which the Cross of Christ is not allowed its true place? that in which "sacrifice", "shedding of blood for the remission of sin", etc., are words only (if owned at all), and not substantive realities?

It has been a portent amongst us that those in office and profession holding the place of Christian teachers have even set themselves to argue against the very books of Holy Scripture which they were bound to maintain, and which are commended to us with all the authority of the incarnate Son of God.* Such attacks had been but little expected, except from those not professing to be under the banner of the Lord Jesus.

Also, in that which professes to be the true spiritual part of Christ's Church, what laxity do we find! All that I said in the conclusion of this volume as to Definite Confessions of faith has a tenfold force now. New things seem so opposed by some who make pretensions to the holding of Evangelical truth as the doctrine of Scripture (so firmly held by the Reformers) of our acceptance in the imputed righteousness of our Lord Jesus Christ. They admit anything rather than that He so

---

\* Under the guise of courtesy we often now find a willingness to concede to opposers almost every vital point: so that *professed* defenders of the authority of Holy Scripture themselves give up, and commend others for giving up the absolutely decisive teaching of the Lord Jesus Christ and of the Holy Ghost, through the Apostles, as to questions of simple fact. Thus one who has professed to vindicate the Pentateuch as to its historic character has been commended in that he "very wisely declines to avail himself of the testimony of the New Testament in his attempt to prove the historic character or Mosaic origin of the Pentateuch. The use that has been made in this controversy of the supposed testimony of Jesus Christ is for the purposes of general criticism wholly irrelevant. It involves certain theological hypotheses which would be rejected by very many who are unquestionably orthodox, and to a reverent piety it is every way offensive. Nothing can be more impolitic (to put the matter on the very lowest ground) than to make the Divine wisdom of our Lord responsible for those canons of criticism and literary opinions which are notoriously uncertain, fluctuating, and progressive", etc. If *professed* defenders can thus write, what line of demarcation remains between truth and error? If our Lord's own statements are but a "supposed testimony", on what can we rely? We have not to make our Lord's Divine wisdom responsible for any uncertain, fluctuating, and progressive canons of criticism, but we have to subject our notions on such subjects to *His* divine teaching. If we are not to believe Him when He said "Moses wrote of me", if we may doubt His wisdom and truth in saying this, then (and not till then) we may be Christians of "reverent piety", though rejecting alike the writings of Moses and the words of Jesus. It is not surprising that those who set aside the reality of our Lord's work of propitiatory sacrifice should contemn first the law in which sacrifice is so taught, and then our Lord Himself as an authoritative teacher.

kept the Law for us that His living obedience is put down to the account of every sinner who is cleansed in His blood. This is one way in which Christ's *real substitution* is set aside: He obeyed for us meritoriously in His life, even as He suffered penally for us in His death. But the reality of His incarnation (as set forth in all the old and orthodox confessions) is opposed by those who either deny the true sacrifice of the cross or who contradict the true doctrine of imputation. The Lord in His life obeyed the Law, and it is in vain to contemn such living obedience by asking if it was "mere law fulfilling": for if Jesus did ever and in all things obey the Law, loving the Lord His God with all His heart and with all His mind and soul, and strength, then was His whole life a righteous law-fulfilling, beyond which He could not go: and by God's grace, "Christ is the end of the law for righteousness to every one that believeth". But in fact those who suggest such doubts seem not to know what is meant by the holiness of God, the law of God, the one obedience by which many shall be constituted righteous; and they only confuse the unwary by some new and false notions on the whole subject of substitution and sacrifice as a sweet savour before God. But the denial of a doctrine of God does not make it the less true and precious, or its maintenance of the less importance.

S. P. T.

*Plymouth, July 9,* 1863.

# CONTENTS

| | |
|---|---:|
| PREFACE | v |
| Note Descriptive of the Maps of the Ancient Empires of Prophecy . . . . . . | xv |
| INTRODUCTION—The Budding of the Fig-tree . | 1 |
| THE IMAGE (Daniel ii) . . . . . | 6 |
| THE GREAT TREE (Daniel iv) . . . . | 24 |
| THE FOUR BEASTS (Daniel vii) . . . . | 30 |
| Note on the Roman Empire and its Divisions . | 51 |
| THE RAM AND HE GOAT (Daniel viii) . . | 75 |
| THE SEVENTY HEPTADS (Daniel ix) . . . | 92 |
| Note on the "Year-day System" . . . | 111 |
| THE PROPHECY CONCERNING THE JEWS IN THE LATTER DAYS. Daniel x, xi, xii . . . | 127 |
| Note on the Rendering and Connection of Daniel xii. 2 . . . . . . . . . | 164 |
| Note on the Interpretation of the former Part of Daniel xi by Past History . . . . | 170 |
| Note on Prophetic Interpretation in Connection with Popery and the Corruption of Christianity | 184 |
| CONCLUDING REMARKS . . . . . | 215 |
| APPENDIX—TREGELLES' LIFE . . . . | 226 |
| Index . . . . . . . . . | 231 |

NOTE DESCRIPTIVE OF THE
## MAPS OF THE ANCIENT
## EMPIRES OF PROPHECY

These maps have been introduced as showing the extent of the territory to which the prophecies of Daniel refer: these ancient empires are exhibited on the same scale, so that they may at once be easily compared.

The limits of the Babylonian monarchy, under Nebuchadnezzar, cannot be defined with certainty; besides the territory which he actually *held*, there was also, in all probability, a large extent of country under his sway and influence, although actually governed by subordinate sovereigns. The territory of the Medo-Persian kings is accurately known. It must however be borne in mind that the Persian empire comprised large districts of mountain and desert, and that the provinces, separated by such regions, often owned a very partial allegiance to a monarch ruling in Susa or Ecbatana. There were also districts which, though lying *within* the Persian monarchy, were governed by vassal kings.

For many years before the reign of the last Darius the Persian empire was materially weakened; whole provinces cast off their allegiance, and if reduced at all, it was to a very doubtful submission. Thus the conquests of Alexander gave him not only a more extensive territory than that of the Persian kings, but also a sovereignty more truly under his sway. The four kingdoms which were formed out of Alexander's empire are defined, page 79.

Of these, that of Seleucus was by far the largest, but much of its extent was not retained by his successors; the eastern provinces became independent, and in other parts, such as Cappadocia, distinct sovereignties were formed.

The Roman empire is exhibited in the map according to its widest extent (as described in pages 12–15). It will exhibit to the eye what the territory is, which, according to Daniel vii, is to be divided into ten kingdoms, out of one of which another king shall rise, who shall conquer three of the former kings, and whose actings are so minutely detailed in prophecy, as carried on against the people of Christ, until He shall have received the kingdom and shall come in the clouds of glory.

These maps were supplied by Bishop D.A. Thompson, as used in his booklet "The Visions & Prophecies of Daniel Illustrated"

# INTRODUCTION

### THE BUDDING OF THE FIG-TREE

"Now learn a parable of the fig-tree: When his branch is yet tender and putteth forth leaves, ye know that summer is nigh: so likewise ye, when ye shall see all these things, know that it is near, even at the doors" (Matt. xxiv. 32, 33).

In this instruction of our Lord to His disciples He shows them the manner in which their expectation was to be directed to coming events. He had told them of the condition of things, in connection with Jerusalem, which should immediately precede His coming in the clouds of heaven; and He then employs this illustration in order to show the real practical use which there was in the things which He had thus unfolded.

Centuries have passed since the discourse on the Mount of Olives, but still the intimations which our Lord gave have not taken place; in other words, the fig-tree has not yet budded. If we then desire to use the truths which Christ then spoke, we have still to turn our eyes to the spot which He has marked out for us, and wait to see the appointed intimations.

It may be said, What use can it have been to the Church to have had to wait for so many years? What profit is there to us in being directed to that which for eighteen hundred years has not taken place? If Christ has commanded it, that is enough—He will always vouchsafe blessing to those who are doers of His will—but further, there is profit which a spiritual mind can apprehend; for if this word had been heeded by saints, it would have kept them from many of those associations and objects which are contrary to the leadings of the Spirit: for thus they would have had before their minds the character and close of this dispensation, and the place of Christ's faithful servants in the midst of the nations, holding the gospel of the kingdom as a witness, but seeing the world's corruption as a thing which flows on unchanged in its nature (while souls are gathered one by one out of it), even up to the coming of the Lord Himself. Had this exhortation been rightly heeded, the hope of the coming of Christ would not have passed away from the minds of saints, so as to be looked at as a thing which, at all events, is not a practical doctrine.

Suppose I were cast upon some uninhabited isle, in a clime in which I could not (from my ignorance of its situation) count the seasons by months; and if the object of my hopes was the summer, and I found a fig-tree, and knew that its budding forth would intimate the approach of that season. I should watch the tree; I should often examine whether it was beginning to bud forth. I might look week after week and see nothing; I might *think* I saw some indications of sprouting, and then find it all come to nothing, but still I should watch on. Now, if I also knew that a ship came to the island at a particular time in the summer, this would be a point of hope to me, for it would hold out the prospect of deliverance; and this would make me doubly diligent in watching and waiting for the budding. Hope would connect itself with those things which indicate its accomplishment. And these things occupying my mind, I should be preserved from the thought of regarding the solitary isle as my abode. I might find long patience to be needful, but at length the buds would come forth; and then, according to the indication of the season, the wished-for vessel.

Thus is it with regard to the Church. God has given us a point of hope, and He has also instructed us with regard to indications of its accomplishment: the point of hope is that to which the soul tends, while the detail of intervening circumstances affords the needed instruction, from which is learned the practical walk of those who possess such a hope. If held in the Spirit, these things cannot take away from the power of the hope—they were revealed for the directly contrary purpose: the early Church knew them, and found them to have a practical and separating power; and in the body of detail with which the epistles (especially the later ones) are furnished, the dark statements of coming evil are given in order that the evil may be avoided, and the bright hope of the glory of the day of Christ might shine through it all and in contrast to it all. Had not the Church been so taught, the taunt, "Where is the promise of His coming?" might indeed be felt as troubling the soul; but when we know that we have been warned of deeeper darkness before the morning, we may indeed feel that the more conscious we are of deepening gloom, the more rejoicingly may we look onward to the dawn.

Nothing gives us any indication of the immediate introduction of the latter day, except this to which Christ directs us; we may see many things to make us expect that the fig-tree would soon bud, but when we see the buds (and not till then) can we speak with certainty as to what is forthwith to come to pass. We might see attempts of the nations to set the Jews in the Holy Land—this ought to make us look carefully to Jerusalem; God might hinder those efforts, or He might allow the fearful closing scenes of this dispensation to issue out of them, as at length He will do.

The importance of the *detail of prophecy* is very great to the believer: it certainly is a sad thing to see this extensive portion of God's truth overlooked and neglected. It is by the detail of prophecy that we learn how to walk in the midst of present things according to God; it is thus we learn His judgment about them, and what their issue will be. Many Christians directed their minds much to this a few years ago; but it cannot, I believe, be denied that this portion of revealed truth has more recently been neglected and overlooked. Those who have done this have surely omitted to see how important its present bearing is on the conscience and conduct: what other portion of revelation shows so clearly the separateness from all that is opposed to the Lord, to which believers are called?

There is such a thing as having held truths and then let them slip; this shows a want of Christian watchfulness. There is such a thing as having set truths before others, and when the time of their application arrives, failing in using them ourselves. Most spiritual minds feel conscious of the power of Satan being great at this time and his workings peculiarly dangerous; but if I see from the word of God that these things are to be, I shall be one of those who know these things beforehand, and this knowledge is to be used as my safeguard, that I be not carried away with the error of the wicked. The voyager who knows from his charts those parts of his course in which danger most exists should be found the most prepared to act in the emergency; it will not take him by surprise.

But it may be said that if results are rightly known nothing more is needed; but surely then we should be using our own thoughts as to all the things connected with those results. The mere knowledge of a coming deluge would never have led to the construction and arrangement of the ark. The knowledge of a result may lead to presumption of the most fearful kind. The whole testimony of the word is our safeguard.

The following Remarks on the Prophetic Visions in the Book of Daniel are intended especially to direct the mind towards some of the important portions of the detail of prophecy with which the Scripture furnishes us. Should they be found helpful to Christians who desire to learn from the prophetic word and to know for themselves what that word teaches, their object will be fully attained. To this end may the Lord vouchsafe His blessing!

# THE IMAGE (DANIEL II)

THE book of Daniel is that part of Scripture which especially treats of the power of the world during the time of its committal into the hands of the Gentiles, whilst the ancient people of God, the children of Israel, are under chastisement on account of their sin.

The first chapter opens with the statement that Nebuchadnezzar, king of Babylon, came up against Jerusalem, that he besieged the city, that "the Lord gave Jehoiakim king of Judah into his hand, with part of the vessels of the house of God, which he carried into the land of Shinar, to the house of his god; and he brought the vessels into the treasure-house of his god". This may, I believe, be regarded as such an introduction to the book as shall guide our thoughts as to its subject; the nation of Israel had departed from God, and He now delivers Judah, that portion of them with whom He had dealt in the most protracted long-suffering, into the hands of Gentiles, to whom He now commits power over His chosen city, Jerusalem. The distinctive object in the book of Daniel is to reveal, at the very period at which this committal has been made, what would be the course, character, and consummation of the power so bestowed.

We may divide this book into two portions—that part which is written in the Chaldee language, and that which is written in Hebrew. While we see that the book has one general scope—namely, Jerusalem given by God for a time into the power of the Gentiles who bear rule—we may regard this in two ways; we may either look at

Gentile power in the outline of its history, or we may look at those things relating to this power in their local connection with Jerusalem. Now, the course, character, and crises of Gentile power are taken up in this book in the Chaldee language, while those things which are limited in their application to the Jews and Jerusalem are written in Hebrew.

There are very few portions of the Scripture which are written in Chaldee; there are some parts of Ezra (chap. iv. 8 to vi. 19, and vii. 12–27) so written, which bring before us the children of Israel as being under the power of the Gentiles; there are some parts of this book; and there is one verse in Jeremiah (x. 11) which contains a message sent to the Gentiles. This verse occurs just as the gods of the nations had been mentioned in contrast with the living God.

It is important that we should so bear in mind the inspiration of Scripture as to recognise that nothing respecting it can be looked on as accidental; there must be in every circumstance a reason as to whatever God has written, and however He has written it, whether we possess sufficient spiritual intelligence or not to apprehend it. Now, in such a case as the present we may be sure that God has not made this difference of language without a very definite object. The Chaldee portion of Daniel commences at the fourth verse of the second chapter, and continues to the end of the seventh chapter: all the rest of the book is written in Hebrew. In the Chaldee portion we see power in the hands of the Gentile presented before us to its character, course, and consummation; and in the latter portion of the book we see the same power localised in connection with the Jews and Jerusalem. The Gentile power is in each part that which is prominently before us, although looked at in different aspects.

We are often instructed in Scripture by having the same set of facts presented before us in different aspects: each aspect may show but a few features of difference, but still enough will be found to evince that the variety is not without its value. As an illustration of this we may take the parables of our Lord, in the thirteenth chapter of St Matthew. He teaches there on one general subject, the effects which would result from the introduction of the gospel amongst men: He illustrates the results, both of good and of evil (from the counter working of Satan), until the day when the tares shall be separated from among the wheat—when the fishes, good and bad, shall receive their respective allotments. Instead of one narrative, or one continuous parable, He uses many, and thus we receive instruction in its individuality as to its several parts, and also in its completeness as to the whole instruction given.

This mode of Scripture teaching, by the presentation of many pictures of the same truths, in order that their bearings and connections may be clearly and rightly apprehended, is especially found in the book of Daniel; in the first chapter of which we see Judah, because of sin, delivered into the hands of their enemies and carried into exile to Babylon.

Thus it is that the prophet is placed in the land of strangers: Daniel had not personally committed the sins which led to the captivity, but as part of the Israelitish nation it was his to share their lot. He and his companions are brought into a place of particular connection with the king's court, and this was an occasion of proving if their hearts were faithful to God or not. Daniel refused the appointed portion of the king's meat, of which he, as an Israelite, could not partake without defilement, and thus in the midst of Babylon was separate unto the Lord his

God. This was nothing in which he sought to bear any ostentatious testimony; in the then circumstances of his nation, rejected by God because of their sins, it was not a time for endeavouring to set forth before the Gentiles that Israel was God's favoured and chosen people, to whom was confided the knowledge of God's truth in the earth. Each had now to stand in a great measure on his own individual responsibility before God. And thus Daniel maintains a separation which was well-pleasing to God, so that in the midst of Nebuchadnezzar's court, and whilst occupied in the service of Gentile kings, his heart was right with God and his actions were directed by a conscience duly exercised. To most he might have seemed but as a faithful servant of the Babylonian king, while the eye of God could mark him as rejecting "the portion of the king's meat", as avoiding those things in which he could not obey God, thus truly owning allegiance and service to earthly sovereigns, but always with the limitation that God's supreme authority should be upheld.

In the second chapter we read of the vision shown by God to the king of Babylon. God appears to be meeting him in the thoughts and inquiries of his own heart. Nebuchadnezzar had seen his own power rising to a great extent, and his own soul was in some measure bent on knowing what the issue of all this would be. We see this from verse 29, "Thy thoughts came into thy mind upon thy bed, what should come to pass hereafter". The extent of his power, so different from that of any who had gone before him, seems to have led his heart to meditate upon the circumstances in which he was set, and the vision declared to him the course and crisis of the power so committed. But although the vision was shown to him, yet he had to receive not only the interpretation, but even the vision itself again, through the instrumentality of the prophet.

In the vision of this chapter the moral character and acting of this power towards God are not stated (except indeed as one who knew the mind of God might gather it from the crisis), but for this we must look for further light in the subsequent visions of the book.

Here all is presented as set before the king according to *his* ability of apprehension, the external and visible things being shown as man might regard them. The vision of Nebuchadnezzar was of a great image with the head of gold, the breast and arms of silver, the belly and thighs of brass, and the legs of iron; in the interpretation all these several parts are taken up, and the symbolic meaning of each is stated. The four metals of which the image consisted represented four kingdoms which should successively bear rule in the earth.

To understand the Scriptures aright we have no occasion to go beyond the limit of the Scriptures themselves. The same passage of revealed truth which tells us of the authority of holy Scripture tells us also of its sufficiency: "All Scripture is given by inspiration of God, and is profitable for doctrine, for reproof, for correction, for instruction in righteousness; that the man of God may be perfect, throughly furnished unto all good works" (2 Tim. iii. 16, 17). Thus nothing can be *needed* by the man of God, in order that he should be "throughly furnished", beyond the inspired writings contained in the Bible. We have then no necessity to go out of the Scripture itself in order to gain information as to those things of which we read in Scripture; we may find many things which are interesting as bearing upon Scripture, but still whatever God looks on as *needful* for the establishment of the souls of His people, and for their spiritual intelligence in His truth, is to be found within the limits of His Scripture. History is not revelation; and we are nowhere commanded to search history to learn the truths found in God's word; although it may be owned most freely that God's word sheds a light upon the things which man has written as history, and that many lessons may be learned from seeing how different are the thoughts of God and of man about the same events.

We have no occasion whatever to go beyond the limits of Scripture to learn what the four kingdoms are which are thus mentioned in Daniel.

*First.* It was said expressly to Nebuchadnezzar that the head of gold symbolised his kingdom (ver. 37, 38): "Thou, O king, art a king of kings: for the God of heaven hath given thee a kingdom, power, and strength, and glory: and wheresoever the children of men dwell, the beasts of the field and the fowls of the heaven hath he given into thine hand, and hath made thee ruler over them all. Thou art this head of gold." These last words fix the first kingdom incontestably to be that of Babylon, which had grown to its greatness under Nebuchadnezzar.

Now, as to the terms in which the extent of Nebuchadnezzar's power is stated, of course we are not to understand that he actually held and exercised this rule over every part of the inhabited earth, but rather that, so far as God was concerned, all was given into his hand, so that he was not limited as to the power which he might obtain in whatever direction he might turn himself as conqueror; the only earthly bound to his empire was his own ambition. This is just what we find also in Jer. xxvii. 5, 6: "Thus saith the Lord of hosts, . . . I have made the earth, the man and the beast that are upon the ground, by my great power and by my outstretched arm, and have given it unto whom it seemed meet unto me. And now have I given all these lands into the hand of Nebuchadnezzar the king of Babylon, my servant; and the beasts of the field have I given him also to serve him." Of course Nebuchadnezzar knew nothing of all this when carrying on his conquests; he had gratified himself without being aware that he was thus the instrument in the hand of God.*

*Second.* He was told, "after thee shall rise another kingdom inferior to thee". To find out what kingdom was intended we have only to inquire what kingdom succeeded to that of Babylon; in 2 Chron. xxxvi. 20 we read of Nebuchadnezzar, "them that had escaped from the sword, carried he away to Babylon, where they were servants to him and his sons until the reign of the kingdom of Persia". And indeed in this book of Daniel itself we find a plain intimation of what the second kingdom should be which should succeed that of Babylon; in chap. v. 28 it is said, "Peres; thy kingdom is divided, and given to the Medes and Persians." Although these

* The extent of Nebuchadnezzar's dominion was, however, very great, far greater than many have supposed. In the course of his conquests he must have become the wielder of most of the powers of the earth, as it then was. We know something of the greatness which Nineveh and Egypt had possessed in previous ages: all this (as the Scripture shows) had now been rendered subordinate to Babylon. We know how the merchandise of the earth was in the hands of Tyre; this, too, we see from Scripture, had become Nebuchadnezzar's. Before this time the Phoenician colonies had extended themselves widely, and these colonies owned a connection with Tyre (and, perhaps, a sort of dependence) in the offerings sent to the altar of the Tyrian Hercules (i.e. Baal). The Phoenician colonies had extended to almost every coast of the Mediterranean, and over these the conquest of Tyre must have given Nebuchadnezzar at least a certain superiority. The early extent of the Phoenician colonies is exhibited in a map and accompanying memoir on the early diffusion of the Hebrew language through the Phoenician colonies in *The Bible of Every Land*. Besides the places mentioned in the "Memoir" as those where Phoenician inscriptions had been found, *Marseilles* must now be added: the Phoenicians appear to have formed a mercantile settlement at that port, before the colony of Phocaeans.

were two nations, yet the Medo-Persian kingdom is regarded as being one, as we also find in chap. viii. 20.

*Third.* In the vision the king had seen "his belly and his thighs of brass" (verse 32), and this is defined in the interpretation to be "another third kingdom of brass, which shall bear rule over all the earth". In chap. viii we learn (verse 21) what this kingdom was, to which dominion was given after that of the Medes and Persians —"the rough goat is the king of Grecia"; this symbolic goat had been previously spoken of as destroying the ram, which was used in that vision as the symbol of the Medo-Persian kingdom. The commencement of chap. xi. tells us the same thing.

*Fourth.* In the vision the image had been seen with "his legs of iron" (verse 33); in the interpretation we read, "the fourth kingdom shall be strong as iron, forasmuch as iron breaketh in pieces and subdueth all things, and as iron that breaketh all these, shall it break in pieces and bruise" (verse 40). We shall not find the *name* of this fourth kingdom in the Old Testament, although we see here, and in other places, its character and description. But we learn from the New Testament what this kingdom is; for we there find another bearing rule over the earth after that of Greece had passed away. Thus in Luke ii we read that there was a certain empire or kingdom which professed to bear rule over the whole inhabited earth at the time when our Lord was born, and in Luke iii we find things so fully spoken of after the Roman arrangement and order that the ministry of our Lord's forerunner is dated "in the fifteenth year of the reign of Tiberius Cæsar, Pontius Pilate being governor of Judea"; thus we see that the empire of the Cæsars had then begun, and that the governor sent by that empire exercised authority for it in the land of the Jews. The same thing is also shown by the reply of our Lord to the question which was put to Him about the tribute-money, and also by the frequent mention made of Rome and Roman power in the book of the Acts.

Thus we may see that it is wholly needless to go to any other source than that of the Revelation of God in order to discover what these four successive kingdoms are—the Babylonian, Medo-Persian, Grecian, Roman.

It must be obvious to the Christian student of Scripture how much more satisfactory it is thus to learn the details of facts from the word of God than from the records of history; the latter may be true, but the former commands our faith, and leaves us with a confidence of certainty which we never can have with regard to facts derived from other sources. It would have been indeed strange if it had been necessary for us to draw from the doubtful statements of profane historians in order to understand prophecy; and we must also remember how many would find it impossible to do this.

The metals which symbolise these kingdoms become less and less pure. A certain process of deterioration appears to be marked out as to power, while passing from one kingdom to another.*

When Nebuchadnezzar received the committal from God it was simply power from Himself, not derived from man, not dependent on the will of others, but put by God into his hand and exercised in responsibility to Him alone, as the only ruler of princes. Nebuchadnezzar might rightly bear, as far as man was concerned, the name of autocrat: his will was law. Now, we can see in part from Scripture how power deteriorated in its character in the

* It may be worthy of observation that the metals in the image lessen in their *specific gravity* as they go downwards; iron is not so heavy as brass, and thus the *weight* is so arranged as to exhibit the reverse of stability, even before we reach the mixture of clay and iron.

other kingdoms. The kingdom of Persia was said to be "inferior" to that of Nebuchadnezzar, and we see that this was the case as to the power of its kings. In chapter vi of this book we find Darius unable to deliver Daniel from the hands of the princes who sought to cast him into the lions' den; not so had Nebuchadnezzar ruled—"all people, nations, and languages trembled and feared before him; whom he would he slew, *and whom he would he kept alive*" (v. 19). In the case, too, of Ahasuerus in the book of Esther, the king and the princes act together, and the king could not undo what they had jointly decreed about queen Vashti. In Ezra vii. 14 we find authority given to that servant of God from the king and his seven counsellors. All this shows us not a king acting in the mere right of his royal prerogative, but a king in a certain sense controlled by counsellors, without whose advice and consent he could not act.

In the continual hindrances thrown in the way of the Jews after their return from Babylon, when they attempted to carry out the edicts of the Persian kings in their favour, we see manifest proof how the governors, and others in authority under the Persian kings, could oppose the execution of the pleasure of the sovereign.

We do not read much in Scripture as to the Grecian power, and therefore details as to the manner of the deterioration are not to be pressed; only the fact of such deterioration of power being intimated should be noticed.

In one respect the Scripture appears to indicate the mode of this deterioration, when it tells us of the divisions of the third kingdom, so that it continued in a fragmentary and not a united form. Babylon and Persia stood as kingdoms and fell as kingdoms; the empire of Alexander continued in broken parts, and these parts were destroyed one by one.

The fourth kingdom is said to be "as strong as iron". As a metal this is in many respects inferior to brass, although possessed of much more strength for certain purposes, and capable of far more extensive application. Strength and force are spoken of, but still apparently deterioration.

It may also be noticed that the deterioration of the fourth kingdom is especially shown in its last state.

Each of the four kingdoms appears as succeeding that which had gone before, not as annihilating it, but as incorporating it with itself—each making, as it were, the dominion of the metal which had gone before a part of itself. Just so do we read in chap. v. 28 of the manner in which the kingdom of the Medes and Persians succeeded to that of Babylon: "Thy kingdom is divided and given to the Medes and Persians"; the kingdom not being, as it were, destroyed, but transferred—that is, the cities and nations were to continue in existence, while the glory which had belonged to them passed into the hand of other powers. Babylon stands as the head of the image, and this headship existing throughout the whole gives the image its identity. The four powers succeeded one another as the actual holders of the dominion, and as they thus came into view, so is their place seen successively in the image.

Babylon may be defined as having been power in the form of absolute autocracy; Persia, power in the hands of the king, while nobility of person and descent were everything—the nobles were the king's equals in rank though not in office. In Greece there was the aristocracy not of birth but of supposed excellence as evinced by the power of the mind of man, and individual influence. In Rome, power had a still lower character, for the emperor was entirely dependent upon popular choice, the soldiers commonly bestowing the imperial dignity upon a successful general—in fact, the very name of "emperor" (Imperator) arose from any commander having been so saluted by his soldiers after a victory if they were satisfied with his conduct; if they did not so salute him, then he could not receive the public honours of a triumph.* Thus we see that in the Roman Empire power actually was derived from the people, and it may also be worthy of observation that the emperors succeeded one another rather in the way of popular military election than in that of hereditary rule.

The committal of power in all the fullness spoken of in verses 37, 38 appears to belong to Nebuchadnezzar personally, or at all events to have been confined to the kingdom of Babylon.

In verse 40 we have rather the character of the Roman power than its territorial extent; this latter subject does not appear to belong to the scope of the present vision, which we have to regard especially as speaking of these kingdoms in their succession from Babylon, and the crisis to which they tend.

The "potter's clay" (verse 41) means, I believe, simply "earthenware"—that which is hard but yet brittle; softness does not seem to be at all the thing pointed out. Now, an image which stood partly upon feet of earthenware would be very stable so long as there was nothing but direct pressure brought to bear upon these feet, while a blow falling upon them would break them to pieces, and that only the more thoroughly from the fact

---

* The senate often made a show of appointing the emperor, but their decree was, in general, simply a needful compliance on their part. So, too, in the case of Vespasian, although the *people* of Rome professed to bestow on him the imperial power (as recorded in the still existing bronze tablets), yet, in fact, they had no real power, for Vespasian already had the military rule in his own hands.

of iron being intermixed with the earthenware; this I believe to be the thought here presented to us.

We see from verse 42 that the part of the feet thus formed of iron and clay intermixed was the toes; and the interpretation which is given is, "the kingdom shall be partly strong and partly broken" (or, rather, "brittle"). In verse 43 the explanation is continued, "they shall mingle themselves with the seed of men"; thus there will be power (in its deteriorated form, iron) mixed up with that which is wholly of man, and which, when put to the proof, is found to be only weakness itself.

Thus we see this fourth empire especially brought before us at a time when in a divided condition, and when thus debased. The number of the toes of the feet appears to imply a tenfold division: this may be taken as a hint given to us here, although the more specific statement of the fact is not told us till farther on in this book. This kingdom is then divided into parts, which we shall see from other portions of the Scripture (especially chap. vii) to be exactly ten. Power in the hands of the people is seen, having no internal stability, although something is still left of the strength of the iron.

Verse 44. Here we see that when the image is fully developed, even to the toes of the feet, then destruction falls on it. In the vision it had been stated (verse 35) that all the materials of the image became, when smitten, "like the chaff of the summer threshing-floors, and the wind carried them away, that no place was found for them". This expression may give us some intimation of the moral character of these kingdoms before God, such as we do not find anywhere else in the chapter; just as we read in the first Psalm, "The ungodly . . . are like the chaff which the wind driveth away."

The expression in verse 44, "in the days of these kings",

is worthy of attention, for it brings before our minds more than had been expressly stated, either in the vision or in the interpretation; namely, that the kingdom which had last borne rule has been divided, and that the toes of the feet do actually symbolise such divided parts. "These kings" cannot mean the four successional monarchies, because in that case the plural number could not be used seeing that they do not *co-exist* as the holders of power. The fourth kingdom is divided into parts (which other Scriptures show to be exactly ten), and "in the days of these kings shall the God of heaven set up a kingdom which shall never be destroyed".

This kingdom is in its character utterly unlike the four which had preceded it; it has nothing springing from Babylonian headship, which may be transferred, and become deteriorated in the hands of men, but it stands in direct contrast to all that has been.

It is important to observe very distinctly what is the crisis of the image: "a stone was cut out without hands, which smote the image upon his feet that were of iron and clay, and brake them to pieces. Then was the iron, the clay, the brass, the silver, and the gold, broken to pieces together, and became like the chaff of the summer threshing-floors; and the wind carried them away, that no place was found for them: and the stone that smote the image became a great mountain, and filled the whole earth" (ver. 34, 35).

Now, what does the stone so falling upon the feet of the image symbolise? It has been sometimes thought that it alludes to grace, or to the spread of the gospel; but surely if the very words of the Scripture be followed, we shall see that destroying judgment on Gentile power is here spoken of, and not any gradual diffusion of the knowledge of grace. The image is standing on its feet, part of iron and part of earthenware; the stone then falls from above upon these feet, and the whole image is destroyed as it were with one crash.

Now, our Lord speaks of Himself as the "stone", and makes reference, or direct citation of, several passages in the Old Testament in which he had been so designated. Thus in Matt. xxi He says, "Did ye never read in the scriptures, The stone which the builders rejected, the same is become the head of the corner: this is the Lord's doing, and it is marvellous in our eyes? ... And whosoever shall fall on this stone shall be broken; but on whomsoever it shall fall, it will grind him to powder" (ver. 42, 44). Our Lord here cites from Psalm cxviii, and alludes to the mention made in Isaiah viii to the stone on which Israel has stumbled and been broken; and he likewise clearly refers to the destroying judgment which takes place when the stone, now exalted at the head of the corner, falls thus upon the fabric of Gentile power—"it will grind him to powder".

"The stone" must be taken as a definite appellation of our Lord. We see this from Psalm cxviii. 22, Isaiah viii. 14 and xxviii. 16, Acts iv. 11, and 1 Peter ii, 4, 6, in all of which Christ is spoken of under this name. Now, this cannot refer to Him as born into the world, because the fourth kingdom was not then in its divided condition —no toes were then in existence. This falling on the feet of the image could not, therefore, have anything to do with our Lord when He was upon earth. Equally impossible is it for this to symbolise the spread of the gospel; for, so far from Christians being put in the place of destroying those that bear earthly rule, they are taught submission to the powers that be as ordained of God, and their place is to suffer, if needs be, but not to rebel.

Thus, it is clear that the Lord Jesus is here referred

to as coming again—in the day when He shall take to Himself his great power and shall reign—when He shall be revealed "in flaming fire, taking vengeance on them that know not God, and obey not the gospel of our Lord Jesus Christ" (2 Thess. i. 8).

It might occur as a difficulty that the Roman empire does not exist as one united body; and hence it might be thought that the stone falling on the image must have been some past event: but observe, the Roman empire is presented in its divided condition. It is true that these divisions commenced about 1,400 years ago, but under the divided parts of the Roman empire we still live,* and its last condition is that in which the stone of destruction falls upon it—a condition in which as yet it has never been.

Now, we may regard "the stone" in three different ways, for we find it in Scripture so spoken of, in connection with Israel, with the Church, and with the Gentile powers. In Isaiah viii. 14, 15 we read that the Lord of Hosts would become "a stone of stumbling, and for a rock of offence to both the houses of Israel, for a gin and for a snare to the inhabitants of Jerusalem. And many among them shall stumble, and fall, and be broken and snared and taken." We see from the words of our Lord already cited from Matt. xxi, and from what Peter says, Acts iv. 11, how Judah stumbled upon Christ according to the words of the Prophecy. We see also from 1 Peter ii. 7, 8 how Israel in their dispersions did also stumble upon Christ as preached unto them—"a stone of stumbling and a rock of offence, even to them which stumble at the word, being disobedient; whereunto also they were

---

* Not only did the monarchies of Western Europe spring up, as each holding a portion of Roman sovereignty, but also in their continued administration this fact has been habitually recognised. Each has regarded itself as holding a portion of *Roman* imperium. See *Note on the Roman Empire and its Divisions*, after Remarks on the Four Beasts, chap. vii.

appointed". Thus *both the houses of Israel* have fallen upon this stone, and they are *broken*, not destroyed—cast off for a time though still "beloved for the fathers' sakes."

How different is the connection of the Church with this stone! "To whom coming as unto a living stone, disallowed indeed of men, but chosen of God and precious, ye also, as living stones, are built up a spiritual house, an holy priesthood", etc. Thus could the Apostle Peter address those who by nation belonged to Israel, who through grace had trusted in the blood of the Lamb, without blemish and without spot. And as the Church consists of "us whom he hath called, not of the Jews only but also of the Gentiles", this blessing is true of the whole family of faith—we are built upon this "stone", this tried foundation; we are thus identified with it, and not with those who have fallen upon it, nor yet with those upon whom it shall fall.

I have already spoken of the relation of this stone to Gentile power, but I would remark further, that the utter distinctness of this power from that which stands in grace is most vividly presented to us in the crisis of this power. The Church is built upon the stone; the image is destroyed by the stone falling upon it. We ought carefully to note the distinctions which God makes in His word, and no line of demarcation which He has laid down is more plain than that which exists between the world and its power on the one hand and the Church on the other. How wondrously does it show the power of Satan in confusing the mind as to things that differ, that it should have been supposed to be possible for the Church rightly to rest upon the power of this world—upon that which the Lord Jesus is going thus to judge!

Let the saints rightly value their place as identified with Christ, as resting upon Him, and then they will see aright how to act as to any connection with the world and its power. A saint who identified himself with the image would be, as it were, so far seeking to put himself in the place of that which will receive destroying judgement. It is quite true that God will keep from final condemnation every soul that He has quickened by the Spirit to believe in Christ; but it would evince a hardihood of mind which seems scarcely compatible with grace for any one deliberately to say, "God will keep me, and so I may put myself in the place where judgment will fall." It is for us to have nothing to do with that upon which the judgment of God will fall, but to realise our union with Him who will execute the judgment, and in whose coming kingdom his people will share.

The second chapter of Daniel may be looked on as the alphabet of the prophetic statements contained in the book; and it is well for the mind to be grounded in the truths contained in this portion of the book, before other parts of it are searched into. We have here the four successive empires, the last of these in a divided and deteriorated condition and then, in contrast to the whole that had preceded, a kingdom, which shall last for ever, set up by the God of heaven—the coming of the Lord Jesus in destroying judgment being the turning point which changes the whole scene; all that had failed in the hand of man then passing away, and that which is kept in the Lord's own hand being then introduced.

If we refer to the 8th Psalm, we shall see the extent of Christ's dominion spoken of in terms very similar to those which in this chapter had been used to describe the power committed to Nebuchadnezzar: we thus see how the power of the earth, entrusted to him, and which failed in his hand, is taken up by Christ, as One who really is able to hold and to exercise aright this dominion in all its wide extent.

# THE GREAT TREE (DANIEL IV)

THE vision in this chapter does not particularly connect itself with the object proposed in these "Remarks", which was to speak of those portions of Daniel which are still, in a great measure, future; it is, however, one of much interest, for here we find, in the past accomplishment of a vision, an earnest of the exact and precise fulfilment which all these visions must necessarily receive.

The *form* of this chapter is remarkable; it is a decree proceeding from Nebuchadnezzar himself, after those things had passed over him which God foretold to him in vision; when he was forced to confess "the signs and wonders that the high God hath wrought towards me. How great are his signs! and how mighty are his wonders! his kingdom is an everlasting kingdom, and his dominion is from generation to generation" (ver. 2, 3). Thus did the king, at length, acknowledge the hand and power of God. After the vision in the second chapter had been declared to him by Daniel, he looked to the prophet as though he were the *source* of the communication of divine truth to him: "then the king Nebuchadnezzar fell upon his face, and worshipped Daniel, and commanded that they should offer an oblation and sweet odours unto him" (ii. 46); he then acknowledged God as the revealer of secrets, although it is evident that his heart was in no way humbled before Him.

And thus, in the next chapter, so far from honouring the living and true God, the king set up his golden image in the plain of Dura, commanding that all should worship the idol; as if he, who was himself the receiver of power from God, could himself possess authority to decree anything as to *who* should or should not be the object of religious worship. The miraculous deliverance of those who refused to obey the king's command to commit idolatry leads to an acknowledgment, on his part, of the God whose power had thus shown itself; so that he made an edict that no one should speak against the God of Shadrach, Meshach, and Abednego, on pain of death.

But still his heart was lifted up in pride; he continued to trust in his own power; and this fourth chapter is his own remarkable declaration *how* God had dealt with him to humble his haughty spirit.

After acknowledging the power of God, he goes on to say, "I Nebuchadnezzar was at rest in mine house, and flourishing in my palace; I saw a dream which made me afraid, and the thoughts upon my bed and the visions of my head troubled me." He then describes (ver. 6, 9) how he sought in vain, from the wise men of Babylon, to learn the meaning of the vision, until Daniel came in before him. To the prophet the king thus detailed his vision: "Thus were the visions of my head in my bed: I saw, and behold, a tree in the midst of the earth, and the height thereof was great. The tree grew and was strong, and the height thereof reached unto heaven, and the sight thereof to the end of all the earth. The leaves thereof were fair, and the fruit thereof much, and in it was meat for all: the beasts of the field had shadow under it, and the fowls of the heaven dwelt in the boughs thereof, and all flesh was fed of it" (ver. 10–12). Such, then, was the tree as seen in its greatness; but the sentence of *God* followed: "I saw in the visions of my head upon my bed, and, behold, a watcher and an holy one came down from heaven. He cried aloud, and said thus, Hew down the tree, and cut off his branches, shake off his leaves, and scatter his fruit, let the beasts get away from under it, and the fowls from his branches. Nevertheless, leave the stump of his roots in the earth, even with a band of iron and brass, in the tender grass of the field: and let it be wet with the dew of heaven, and let his portion be with the beasts in the grass of the earth." The next verse shows that even the dream intimated that the tree symbolised *a person*: "Let his heart be changed from man's, and let a beast's heart be given unto him, and let seven times pass over him. This matter is by the decreee of the watchers, and the demand of the word of the holy ones; to the intent that the living may know that the Most High ruleth in the kingdom of men, and giveth it to whomsoever he will, and setteth up over it the basest of men."

Having thus narrated the dream, the king sought the interpretation from the prophet. Daniel shows us that the communication of truth from God, or a place of special service to Him, does not at all interfere with the full action of right human feelings. He saw that the vision foretold a solemn chastisement from God which should fall upon Nebuchadnezzar, and therefore he felt deeply his own position as being thus the communicator of evil tidings. "Then Daniel, whose name was Belteshazzar, was astonied one hour, and his thoughts troubled him. The king spake and said, Belteshazzar, let not the dream, or the interpretation thereof, trouble thee. Belteshazzar answered and said, My lord, the dream be to them that hate thee, and the interpretation thereof to thine enemies." He then, after describing the tree in all its greatness, adds: "It is thou, O king, that art grown and become strong: for thy greatness is grown, and reacheth unto heaven, and thy dominion to the end of the earth." He then applies the judgment on the tree to the king: "They shall drive thee from men, and thy dwelling shall be with the beasts of the field, and they shall make thee to eat grass as oxen, and they shall wet thee with the dew of heaven, and seven times shall pass over thee, till thou know that the Most High ruleth in the kingdom of men, and giveth it to whomsoever he will." But still the king was told that his kingdom should be sure unto him, after he knew that the heavens do rule. Daniel's feeling towards the king did not allow him to rest with merely delivering the prophecy of chastening; he exhorts the king as having a true and earnest desire for his welfare: "Wherefore, O king, let my counsel be acceptable unto thee, and break off thy sins by righteousness, and thine iniquities by showing mercy to the poor; if it may be a lengthening of thy tranquillity."

A year passed on: the king's heart was not humbled; he still looked on his power and might as his own, and did not confess that rule and authority are from above, and not from beneath. He was walking in the palace of the kingdom of Babylon, and his haughty utterance was, "Is not this great Babylon that I have built for the house of my kingdom, by the might of my power, and for the honour of my majesty?" According to the thoughts of man this was only natural: it was Nebuchadnezzar who had made Babylon what it was in its greatness and vastness, not merely politically, but also as to the actual, visible, edifices.* At once there came to him a voice from heaven declaring the immediate accomplishment of the prediction, which was fulfilled the same hour.

* It was reserved to our day to bring out to light an abiding record of the extent of the works of Nebuchadnezzar: the inscription in the arrow-headed character, found on the *bricks* in every part of the plain of Babylon, is "*Nebuchadnezzar, the son of Nabopolassar*". Turned to so many new uses, they still speak of the establisher of Babylon's greatness.

The appointed seven years were at length accomplished in the king's humiliation, and then (he says), "At the end of the days I Nebuchadnezzar lifted up mine eyes unto heaven, and mine understanding returned unto me; and I blessed the most High; and I praised and honoured him that liveth for ever", etc. (ver. 34). And then, according to the word of the Lord by Daniel, his kingdom was restored to him, and "excellent majesty was added to him." He whose earthly power had been so great had now learned to "praise, and extol, and honour the King of heaven, all whose works are truth, and his ways judgment: and those that walk in pride, he is able to abase".

This is an instructive lesson of the exactitude with which prophecy is accomplished: it may teach us *how* we should expect the fulfilment of what is yet future. These things took place under the head of the first of the four great monarchies, and thus they might have been regarded as a warning to those possessed of the power of the earth, that they might learn *who* gives them their power, and *who* it is that ruleth among the children of men.

How little this was heeded is shown us in the next chapter, where Belshazzar, unmindful of what he had *known* (chap. v. 22) of the actings of God, went on in a course of unhumbled blasphemy. The neglected warning made the condemnation all the greater. The kingdom of Belshazzar was numbered and finished; he was weighed in the balances and found wanting; to him there was no ulterior promise of restoration, for he had sinned wilfully after having had the lesson of God's dealing set before him.

Thus has God, from the beginning, shown us what the result is of power in the hands of the Gentile monarchs:

the Giver of authority has been continually forgotten; it has been regarded as something not received, or else it has been attributed to wrong sources.

In the sixth chapter of Daniel we find one remarkable exemplification of what man may do when possessed of authority: Darius was led by the craft of the presidents and princes to decree that no petition should be asked for thirty days of any God or man save of himself only. He seems to have thus unwittingly put himself in the place of God, and thus became an aider of the evil design formed against Daniel—a design which, by the miraculous interposition of God, issued in the destruction of those that formed it.

All the results set before us in this book show that power will never be held as from God, and for God, until Christ takes it into his own hand. God dealt with the first head of Gentile power for the instruction of those who should come after ("to the intent that the living may know that the Most High ruleth in the kingdom of men"); but the result has only been farther and yet farther estrangement from God, until this shall be fully exhibited in the last head of Gentile power.

## THE FOUR BEASTS (DANIEL VII)

THIS chapter contains a prophetic vision, and its interpretation given to the prophet, in which the objects are presented not merely according to their external aspect (as had been the case in the second chapter, in the vision seen by the king), but according to the mind of God concerning them.

In this vision we not only have again four successive kingdoms upon earth, and an everlasting kingdom set up by God on the destruction of the last of these, but we find also distinct details as to moral features, as regards God and those who belong to Him.

This vision was seen in the first year of King Belshazzar, when the power of Babylon, which had risen to its height under Nebuchadnezzar, was about to pass away, the warnings given by God to that king having been wholly disregarded by his successor.

In speaking of the origin of these four kingdoms we read (verse 2) of "the great sea" as the scene from which the four symbolic beasts arise; this is not, I believe, an expression which we should overlook, for the "great sea" is always used in every other passage of Scripture in which the phrase occurs as meaning distinctively the Mediterranean Sea. This, I believe, presents that sea before us as the centre territorially of the scene of this vision.

Four beasts arise out of this sea (verse 3), and these are (verse 17) interpreted to be "four kings which shall arise out of the earth". From the words of verse 23, "The fourth beast shall be the fourth *kingdom* upon earth", it is clear that the words "king" and "kingdom" are used, in passages of this kind, almost in an interchangeable sense—a kingdom is sometimes looked at as headed up in its sovereign, whose name is used; at other times the name of the kingdom is used in speaking of the power, designs, etc., of the sovereign. This must be borne in mind just as much in reading prophetic narrations as in the common language of life.

We may thus, interchangeably, speak of the Babylonian, Medo-Persian, Grecian, and Roman empires, or of those of Nebuchadnezzar, Cyrus, Alexander, and Augustus.

The distinct scriptural proof of what these four kingdoms thus succeeding each other must be has been given in Remarks on the Great Image, chap. ii, pp. 12.15: it is needless to repeat it here; but it may not be amiss to add that the four individuals regarded by God as the heads of these several monarchies are all of them definitely brought before us in Scripture, either in historical account or else in distinct prophecy as to their persons, or both. Of the four personal heads, Alexander alone is not a subject of Scripture *history*, as well as of prophecy.

Now while I believe it to be most important for us to remember that, for the real spiritual understanding of the word of God, and for its use as bearing on our consciences, we need no knowledge but that which the Spirit has given us in the word, yet we may often find truths intimated in the prophetic Scripture, which throw much light upon what we learn as facts from other sources. This is a very different thing from using history in a manner for which God has given us no warrant, as though the world could be illuminated by any such doubtful, defective, and glimmering light of man's kindling.

Now, in looking at "the great sea" as the territorial scene of the vision, we must also remember that the time to which the visions in Daniel belong is that of Gentile power ruling over Jerusalem and the Jews, and also that the powers are defined (verse 17) to be monarchies; we thus find that each of these beasts symbolises a monarchy bordering on the Mediterranean and having Jerusalem under its dominion. Now, in point of fact, we find that this was the case with regard to these powers; each stood as symbolised by a beast, and it superseded the one that had gone before it, when these three particulars were true of it, and not before.

Babylon had existed as a monarchy originally under Nimrod, and again afterwards in the days of Hezekiah, but it did not border on the Mediterranean, nor bear rule over Jerusalem, until the time of Nebuchadnezzar, and then both of these things took place simultaneously; its empire extended along the eastern coasts of that sea.

Persia had been a monarchy previously, but so soon as the empire of Cyrus reached the Mediterranean, the empire of Babylon passed into his hands, and Jerusalem became part of his dominions; this empire encircled more of the Mediterranean, from the Hellespont to Cyrene.

Greece, although locally situated on the Mediterranean Sea, had not been a monarchy previous to the time of Alexander; but so soon as this took place the power of Persia passed away before it, and Jerusalem became a part of the new empire. The Grecian monarchy surrounded yet more of the Mediterranean; for it added all the coasts of Greece to that part which had been held by Persia.

Rome, too, was locally a Mediterranean power, but not a monarchy. Three things took place, however, at the same time: the last of the four parts of Alexander's empire (symbolised, even in this vision, by the four heads of the third beast) passed into the hand of the Romans, Jerusalem became a mere dependency, and Rome became a monarchy under Augustus—this fourth empire surrounding all the coasts of the Mediterranean Sea.

This, as it appears to me, is what we have presented before us in the territorial allotment of the sphere of this vision.

The brief interpretation of the vision is given in verses 17, 18: "These great beasts, which are four, are four kings, which shall arise out of the earth: but the saints of the most high [places] shall take the kingdom, and possess the kingdom for ever, even for ever and ever." This gives us the general outline of the truths here taught us—the succession of the monarchies, and a kingdom which should arise in contrast to the earthly empires.

The first of these four kingdoms is here symbolised by a lion (verse 4) with eagles' wings: the prophet beheld it until the wings were plucked—until (I suppose) its ability for widespread conquest had passed away; it was made to stand on its feet as a man, and a man's heart was given unto it. These words seem to me an intimation of what had taken place with regard to Nebuchadnezzar, who was taught by the remarkable discipline of God that the Most High ruleth in the kingdom of men.

The second monarchy was symbolised by a bear: this beast made for itself "one dominion" (for so I believe we should render the expression which stands in our version "one side"). The Medes were an ancient people, and the Persians were a comparatively modern tribe; neither of these could be looked on as likely to overturn the power of Babylon; but by the expression "one dominion" there seems to be a hint of the second kingdom being a *united* power, so that the one dominion should be a combination, and thus it stands in contrast to the third and fourth monarchies which were at first united and afterwards were divided. The three ribs seen in the mouth of the bear seem to indicate the conquests which it was devouring, according to what was said to it, "Arise, devour much flesh."

The four-headed winged leopard, which symbolised the third kingdom, seems to indicate the rapidity of the conquests of that power, and the fourfold division which was its after condition.

But it is impossible to read this vision without seeing that the fourth kingdom is the principal topic brought before us, and that the other three simply appear as introductory. We see from verse 19 that this was the impression made upon Daniel's mind by that which was exhibited to him in symbol. But not only was the fourth beast the most conspicuous object, but it was while in a certain condition that the details concerning it are given, we look in fact rather at the *crisis* than the *course* of its history. The description of the beast is given in verse 7: "After this I saw in the night visions, and, behold, a fourth beast, dreadful and terrible, and strong exceedingly; and it had great iron teeth: it devoured and brake in pieces, and stamped the residue with the feet of it: and it was diverse from all the beasts that were before it"; this is the general description, and then there is added, "and it had ten horns," and then another horn is spoken of as springing up amongst the former ten. Now, it is clear that it is the actings of the beast when possessed of this horn, or rather perhaps of this horn as concentrating the power of the beast, with which in this vision we have to do.

In the statement which was made to Daniel we find a

## RISE OF THE LITTLE HORN

very distinct explanation of these things: it was said to him (verse 23), "The fourth beast shall be the fourth kingdom upon earth, which shall be diverse from all kingdoms, and shall devour the whole earth, and tread it down, and break it in pieces: and the ten horns out of this kingdom are ten kings that shall arise." Thus we see that the horns symbolise what this kingdom would become at a particular point of time, namely, when that empire, which was once united as a monarchy under the power of the Cæsars, should be divided into ten kingdoms. An intimation of this had been given in the number of the toes of the image in chap. ii, and the same thing is found both in symbol and in direct statement in the book of Revelation (see, for instance, chap. xiii. 1, and xvii. 12).

This, then, must be the state of the Roman earth at the time when another king, whose actings are here detailed, arises in the midst of the other kings.

This king is at first symbolised by "a *little* horn": this is not his designation when acting in blasphemy and persecution, for then the symbolic horn had become very great, "his look was more stout than his fellows"; but at first he rises like "a *little* horn" in the midst of the other horns, and then so increases in power as far to surpass them all.

The rise of this last horn was thus shown in the symbol: "I considered the horns, and, behold, there came up among them another little horn, before whom there were three of the first horns plucked up by the roots: and, behold, in this horn were eyes like the eyes of man, and a mouth speaking great things" (verse 8). This is explained, in verse 24, to be another king rising after the first ten, "and he shall be diverse from the first, and he shall subdue three kings": and then his persecution and blasphemy are mentioned.

As spoken of at first, we meet with nothing but his blasphemy against God, and then (verse 11) judgment from God falling upon the beast because of this blasphemy; but when Daniel is making inquiry as to what all this might mean, some further particulars are brought before us: "I beheld, and the same horn made war with the saints, and prevailed against them; until the Ancient of Days came [as had been shown in the previous vision, ver. 9], and judgment was given to the saints of the most high [places]; and the time came that the saints possessed the kingdom" (verses 21, 22). This is explained (verse 25), "And he shall speak great words against the Most High, and shall wear out the saints of the most high [places], and think to change times and laws: and they shall be given into his hand, until a time and times and the dividing of time."

Thus, we see this king using his power in a twofold form of opposition to God—in open and direct blasphemy against Him, and in the persecution of his saints. We also find that this opposition continues to the end of his reign, and that this is consummated by the direct judgment of God.

While the scene presented on earth is the beast energised by this last horn, wearing out the saints and blaspheming the name of God, we have also the veil so withdrawn as to unfold to us what at the same time takes place in heaven. In verses 9 and 10 we have this displayed to us; a court of judicature is set in heaven, where God judges, and, in consequence of His judgment, the sentence which is pronounced above, unseen by any eye save that of faith, is executed upon the earth: "I beheld till the thrones were cast down [or rather *were set*], and the Ancient of Days did sit, whose garment was white as snow, and the hair of his head like the pure wool: his throne was like the fiery flame, and his wheels as burning fire; . . . the judgment was set, and the books were opened"; and then the effect on earth of the judgment in heaven is thus spoken of: "I beheld then, because of the voice of the great words which the horn spake; I beheld, even till the beast was slain, and his body destroyed, and given to the burning flame." Verse 12 must be regarded, I think, as a kind of parenthetic statement of the manner in which the dominion of the three former beasts had passed away, not by any destroying judgments from God, but by each being superseded by its successor. But here there is the direct judgment of God upon the fourth beast, because of the matured evil of its last horn.

There is a particular and interesting portion of the heavenly scene in verses 13, 14. There we find "one like the Son of Man" coming to the Ancient of Days in the place of judicature, and there receiving investiture of a certain kingdom. This is in fact very similar to what we read in Psalm cx, where it is said, "Jehovah shall send the rod of thy strength [Messiah's strength] out of Zion: Rule thou in the midst of thine enemies." We must avoid regarding the events of these two verses, namely 13 and 14, as being actually subsequent to the destruction of the fourth beast, because of the voice of the great words which the horn spake; it is rather a part of the heavenly scene coinciding in point of time with the secret judgment which had been just before mentioned, the delivery of the kingdom into the hand of the Son of Man in heaven being in fact the immediate introduction to his coming forth to execute that vengeance in which the last horn is destroyed.

It is impossible for us not to call to mind the various passages in the New Testament which speak of the Lord Jesus coming "with clouds", even as when He ascended "a cloud received him out of their sight": to instance one of these places:—when our Lord stood before the high priest, He said, "Hereafter shall ye see the Son of man sitting on the right hand of power, and coming in the clouds of heaven" (Matt. xxvi. 64). Now, in the expression "sitting on the right hand of power" He clearly referred to Psalm cx. 1 (see also Psalm lxxx. 17), but in speaking of the clouds of heaven He as manifestly alluded to this place in Daniel: the one passage of the Old Testament brings before us the place into which He, who has thus been rejected by men, is received by God; the other brings before us the glory which shall be manifested in His coming and taking the rule into His own hands.

But there is this difference between the mention made of "the clouds of heaven" in Daniel from that in the New Testament, that here we have not the coming forth of Christ spoken of, but that which immediately precedes it; I say advisedly *immediately precedes*, because He sits at the right hand of Jehovah *until* His enemies are made His footstool, and when God has accomplished that, then this kingdom is given in actual investiture to the Son, and He comes forth to crush His so prepared footstool beneath his feet.

But though this scene, in which the clouds of heaven are mentioned, is not identical with the actual *coming forth* of Christ, yet even this passage might be taken as intimating the very close connection between the two things —for the court of judicature set in heaven is, so to speak, the intermediate point between His seat in glory, where He now is, and the manifestation of His person, when "every eye shall see him"; He has with Him the same adjuncts that He will have when He returns to this earth.

## THE HORN OF BLASPHEMY

We have then as the parties before us in the crisis of this chapter—

Upon earth: 1. The last horn of the fourth beast, persecuting the saints and blaspheming God.

2. The beast itself with ten horns (three plucked up before the last horn), so connected with the horn of blasphemy that it is involved in the judgment on that horn and is in several important senses responsible for its acts.

3. The saints worn out and warred against by the horn of blasphemy.

In heaven: 1. The Ancient of Days taking the place of judicature and condemning the fourth beast because of the words spoken by the horn.

2. The Son of Man brought before Him with adjuncts of heavenly glory, and receiving above a kingdom which He will exercise in government upon earth.

If we learn simply from Scripture, I think that there can be no question as to who or what the fourth beast symbolises—that has been considered already—but with regard to the horn of blasphemy, it is very important for us distinctly to see from the word of God whether this be a power past, present, or future. One thing is clear, that his dominion and actings in blasphemy and persecution continue up to the coming of the Lord, because it is then the saints take the kingdom and not before, and *till* they take the kingdom he wears them out.

Thus, if he be a power whose rise is past, he must also be present, and some of his actings must be future. And, further, if his wearing out of the saints has begun, it must also be now going on and must still continue until the judgment of verse 10. It might also be left to the consciences of Christians to say whether they are now at this time enduring active persecutions of this kind, or whether they are in most places permitted to dwell in external rest and tranquillity.

We cannot, then, possibly speak of this horn of blasphemy as already past; just as manifest is it that his dominion is entirely future. The considerations just stated appear to prove this point.

But, further, it is said (verse 25), "And he shall speak great words against the most High, and shall wear out the saints of the most High [places], and think to change times and laws: and they shall be given into his hand, until a time and times and the dividing of time." Here then we have a chronological statement, to which we shall do well to take heed. It is true that this is a period reckoned backward, and thus we can form no calculation of our own upon it as to times or seasons, but for the purpose for which God has revealed it, it is so stated as fully to meet the object; it is a period which runs on to the coming of the Lord Jesus, and must be reckoned backward from that time. This then gives the limit of the distinct actings of this horn in blasphemy and persecution; it commences at the beginning of the "time, times, and a half", and runs on to the coming of Christ without any intermission.

This period has been commonly taken (and I have no doubt rightly so) as signifying three years and a half. Now, we know that it must mean a period exactly defined, and not *about* such or such a time; for had it been merely an indefinite statement, the mention of "half a time" would be useless. It is impossible to be definite and indefinite at one and the same time. The word rendered "time" is that which denotes either a stated period or else a set feast, or else an idea blended, as it were, of the two, namely, the interval from one of the great set feasts to its recurrence, i.e. a year; thus then we find *a time*, i.e. one year; *times* (the smallest plural, as the statement is *definite*), two years, and half a year, i.e. three years and a half.

The word "time" is similarly used in chap. iv, where it was foretold to Nebuchadnezzar that he should be driven from men until "seven *times*" should pass over him, i.e. seven years; also in Lev. xxiii, where the feasts are mentioned, the Hebrew word which corresponds to the Chaldee word here used (and which itself is found in chap. xii. 7) is employed in the sense of denoting a set feast, or the period from one recurrence to another.

Thus then the period at which the especial blasphemy and persecutions of this horn begin is three years and a half before the coming of the Lord Jesus—a short time, during which evil will be allowed greatly to prevail, but then in consequence of its full development the judgment of God will come in.

This then is briefly his history as given in this vision. The Roman earth is found divided into ten kingdoms: another king arises who destroys three of the former kings: for three years and a half he acts in open defiance of God, and in persecution of his saints: the whole Roman earth is so connected with his deeds as to share in the judgment which comes from the hand of God upon him, and this occurs at the very time when the kingdom is given into the hand of the Son of Man, and when the saints take it with Him.

But many may object, Is not the horn here spoken of the Papacy? Does not history warrant us in charging these blasphemies and persecutions upon that power?

To this I reply, No appeal to history can be of any avail in opposition to direct testimony in the word of God. Thus, unless this power be wearing out the saints continuously up to the coming of the Lord, the chief point in supposed resemblance is lost. And even further, if any one chooses openly and fairly to appeal to history, he will find discrepancies at every point—for instance, the tenfold division of the Roman earth of which mention is here made has never yet taken place, and therefore, of course, the horn which was to arise after the others has not yet come into existence. It is quite true that many have given lists of kingdoms which arose in the fifth and sixth centuries out of the broken parts of the Roman empire, but these have all been sought merely in the west, as though the eastern half were not to be considered, when in fact the existence of the eastern empire was protracted for a thousand years after that period.* And further, whatever lists have been made out of ten kingdoms, they have all varied widely both as to the kingdoms themselves and also as to which were the three which the Papacy overcame. It has also been entirely forgotten that the Papacy existed *before* the breaking up of even the *western* empire, instead of being a horn springing up *after* the other ten.

But it has been said that this horn must be a power existing through a long period of time, and not a single king; because it is alleged that in prophetic language a day is used as a symbol of a year, and therefore a year as that of three hundred and sixty days (twelve months of thirty days each), and thus the whole time of the persecution of this horn is twelve hundred and sixty years. This question is one into which, in its full statement, I cannot enter in this place, but the reader will find it examined elsewhere more fully.† I will only here remark, that if this canon of interpretation were sound the period of Nebuchadnezzar's madness ("seven times")

---

* Till May 29, 1453, when the Turks took Constantinople and the last Constantine fell.

† See Note on the Year-day System, after Remarks on The Seventy Heptads (Daniel ix).

would be still continuing; and not only should we be left in utter uncertainty in every prophecy in which time was mentioned, but in some we should even find inextricable incongruities and contradictions. What, for instance, could we make of the three days during which our Lord was to lie in the grave? But the comparison of the "seven times" which should pass over Nebuchadnezzar is sufficient in this place: the dominion of this horn is half of that time, both are prophetic statements, and thus the allegation is utterly groundless, that we have here a period predicted of 1,260 years. The accomplished prediction of chap. iv is *authority* to us for understanding the expressions of chap. vii. Let us take it simply as being what it states—three years and a half, a short period, immediately followed by the coming of the Lord Himself.

The same considerations which show the non-applicability of this horn to the Papacy will equally evince that it cannot be any other power whatever which has as yet come into existence; we have yet to see the tenfold division of the Roman earth before it can arise.

If we look on corrupted Christianity as the worst form of evil, we should fail greatly in estimating aright those things of which the Spirit teaches us in the word. Corrupt Christianity—the introduction of other things as the ground of peace with God besides faith in the one sacrifice of Christ once offered, the admixture of idolatry with the worship of God, even as the mixed multitude did in the cities of Samaria (2 Kings xvii)—these are indeed abominations; but our eyes are directed to see "greater abominations than these". The consequence of the non-reception of the truth will be the solemn act of God in sending upon men "strong delusion", so that they will receive, own, and honour, in the place of God, that person "whose coming is after the working of Satan, with all power, and signs, and lying wonders". God will act in this manner to prepare the foes of Christ to be crushed by His feet (see Psalm xcii. 7). Corrupt Christianity may obscure every fundamental truth of God's revelation, but it would cease to be Christianity at all (whether in substance, form, or name) if the God whom we own should be denied and counselledly rejected, both in heart and also in word—and yet this will be done. He will "deny the Father and the Son".

Let then our thoughts of the evil of corrupt Christianity be what they may, let us form a just estimate of its awfulness from its contrast to that which God reveals as His truth—*here* is something which goes beyond it: it is true that it issues out of it, but still it is not to be measured by its precursors. If then we apply these solemn truths to things past or present, we lose the true purpose for which God has revealed them, and blunt (so to speak) the edge of His truth.

There is one point in the vision and interpretation which must not be overlooked: in the vision (ver. 13, 14) the Son of Man takes the kingdom; in the interpretation (verse 18) it is said, "the saints of the most high [places] take the kingdom". How simply does the light of New Testament truth explain to us that which at first sight might seem a contrast instead of a connection! This is one of the passages of the Old Testament Scripture which may be taken as an intimation of that union which was afterwards to be declared as existing between Christ and His people—the union which was brought out in His death and resurrection. That which had been said of Him in the vision is said of them in the interpretation.

In verse 27 it is said that the kingdom, etc., "*under* the whole heaven shall be given to the *people* of the saints of the most high [places]". This appears to me to be a different statement, informing us that a certain kingdom, not co-extensive with that of the Son of Man, will be given to a certain nation. Who then can this nation be? Now, it is clear from many Scriptures that Israel will, after they are set in grace, and their blindness and consequent rejection are ended, be the head of the nations, and bear rule over the earth. In chap. viii. 24 we find the expression "the mighty and the holy people", or, more literally, "people of the holy ones", or "people of the saints", this Hebrew phrase answering pretty accurately to the Chaldee used in the passage before us. Now, as in chap. viii, the Jews are clearly the nation denoted, so do I consider that they are intended here. But it may be asked, Why are they so called in this place? and why are the saints of the most high [places] thus connected with them? To give a complete answer to these inquiries in all their branches would involve the consideration of very many portions of Scripture; reference to a few passages may suffice to guide the mind aright.

In Rom. ix. 24 we read concerning the saints of God, "us whom he hath called, *not of the Jews only*, but also of the Gentiles". In Rom. xi. 24 we read of "their own olive tree" (Israel's) as being that into which Gentile believers are graffed. Now, I believe that if we would give a Scriptural definition of the Church of God, we should say that they are *Abraham's seed*: if we would define the Church as it now exists upon this earth, from the time of Christ's first coming, resurrection, and ascension, to His second coming, we should say that they are a body "blessed with all spiritual blessings in heavenly places in Christ" (Eph. i. 3), including believing Jews, during the time that the nation at large is under blindness, with whom God in sovereign and marvellous grace has associated believing Gentiles, making all one body, joint heirs, etc. Thus, although on every side we see many Gentiles professing or holding the faith of Jesus, and very few Jews, we must not forget that at Pentecost the gathered company was entirely Jewish as to nation. Hopes, thoughts, and glory were opened to them *beyond* those of their nation: they were instructed to look upwards to a risen Messiah, waiting at God's right hand till His foes should have been made His footstool (Acts ii. 33–35), they were told of blessing while their nation was in blindness (verse 40), and they heard of judgment as necessarily preceding Israel's earthly blessing, but still they were Jews; and most gradual was the opening to them of the possibility of Gentiles sharing in the new fellowship, hopes, and glory, which they learned to be their true portion. Gentiles were one by one brought into this believing body; and thus we see the meaning of the words "us whom he hath called, not of the Jews only, but also of the Gentiles". Whatever the Church on earth may seem to us now to be, it is still, as to its constituent parts, a company comprising Jews, partakers of grace, with whom God has brought in certain Gentiles, setting them on the same ground as to essential blessings, even as all the redeemed of every age are essentially one in the relations in which they are set.

In Isaiah viii. 18 Christ speaks of His brethren—God's children given into His hand to be redeemed—"Behold, I and the children whom the Lord hath given me, are for signs and wonders *in Israel*"; this can only be from their having that connection with Israel of which I have been speaking. God's faithfulness to the Church is the pledge and security of His faithfulness in His promises to Israel, but it is also more; His continuing faithful to His Church is actually the continuance of His faithfulness to Israel; it is thus that the Apostle Paul argues in Rom. xi. 1.6. God had not cast off His people, for Paul was not cast off—the believing branches yet remained in "their own olive tree"; and, as the branches graffed in with them were made one body, so His faithfulness to this one body was actually His faithfulness to Israel (exemplified yet more than had been the case in the days of Elias), and also the pledge of their future national blessing, as had been promised of old (verses 26–29).

Thus, then, may we understand how in this chapter of Daniel we find the expression "people of the saints of the most high [places]"—that nation to which the saints stand in some peculiar relation, although they themselves may, for the most part, be of other origin, according to the flesh. But it may be thought that Daniel could have no apprehension of saints who were not Jews; let this be granted, but what then? The meaning of the statements in God's revelation must not be limited by the thoughts of those to whom they were addressed; for if we were to interpret Scripture in this manner, we should be continually bounding the truth of God by the finite apprehension of man. The oneness of the body, jointness of the inheritance of those who are made partakers of grace, whether Jews or Gentiles, was a truth which God purposed in after times to reveal; but while this is fully admitted, we must avoid the dangerous error of excluding from Old Testament statements those whom we learn from the New Testament to have been included in the mind of God in the promised blessings. If we had to look at any of those things according to Daniel's apprehension of them, what, we might ask, could he have known of the Son of Man taking the kingdom in the vision, the saints taking it in the interpretation? What could he have thought of their being designated "saints of the most high [places]"?—a name which so clearly refers to the position above, which belongs to those who have a portion in Christ. Christ was not yet risen and ascended, and therefore the saints (see Eph. i.) were not risen and ascended *in* Him, and yet the Holy Ghost could beforehand make use of such terms as these.

The chapter concludes by telling us, "As for me, Daniel, my cogitations much troubled me, and my countenance changed in me: but I kept the matter in my heart." This seems to intimate that the mind of the prophet was as yet enabled but little to apprehend intelligently the things which he saw and heard. Their significance therefore must most assuredly not be limited by the thoughts which occupied Daniel's mind.

We have then "the people of the saints of the most high [places]" as one of the parties to partake in the blessing to which this chapter leads us on.

I believe that it was intended that our minds should rest very particularly upon the brief interpretation given in ver. 17, 18.

There we have in contrast "four kings which shall arise out of the earth" on the one hand, and "the saints of the most high [places]" who "shall take the kingdom", etc., on the other. The issue of earthly power is told us here: to what does it all lead?—to greater and greater opposition to God, so that the last state of the fourth beast (the period when earthly power has had before it the light of Christ's gospel, and has rejected it) is found to be of the most malignant character of evil against God and His saints; but all this ends in "the burning flame"!

On the other hand, we have saints whose portion is found to be one of deepest suffering during this very period, and God allows them to suffer; but they belong to the most high places, not to the earth from which the four beasts have arisen, and the end of the whole matter to them is, reigning with Christ—with Him whose precious blood is their title to glory, for whom they have been allowed to testify in suffering, and by whose continuous grace they have been sustained.

This chapter of Daniel teaches us some of the *characteristics* of our own dispensation—Jerusalem under Gentile power, the fourth beast bearing rule, the saints called to a place of testimony. The *characteristics* of such a period as the present must not be confounded with its *blessings* and *privileges*. We have to look at that which stands in *contrast* to other periods.

Now, is it possible to be identified with the actings of this fourth beast and yet to be one of these saints? The question might seem needless, but, practically, men have said that the two things are compatible and consistent.

Again, is it possible that it could be according to the pleasure of God that those who now bear earthly rule should also take the superintendence of His Church? In other words, can authority in the Church rightly spring from the fourth beast—the throne of the Cæsars? If this can be so, then let the wolves be the shepherds, instead of their being the adversaries into whose midst the sheep are sent forth. Also, let us remember that the horn of persecution and blasphemy will be the last holder of the power of the fourth beast: can he be the source of power in the Church? and if not, can his predecessors? Could Tiberius or Nero be this? The present state of the fourth beast lies between these two points.

How rarely do men make such confusion as this in natural thingss—then, should real Christians make them in the things of God? In matters of civil government it is our place to *obey* the powers that be, to own them as set of God, but never to forget the Supreme Lordship of Christ over us: and for the right discerning of these things it is our place to take heed to the word, doctrinal, preceptive, and prophetic, knowing that it is thus the Spirit of God instructs us.

As believing in Christ we ought to esteem it a high and wondrous blessing that we are not only cleansed in His precious blood, and made heirs of glory with Him, but that we are instructed *now* as to things around us and before us, that we may judge of them according to His mind.

May we be taught, as one part of our Christian walk and discipleship, to understand how opposite is earthly authority in its course and issue to all that to which we are called; and, especially, to see the Church so contrasted with the power of the world that the one cannot possibly be the source of office or authority in the other!

We see grievous confusion around us: the word of God teaches us that it will increase—how blessed and cheering it is to our souls to look on the coming of Christ as beyond it all, our point of hope and joyful expectation! What though the wearing out of the saints will intervene?—it is only until the judgment of the Ancient of Days, when the Son of Man takes the kingdom, and we take it with Him. "Sorrow may endure for a night, but joy cometh in the morning."

# NOTE ON THE ROMAN EMPIRE AND ITS DIVISIONS

OF the four monarchies, symbolised by metals in the image and by beasts in the vision of Daniel vii, that which is chiefly of interest to us is the *fourth*; for under it, during its changes and processes of division, do we now live. I shall therefore state the extent, etc., of that empire when it stood in its entirety, and then show (what to some minds is difficult to be understood) that this empire is that which still bears sway, though in a divided condition.

Let it be observed that I do not say that it is of absolute necessity, for our spiritual apprehension of the vision, that we should know the detail of geographical and historical facts; but surely we are, if we possess the opportunity, to compare such facts with Scripture, and thus use Scripture as giving us right thoughts as to the facts. If God gives us a prophecy in Scripture concerning Egypt or Tyre, we are of course to use those powers of observation with which He has furnished us so as to know what and where Egypt and Tyre are; how much more, then, must this be the case as to territories and nations with which we are ourselves concerned?

The power of Rome was of very gradual rise; the city, which at the first bore the name of *seven-hilled*, not from its being built on seven *different* hills, but only from seven ascents or points of hill on which it stood,* ex-

* The seven *hills* which originally gave the well-known designation to Rome were Palatium, Velia, Cermalus, Cælius, Fagutal, Oppius, Cispius.

panded as to its own circumference, and as to its dominion, until it became the metropolis and mistress of the civilised earth—until her sway extended throughout the East and the West alike.

The internal changes of the Roman commonwealth had been equally great: the stern republic of patricians, who, on the one hand, had expelled their kings and, on the other, had pressed down the plebeians, had been gradually compelled to admit all its citizens into almost every office of honour, trust, and power. The early course of Roman government, after the expulsion of the Tarquins, was in many respects like that which the state of Venice actually succeeded in establishing and perpetuating to the end of its independence of thirteen hundred years. Not so was the course of events as to Rome: plebeians and patricians, in the latter days of its republic, were alike holders of power; and if certain honours in religious rites were the exclusive possession of the latter of these bodies, the substantial powers of the office of tribune belonged entirely to the former.

From this latter condition of the republic arose that

---

[So Niebuhr.] The three first of these belonged to the *Palatine*, the two next to the *Cælian*, and the other two to the *Esquiline*; being thus, in fact, so many ascents, and not distinct hills. The name of Septicollis having been applied to Rome in its early form, was retained long after it ceased to be applicable in its original connection. After Rome had extended, it was supposed by some to relate to seven distinct hills: and thus the *number* was made to correspond by counting the Palatine, Capitoline, Quirinal, Esquiline, Cælian, Aventine, and the trans-Tiberine Janiculum. In this arrangement the Viminal (which lies between the Quirinal and the Esquiline) was omitted, in order not to exceed the number; in another arrangement, Janiculum, as being on the right side of the Tiber, was excluded and the Viminal reckoned: the seven hills were thus arbitrarily restricted to the left bank of the river, although the hill on the other side is the highest of the whole. In the days of Augustus and his successors, a large part of Rome had extended far beyond the hills and the intervening hollows, into the flat plain of the Campus Martius, which is the site of the greater part of the modern city of the popes.

imperial rule which was prefigured by the fourth beast seen in Daniel's vision.

At the time of this prophecy the power of Rome was in an undeveloped condition: this vision was seen about half a century before the expulsion of the kings, an event which was followed by a long period of diminished power. At this very time the third monarchy (although the elements of which it was to be constructed were occupying a prominent place) had no formed nucleus, so utterly was all that God now revealed irrespective of the ideas of the future which human sagacity might form. God's *anticipative history* was *now* written as to the outlines of the monarchies of the earth, a century before the time of Herodotus, the father of profane history.

Rome had, in its republican days, added to its territories the kingdoms of several of Alexander's successors; the Egyptian sovereignty, however, still continued, and in it there was a perpetuation of the third great kingdom until the time when Rome should be a monarchy. This *almost* took place when Caius Julius Cæsar made himself the virtual master of the Roman world: this same conqueror, besides what he added to the Roman territory in the west, so connected himself also with Egypt as to bring that last fragment of Grecian sovereignty under Roman influence. After the assassination of Julius Cæsar, changes of a few years' duration followed: the western territory was in the hands of Octavius, the nephew and adopted son of Julius; while in the east, Antonius had leagued a portion of the Roman power with Cleopatra, queen of Egypt, the last representative of Alexander's empire.

The battle of Actium (September 2, 31 B.C.) decided two things at once; it placed the sovereign authority of the Roman earth in the hands of Octavius, and it destroyed the power of the Egyptian kingdom. The two events occurred by a kind of necessary connection: Rome received the obelisks of Egypt to adorn the shores of the Tiber, and, acknowledging the imperial power in the hands of Octavius, bestowed on him the dignified designation of Augustus.*

At the commencement of the rule of the fourth

* The following extract from Spalding's *Italy* (vol. i, p. 96) describes the kind of authority which was exercised by Augustus:
"The title by which Augustus pretended to the sovereignty was that of a free election by the people, renewed from time to time. All names, forms, and ceremonies, which the free constitution held illegal, were carefully shunned; and all that the spirit of liberty had honoured were protected and brought paradingly forward. But the republicanism was a wretched mask through which every man of information saw distinctly, though none was strong enough to tear off the disguise. From the very commencement of the first reign all the powers, both of the senate, the popular conventions, and the magistracies, were virtually and effectually secured to the emperor. The new prince united by degrees in his own person all the ancient offices of state; or, at least, though he allowed the appointment of colleagues, he entrusted to them no share of the real administration. He founded, on his assumption of the tribuneship, a claim of personal inviolability, and his title of Imperator, which we translate Emperor, a prerogative of absolute military command, not only beyond the city, which was the republican rule, but also within it—an extension of powers which directly contradicted the old constitution. *His generalship of the armies, indeed, aided by the official weakness and personal subserviency of the senate, constituted the true ground on which his monarchy rested.* But, in appearance, he was only the first of senators; the august forms of the assembly were treated with profound respect; and the sovereign sheltered his ordinances under its name."

Such was the nature of Roman monarchy: it comprehended the absolute *military* Imperium beyond the city; to this it added a similar Imperium, not so confined, decreed by the senate; and, as a third element, it comprehended the Tribunitian power derived from the *people*—the long-cherished prerogative which the plebeians had earned for themselves on the day of their secession to the Mons Sacer.

Julius Cæsar had endeavoured, like Sulla, to rule as perpetual dictator, a *name* of ancient historic importance in Rome, but utterly deprived of its old significance by the adjunct of *perpetual*. When Cæsar fell beneath the daggers of conspirators, staining with his blood the statue of Pompey, the name and office of *dictator* were abolished by the senate. It was therefore no longer available for his politic nephew when he rose to supreme power: in the three-fold relation in which he stood as connected with the army, the senate, and the *plebs*, he combined that substantiality of power which he never could have done had he, like his uncle, depended on mere military prowess or on the support of one class.

monarchy it possessed in Europe, Italy, Gaul, the Spanish peninsula, Greece, Macedon, Thrace, and Illyricum, so that its boundary was pretty nearly the line of the rivers Rhine and Danube; in Africa it possessed the northern coasts and Egypt; and in Asia, Syria, and Asia Minor, the Euphrates being about the limit. Judæa, which formed at this time a dependent kingdom, became, during the reign of Augustus, a Roman province.

Such, then, was the original *empire* of the fourth beast. Under the successors of Augustus other conquests were made. Britain, which had been invaded by Julius Cæsar, and which for many subsequent years maintained only a commercial connection with Rome, was made a part of the empire, so far at least as the line of forts carried from the Clyde to the Forth.* In Germany the Roman boun-

* *Roman Britain.*—The first invasion of this island by Rome was conducted by Julius Cæsar, who, on the 26th of August, 55 B.C., in the consulship of Pompey and Crassus, planted the standard of the eagle on our shores. But Cæsar founded no permanent dominion in Britain; he left no garrison, and added no territory to the Roman state. However, from that day, Britain was known to the Romans; and in the reign of Augustus not a little commercial intercourse had sprung up: hence parts of the island were Romanised before they were at all brought under the sway of Rome. The subjugation of the island was undertaken by Claudius a century after the expedition of Julius Cæsar. The exports of grain from Britain had rendered its possession an object of importance in the eyes of Rome. Of the Roman legions, originally sent into Britain by Claudius, the *second* was stationed at Caerleon-upon-Usk and the *twentieth* at Chester; these, together with the *sixth*, brought over by the Emperor Hadrian, and stationed at York, formed the permanent garrison of our island. Besides these troops, however, there were also military colonists out of almost every conceivable part of the Roman empire, placed at different stations. Amongst other names we find those of Thracians, Dacians, Spaniards, Moors, Dalmatians, Batavians, Sarmatians, and *Indians*: these heterogeneous tribes introduced their own forms of idolatry; so that under the Roman dominion there was hardly a single kind of worship then known which did not flourish: this fact is attested by inscriptions and altars still extant. Under the Roman rule Christianity had penetrated into Britain, and that, probably, at an early period, so that the Roman dominion was instrumental in spreading the gospel of Christ. There is even reason for supposing that some of those whose names occur in the end of the 2nd Epistle to Timothy were Britons; at least the names of Pudens, Linus, and

dary was carried by a defined rampart from the Rhine near Bingen, along the Taunus mountains, then in a direction mostly south-east until it reached the Danube at the most northern point of that river. The Emperor Trajan added the province of Dacia, north of the Danube: the western boundary of this conquest was marked by a fortification skirting the extensive marshes which lie to the east of the river Theiss. The northern limit of Dacia crossed the Carpathian mountains to the river Dniester. In the east Trajan made many conquests beyond the Euphrates, but few of which were attempted to be retained as possessions; they might however be considered as belonging to the Roman empire in its widest extent. To the countries which have been mentioned must also be added the southern coasts of the Crimea.

Besides the conquests of Trajan, which were at once resigned, Rome withdrew, in the reign of Aurelian, from the province of Dacia: the *name* was thence forward given to a district south of the Danube. In other points also there was afterwards some contraction of boundary: the Rhine from the lake of Constance and onward had be-

---

Claudia were at that very time borne by three of a family in part British. The Diocletian persecution found some of its martyrs in Britain, of whom *Alban*, who suffered at Verulamium (the metropolis of Cassivellaunus in Cæsar's days), was the first. That persecution however was greatly restrained in the western countries which were under the rule of Constantius Chlorus. At the Council of Arles, in 314, we find the subscriptions of three British bishops; and before the close of the fourth century Britons joined with others in the vain pilgrimages to Jerusalem.

Amongst the more important events during the Roman occupation of Britain were the deaths of Septimius Severus, at York, in 211, and of Constantius Chlorus, in 306, at the same city; this caused his son Constantine to assume the imperial purple, which led to the cessation of all persecutions of Christians. The extent of the Roman dominion in Britain varied at different times: the rampart of Hadrian (the Picts' wall, as it is often called) crossed the island from Carlisle to Newcastle; but the vallum of Antoninus included a greater extent of country, running as it did from the Forth to the Clyde; while even farther north there were Roman towns.

come the limit; from that lake the line was drawn northward to the Danube. Such was the extent of the Roman earth at the time of the division into East and West.

Before the formal division of the imperial power there had frequently been a partition of the sovereign authority of Rome. Thus Augustus, the first emperor, associated with himself, in his later years, Tiberius, who became his successor. In the second century the principle of association in the imperial rank and authority became frequent in the time of the Antonines, but still the empire was not divided as to its *territory*. This was almost the case in the latter part of the third century, when Diocletian, two years after his assumption of the imperial dignity, took (in 286) Maximian as his associate in the empire; from this time the *administration* was divided, and the one emperor making Nicomedia, in Bithynia, his place of government, and the other Milan, Rome itself ceased as much to be the actual seat and centre of empire as Macedon had in the latter days of Alexander's successors.

Under Constantine there was again an united empire, but this monarch, by founding the city which still bears his name on the side of the ancient Byzantium, gave a principle of permanence to the territorial division, for he thus established what has been from that time and onward the metropolis of the eastern empire. Constantine at his death (in 337) divided his dominions amongst his *three* sons, a form of partition which lasted but three years.

After the death of the last surviving son of Constantine, and the short reigns of his two successors, the formal division of the government of the empire into East and West took place. In the year 364 Valentinian I retained the West for himself and invested his brother, Valens, with the empire of the East; the line of division was nearly that which separates Thrace from Macedon, continued northward to the Danube; Crete with some of the islands of the Ægæan sea were appropriated to the West; and in Africa the western limit of Cyrene was the boundary.

In *this* division it was intended that the West should be the more important empire. However, in 395, when the East was appropriated to Arcadius, the eldest son of Theodosius the Great, and the West to Honorius, his younger brother, the boundary was so changed as to unite the greater part of what is now European Turkey to the East. The boundary left the shores of the Adriatic, between Ragusa and the mouths of the Cattaro, and running northward till it approached the river Save, reached that stream by a bend to the east.

In the year 425, when Theodosius II took Valentinian III as his associate in the empire, he united a still further portion of territory to the East; the West (of which the seat of government was now Ravenna) no longer retained the provinces east of Venetia and Rhætia. The boundary was thus formed by the Julian Alps, then by a line drawn to the river Inn just where its course turns to the north (at the point where it now flows from the Austrian into the Bavarian territory), and then by the course of the Inn to the Danube.

This was the definite line of demarcation by which the Roman earth was fully divided into East and West; the separation was occasioned by internal as well as external causes. Within, the empire had consisted of elements utterly distinct, mentally and morally; it needed a strong hand to cause such contrary materials to coalesce; and when the Parthian power on the east and the vast immigration of tribes from the north pressed on the Roman territory, a separation of administration was almost the necessary result: thus the long-admitted principle of association in the empire now assumed the form of distinct and separate government.*

The western empire soon became a prey to the northern invaders, so that in 475 the succession ceased in the person of Romulus Augustulus: not so, however, at Constantinople, where, with varied circumstances and a circumscribed territory, the imperial dignity continued, until it expired with the last Constantine, when (in 1453) the eastern metropolis passed into the hands of Mahometan invaders.

This, then, is the empire whose whole extent is marked out in prophecy as that which shall be divided into *ten* kingdoms, just as the dominion of Alexander was separated into four.

It may be questioned whether, with regard to this division, the empire must be looked at as it existed under Augustus, or in its widest extent, or according to its limits when the complete division took place of East and West. The first of these limits is not, I believe, the true one (reasons for this opinion will appear presently), and as to the second, it may be doubted whether terri-

* The Roman hold on Britain was almost entirely relinquished at the time of this ultimate division of empire. In the year 383, when the usurper Maximus endeavoured to establish his authority in the west, he left Britain with all the military force that he could raise. This army never returned, and as its place was not supplied, and as Roman policy had put the defence of the provinces into the hands of strangers, or of military colonists, the Britons were left almost unprotected; they had to oppose the northern Caledonians and maritime marauders. Only about twelve years had elapsed before the Britons were compelled to apply to the court of Ravenna for aid, when they received inadequate succours. The sack of Rome by Alaric, in 410, shook the imperial power in distant provinces, and this event virtually closed the Roman rule over Britain. At the beginning of this century we find the twentieth legion no longer in the island, the second was removed from Caerleon to Richborough in Kent (Rutupiæ), while the northern defences of the sixth legion at York, and the troops on the wall of Hadrian, still continued. In 418 there was a great migration of the Roman population from Britain, and the final abandonment by Roman troops took place in 436.

tories which Rome voluntarily resigned could be regarded as integral parts of the empire; hence it seems to me that we should include Southern Britain, and take on the Continent the line of the Danube and Rhine in a general sense.*

In this territory, according to the terms of Daniel's prophecy, written before Rome rose to be a mighty power, and according to the Apocalypse, seen when that power had almost approached its height, we may expect a division to be found into ten kingdoms.

We have, in accordance with Scripture, to look at all the present period as one in which changes and divisions take place within the Roman earth, prior to that tenfold development into kingdoms which shall precede the rise of the terrible but transient horn of blasphemy.

Does this seem difficult to any mind? If so, let it be considered that in the vision of Daniel vii the fourth beast is regarded as reigning *until* the Son of Man takes the kingdom and His saints take it with him. If this has not taken place as yet, then the fourth beast still bears rule, however changed may be the form of his power.

The example of the third beast may illustrate this: the united empire of Alexander began to dissolve at his death; but still as long as any of its great divided parts remained as sovereignties (whatever changes they had undergone) any person would have been living under the third beast. This would have been true before the battle of Ipsus (301 B.C.) effected the fourfold division; it would have been equally true when that great division had in many respects changed, and until the fourth beast

---

* The Emperor Caracalla (whose reign began in 211) extended the privilege of Roman citizenship to all persons born within the empire who were not slaves. This was done for the purpose of raising an increased property-tax; it had, however, a very important effect in giving a certain unity to the races within the empire.

had by the conquest of Egypt superseded the last of the four Grecian sovereignties.

In one respect the third and fourth beasts stand in definite contrast: the fourfold division of Alexander's empire took place without any great interval of years after his death; and then other changes ensued: the territory of the fourth beast, whether intermediate divisions had taken place or not, was to be found separated into ten kingdoms *just before its utter destruction* by the Lord Himself. Thus, unless we can say that Christ has taken *His* kingdom and destroyed the divided sovereignties of Rome, we are still living under this fourth monarchy, and its tenfold division is what we must expect.

How fully the *Roman* character has been impressed on the sovereignties formed within its territory is shown by the circumstances of their rise. They were in general founded by some king or chief of an invading tribe, who succeeded in planting his people within the imperial territory; over his own followers he possessed a defined military authority. To the Roman provincials it was a very indifferent matter *who* their sovereign might be: they were heavily taxed and dispirited, so that to the greater part of them it seemed preferable to be ruled by a military conqueror who from local connection might be interested in improving their condition, than by an emperor who secluded himself in the luxury of Ravenna, or one who, reigning on the shore of the Bosphorus, cared only for the eastern provinces. The provincials, too, had seen examples enough of barbarian rule during the days of the united empire not to object to any sovereign because of his birth or nation. Thus they acknowledged their new rulers as holders of Roman *imperium*, and regarded them as possessed of that absolute power which the Roman emperors had claimed and exercised.

The new rulers willingly accepted the acknowledgment of the provincials, and thus, without exchanging their kingly titles for the imperial *name*, they governed as holding an associated authority within the empire. The twofold power which they thus possessed, that over their original followers and that over the provincials, led to the development of new forms of government containing opposing principles. The followers of the invading chiefs owed them but a kind of limited allegiance, they possessed privileges which were as indefeasible as was the power of the sovereign; the new subjects, on the contrary, knew of no relations between the governed and those governing, other than had been recognised by Roman rule.\* The municipalities, indeed, had possessed certain privileges, and when permanent conquest and not mere devastation was the object of the invaders, they found it to be for their own interest to preserve such bodies. It was by means of the municipalities, with

---

\* Thus it has been said that the Franks occupied the soil of Gaul for three centuries, without any amalgamation having taken place between the new dominant body and the old Roman provincials; the terms might seem to be borrowed from what Daniel ii says of the iron and clay.

From the relation in which the followers of the invading leaders stood to them sprang much of the notion of modern European *nobility*. The almost *independent* ground which this class could assume, seven centuries ago, shows what a limited allegiance chiefs *even then* rendered to their sovereigns. Thus the original form of the homage of the Aragonese nobles to the sovereign ran thus: "*We who are as good as you, and together are more than you, will be faithful to you as our king and lord, if you govern us well and truly,* IF NOT, NOT." The privilege of remaining covered in the presence of the sovereign is all that the Spanish nobles *now* retain of these high-sounding claims. So long as the ancient office of hereditary Lord High Steward of England continued, the sovereign was treated, *in word*, with as much independence. This officer, at the coronation of a king, receiving from his hands a sword, addressed him thus, "With this sword I will defend thee, so long as thou governest well, as thou hast sworn; but with this sword I and the people of England will depose thee, if thou governest contrary to thy coronation oath." After the attainder and execution of the Duke of Buckingham, in the reign of Henry VIII, this office and ceremony ceased.

their local organisation, that much of what had been Roman floated above the wreck of ages down to our days.*

The twofold relations of the new sovereigns seem to have occasioned what we should now call constitutional governments, in which, however, almost all that controlled the king was to be found amongst his original followers. From the greater submission of the provincials, the kings had an interest in bestowing on them such privileges as might check (what might be termed) the military nobility.

In some cases the kings, whose power had arisen within the Roman earth, sought and obtained imperial recognition from Constantinople. This was the case in England, where, during the days of the Heptarchy, one sovereign bore supreme rule, being acknowledged as an associate in the empire by the reigning emperor in the East. Hence, we find on Saxon coins the title of *ΒΑΣΙΛΕΥΣ*, as borne by the Greek Emperors, and the she-wolf with Romulus and Remus. Thus did the invading rulers, who had established themselves in this country, identify themselves with the authority, the institutions, and with the historical associations of Ancient Rome. This fact indicates (as it appears to me) that we are not to exclude from the prophetic history

* In this country, London held a remarkable place as a municipality. It seems to have risen to its importance through traffic, between the time of Julius Cæsar and the Roman occupation under Claudius. It afterwards became the capital of the country, though not a military station. After the departure of the Romans, it maintained a kind of municipal independence; and it was not until the consolidation of the Saxon kingdoms that it submitted to the supreme state, without however giving up its own privileges. Thus, in the changes of dynasties, religions, and races, London, as a municipality, has been the most stable of the links of connection between the present hour and the time of Roman rule. The whole history of the municipalities has thrown (by means of modern research) no small light on the permanence of Roman institutions.

of the Roman earth such territories as were not included within its limits in the days of Augustus.*

Although from the year 476 there ceased to be an emperor reigning in the West, the authority of the imperial name was not finally extinct in its original centre of dominion. Odoacer, the king of the Heruli (a tribe issuing from the shores of the Baltic), who in 476 had deposed Romulus Augustulus, was invested, at the request of the Roman senate, with the title of Patrician by Zeno, the eastern emperor, and under this designation he exercised sovereign power. Theodoric, the king of the Ostrogoths, by whom Odoacer was displaced and slain (in 493), had been educated at Constantinople, and it was as a province of the empire, and under the (disregarded) condition of tribute, that he received the grant

---

* Sir Francis Palgrave in his *Anglo-Saxon Commonwealth* has done much to show the relation in which sovereignty within the Roman empire, and in particular in Britain, was connected with imperial recognition and association.

The rise of Saxon rule, however, was marked by some peculiarities. At the departure of the Romans, three races occupied the country: First, the non-Romanised Britons, whose abode was principally to the west of the Severn and Exe. Second, the Romans and the mixed population which had become Romanised. The districts *especially* Romanised were the country from Bath and Cirencester, north-eastward as far as Northamptonshire, and south-eastward as far as Sussex. Third, the Saxon population, which thus early had established themselves: this body of inhabitants were probably confined to the *littus Saxonicum*, from the south of Kent to the edge of Lincolnshire. The settlement of this Teutonic race seems to have originated in their mercantile and predatory expeditions, which led to their being encouraged by the Romans, in the hope, probably, that they would guard the exposed coast. It was apparently the frequency of piratical attacks which caused the removal of the second legion from Caerleon to Richborough.

After the withdrawal of the Romans, sovereignty became independent amongst the non-Romanised Britons; while the Roman population sought weakly and vainly to maintain their authority in the island. The dominion of the Saxons arose, not by breaking down Roman authority, but by occupying the ground which Rome had left vacant. Successive bodies of Saxons, Jutes, and *Angles* (the last being the race whose *name* was to be perpetuated) planted themselves in Britain, and the only independence from their sway was found by withdrawal to the non-Romanised Britons

of Italy from Zeno. In the middle of the following century the victories of Belisarius and Narses united to the empire of Justinian the Carthaginian provinces, Italy, and the islands of Sicily, Sardinia, and Corsica. That part of Italy which continued to belong to the Empire after the Lombard invasion was ruled by a governor bearing the title of *Exarch*, whose abode was at Ravenna. Thus was the direct authority of the emperors maintained over Rome, and other portions of the West, till the year 731.

Seventy years had not passed from that date when Charlemagne, the monarch of the Franks and the German tribes, was (in the year 800) solemnly crowned emperor, at Rome, by the pope. This has been regarded by some as though he thus became the *remote* successor of Augustulus: it was, however, rather as the associate of Irenè, then ruling the eastern empire, that the imperial dignity and name were conferred on the Western conqueror.

In his family the imperial title continued with diminished lustre; at Coblentz, in the church of St. Castor, his descendants agreed to divide his territories; and after various vicissitudes, the title of Roman Emperor, together with the supremacy over Italy (*real* at that time), was appropriated, in the person of Otho, 962, to an elective German monarch. But though his rule was *principally* beyond the Alps, yet for ages it was considered that the imperial title was not rightly his until he had been crowned in Rome as Emperor of the West.

---

in Wales and Cornwall. The partially-received Christianity was so extinguished, except in those districts, that on the arrival of Augustine the Monk, in 596 (one hundred and sixty years after the final withdrawal of the Romans), not one Christian, whether Roman or Saxon, could he find —and that in a land whose bishops had assisted at early councils, and where Christian profession had so far extended that important doctrinal differences were widely discussed, and much pains bestowed for rooting out errors and teaching dogmatic truth.

The latest traces of the power of the eastern emperors in the West are to be found in the Italian islands and the territory of Naples. Much of the latter was conquered from the Lombards, in 891, by the generals of the Emperor Leo; and even after the Norman kingdom of Naples had arisen in the eleventh century, the claim of Constantinople was not withdrawn; nor was it till 1157 that William of Naples was acknowledged as king by the Greek emperor.

Thus it was by gradual steps that changes took place in the Roman earth; and thus plain is it that the sovereignties of South-western Europe not only *were*, but *were considered* to be, perpetuations of Roman power.

This sometimes led to *formal* transactions resembling the ancient assumption of an associate in the empire. Thus, in November 1337 the Emperor Lewis, the Bavarian, met Edward III of England at Coblentz, and there at the church at St. Castor, where the empire had been divided five hundred years before, he constituted him Imperial Vicar of all territories and peoples on the left bank of the Rhine, with authority to coin money in those districts—an authority on which he acted at Antwerp. This imperial title was distinctly declared in an Act of Parliament in the time of his grandson Henry IV, and it explains part of the ceremonial observed in the threefold coronation of Queen Elizabeth, first as Queen of England, second, Queen of Ireland, third, "Sovereign Lady and Empress of all Nations and Countries from the Islands Orcades to the Mountains Pyrenees".

Thus, though the Ottoman arms destroyed the imperial name and power in the East in the fifteenth century, its different western branches have continued, whether as bearing imperial or royal names. It was common to consider France as *successionally* perpetuating the empire in the West,* while even to our days the head of the Germanic body was styled Roman emperor and successor of Augustus.

It may be questioned whether the tenfold division of the Roman earth must be precisely in accordance with its geographical boundaries: but at all events it seems clear that the *seat* of all the kingdoms must be *within* the Roman bounds as well as the main body of the territory: further than this it may not be safe to venture an opinion. The Romans *conquered* far beyond the limits which they retained: the Eyder, between Holstein and Schleswig, appears to have been the line to which they penetrated in that direction: they also occupied military positions beyond the boundaries of the empire, just as Napoleon held Magdeburg and other places which were no part of his territory. Thus there may be districts beyond the Roman earth which will be connected with parts of the ten kingdoms. It is "*out of*" the fourth kingdom that ten others arise, whatever exterior territory any of them may possess or conquer.

From the vision of Daniel ii, and that of chap. vii, we may see that the ten kingdoms do not arise until a certain process of deterioration (the mixture of clay with iron) is complete; and that these kingdoms, when all developed, have not any protracted course before them. Just as the sovereignty, out of which they sprung, was secular, so of course are they also secular. Whatever have been the changes in the Roman earth, as yet we have not seen the definite tenfold division; indeed, had we seen it we could have expected nothing other than

---

* This was done partly through the strange transaction between Andreas Palæologus and Charles VIII in 1494; the latter, in 1495, when in possession of Naples, formally received and bore the title of *Emperor*; he seems to have considered himself as then holding part of the *Eastern* Empire.

the appearance of the last horn and the judgment of the Son of Man at his coming.

To suppose this last horn to be the Papacy would interfere with almost every point that the visions in Daniel teach us; it would involve us in the supposition that before the rise of the Papacy the imperial power had passed away, and that its territory was in the hands of ten definite kings. If so, those kingdoms must continue as such (unless the *three* which fall before the last horn be excepted) until the coming of Christ: whereas we know how change after change has passed upon Europe since the Popedom began. The *time* at which many have sought for ten kingdoms has been the fifth and sixth centuries, and they have mostly sought them in the invading hosts. But although Rome had been severed for a time from the imperial sway, and though many provinces had become independent kingdoms, the dignity of emperor still continued, and the power of those who held it was again to be exercised over *Rome itself* for two centuries. This might have been an intimation that it was vain to look for the defined division, *even of the West* at least before the year 731. But of course we ought not (if we follow the terms of the vision) to exclude the East, even after that year: five toes were on each foot of the image. And thus we are led on, so as to find that no point of time *prior* to the extinction of the imperial name and power at Constantinople (1453) *could* be assigned for any such division.

The tenfold division of the Roman empire (even if we had a right to exclude the eastern half) could never be definitely pointed out, whether in the early centuries or since. The lists differ exceedingly, and very frequently countries wholly disconnected with the Roman empire are introduced simply because in later days they have been upholders of the Popedom.* But even *if* the lists of kings could be made out, and *if* the commencement of the divisions of the empire were the proper time, and not a little before the second advent of Christ, it would still remain to be shown *how* the Popedom then rose after the ten kings, and how it destroyed three of the former kings, and *what three*.

Some place the rise of the Papacy, as the little horn, in the reign of Justinian, in the middle of the sixth century; at that very time, however, the Popedom, both in temporal and spiritual things, was ruled over by Justinian: Vigilius, the weak and vacillating Roman bishop, who, according to circumstances, adopted or renounced the monophysite heresy, possessed no temporal authority; and in doctrinal points he bound himself by oath to the emperor. As if to reverse the relations in which things afterwards

* The following note, from [the late] Mr. Conder's *Literary History of the New Testament* (p. 576), shows what ideas have been advanced as the division of the Roman empire into ten kingdoms:

"At the epoch of A.D. 532, which is fixed upon by Mr. Elliott, there existed on the platform of the western Roman empire the following ten kingdoms: the Anglo-Saxons, the Franks, the Allman Franks, the Burgundians, the Visigoths, the Suevi, the Vandals, the Ostrogoths, the Bavarians, and the Lombards. Notwithstanding many intervening revolutions and changes in Western Europe, ten has generally been noted as the number of the Papal kingdoms. Thus Gibbon, speaking of Roger, first king of Sicily, A.D. 1130, says: 'The nine kings of the Latin world might disclaim their new associate unless he were consecrated by the authority of the supreme pontiff.' The nine kings were those of France, England, Scotland, Castille, Aragon, Navarre, Sweden, Denmark, Hungary."

I do not discuss the points stated as historical facts (such as whether there was *one* united Anglo-Saxon kingdom in 532); the kingdoms being sought in the *West* alone is sufficient to show the fallacy of the scheme which ignores the eastern empire; the date, too, is not a fortunate one, as it is just before the eastern emperors again extended their influence over the West. But what relation has the extract from Gibbon to the matter in hand? If we are to seek for ten kingdoms in the Roman empire, to the Roman empire let us confine ourselves. On what principle are we to bring in countries never Roman, such as *Sweden* and *Denmark*? And if we take the *West* Roman empire, why wander as far as *Hungary*, which never did or could pertain to it? [See note on Luther's enumeration at the end of this chapter.]

stood, the emperor declared the pope, when unsubmissive, to be excluded from the fellowship of the Church.

Others regarded the Papacy as thus arising when Boniface III was addressed by the Emperor Phocas in 606 as "Universal Bishop".* That the secular authority of Rome, then, belonged to the emperor we have proof existing in the Roman Forum itself, where, in our days, excavations around "the nameless column with the buried base" have caused the base to be no longer buried, and the column to be no longer nameless, since the inscription on the pedestal shows that it was erected to the honour of this very Phocas by his Italian representative. How completely the popes were *subjects*, at a later period, is shown in the case of Pope Martin I, who, for his firm opposition to the monothelite heresy, was seized at Rome, in 653, as a *traitor* to the emperor, and, after having been conveyed to Constantinople, ended his days in banishment at the ancient Cherson in the Crimea.

It is to the age of Pepin and his son Charlemagne that we must descend before we find the popes as holders of temporal sovereignty. This, however, they held as feudatories of the western emperors, so that Leo III was required by Charlemagne to vindicate himself from treasonable charges.

* The title of "Universal Bishop" had been used for some time in the East as a complimentary title: it was not intended to signify that the person to whom it was applied excluded the jurisdiction of other bishops, nor yet was it so understood as if it could belong to *one* only. In England the legal designation of the Archbishop of Canterbury is "Primate of ALL England"; but this is not designed to interfere with the jurisdiction of the Archbishop of York, within his own province, who is styled "Primate of England". This may illustrate the complimentary character of this high-sounding title. Complimentary designations, when expressed by *superlatives*, are never *strictly* interpreted.

More has been made out of the title of "Universal Bishop" than it really involves. Boniface III accepted a title which the cooler judgment of his predecessor, Gregory I, had rejected. The *title* gave no added jurisdiction, spiritual or temporal.

In later days popes did indeed claim a power of conferring sovereignty, as though all the kingdoms of the earth were theirs, but this was not through the territorial dominion which they held, but as a supposed attribute of their spiritual jurisdiction. As yet they claimed no part of the dominion of the Cæsars, for even in the districts of Italy ruled by the popes the inhabitants swore allegiance to the emperors. It was not till the accession of Rudolf of Hapsburg, 1273, that the popes claimed *independent temporal* rule: the claim was admitted by the emperor, more occupied with transalpine than Italian objects; and thus, from 1278, the oath of allegiance to the emperor was not imposed in the territory of the popes, who thus became independent secular sovereigns—an accession of dignity which was soon marked by a double crown, and then by the triple, as still borne.*

But the actuality of a secular kingdom did not increase

* How *gradually* the popes acquired independent temporal sovereignty is shown by their transactions with the emperors.

"Since the revival of the Roman Empire under Otho the Great [962], the emperors had regularly placed in Rome a prefect or legate, who swore allegiance to them, and exercised a control over the civil administration. . . .

"At home the pontiffs were weak, often despised, and sometimes expelled; but abroad their name grew and flourished. . . . The minority of Frederick II enabled the resolute Innocent III [1198–1216], a middle-aged Roman noble, to fortify the temporal sovereignty of the holy see over a large district of Central Italy. He revived, and, partly by force, partly by the submission of the principal towns, was able to bring into effect that famous donation by which, in the times of Hildebrand and his successor, the Countess Matilda of Tuscany had bequeathed to the Papal see her extensive fiefs, the Duchy of Spoleto and the March of Ancona."—Spalding's *Italy*, ii. 103, 105.

The entire *independence* of the Papal states was secured in 1278: during the secession to Avignon (1305–77), however, and the subsequent schism of the West (1378–1417), the power of the popes over them was weakened and in part destroyed, so that it was not till after the French occupation of Italy, in 1494, under Charles VIII, that the Papal territorial rule was reconsolidated. From that time it received various additions till the year 1644. In modern days the whole of the Papal dominions have been swept

the Papal influence in temporal things. Boniface VIII sought in vain to bestow kingdoms and to resume them, as Innocent III had done a century before. From that time, in temporalities, the popes became petty Italian sovereigns, while in spiritual things their authority was equally recognised as before. Such were the steps by which the popes gained secular sovereignty: for which *secular* sovereignty alone we are now concerned: it was that, and that alone, which had belonged to the Cæsars, and the divided parts of their dominion could not be something differing entirely in kind from the dominion itself.

Thus there is really no point of time at which we could apply the vision of Daniel vii to the Papacy. We must look at the Roman power still continuing in its divided parts, and expect that its ultimate condition will be a tenfold division into kingdoms in which strength and weakness will be combined, when—three years and a half before the second advent of Christ—a power of blasphemy and persecution will arise who will overthrow three of the former kings.

The spread and use of the Roman law illustrates the continuance of the Roman power. Throughout the Roman earth, Roman law became the basis of all jurisprudence, and though modified by custom or direct enactment, it still furnishes a body of principles of wide and various application. The Corpus Juris Civilis itself

---

away from their priestly sovereigns, and all (with the exception of Avignon and its territory) have been again restored and confirmed. [Since this was written, other changes have caused a loss of a large portion: all, indeed, except what is held through French aid. And thus it has been increasingly shown that the temporal power is not essential to the Papacy. 1863.]

THE AUTHORITY OF SCRIPTURE 73

supplies evidence of the continuance of Roman power and institutions, for there we find enactments of the Henrys and Frederics of the house of Hohenstaufen, as co-ordinate with those of Severus, Constantine, Theodosius, and Justinian. The same imperial authority attaches to the decree of Henry VII of Luxemburg (in which he styles Constantine "our illustrious predecessor"), dated in 1313 from Pisa, as to the Pandects of Justinian, the ancient *Pisan* MS of which\* was the instructor of the dark ages, and laid the foundation of that maritime law which all civilised states alike recognise.

What does this long statement of facts teach? Does it supply us with new light as to the bearing of Daniel's prophecies, different from what we should have learned from the Scripture itself?

To the Scripture we may adhere simply: facts, or supposed facts, can never alter the force of what the Spirit of God has caused to be written. This statement of facts is intended (and I trust it may serve) to show that *objec-*

\* The Pisan Codex is said to have been brought thither from Amalfi: after the subjection of Pisa to Florence this MS became one of the spoils of the victorious city, where it is still preserved in the Laurentian library.

In connection with Roman law it may be observed that Britain seems to have profited not a little. York was the place where Papinian, the celebrated jurist, presided in the early part of the third century: the law school in that city continued to flourish after the Saxon occupation had driven the name of Christianity out of the most part of England, and after the labours of Roman missionaries had again triumphed over idolatry. We find proofs of the existence of this school of Roman law from the seventh to the ninth century.

[Luther gave an enumeration of ten kingdoms which did not exclude the East: but then he supposed the power which destroyed three of them to be not Papal but Mahometan. "The Anti-Christian power spoken of in Dan. xi. 39, etc., was the Pope; that of Dan. vii. 8, etc., the Turk. The Ten Horns of the last or Roman kingdom were Spain, France, Italy, Africa, Egypt, Syria, Asia, Greece, Germany, etc. The Little Horn coming up among them, or Mahomet, plucked up three of them by the roots, viz. Egypt, Asia, [? Africa,] and Greece. Walch. xx, p. 2691, etc." *Life of Martin Luther*, by Henry Worsley, M.A., ii. 184, *note.*]

*tions* to the simple reception of Scripture teaching, *when based on facts in their supposed bearing,* are manifested to be groundless, so soon as the facts themselves are correctly presented. History thus possesses a *negative value*, and enables us to cast aside difficulties with which some would obscure the force of God's word.

# THE RAM AND HE GOAT (DANIEL VIII)

THE prophetic scene becomes narrowed before us in this chapter; one definite portion of future history is here anticipatively written for us by God. The same is the way which God has taken in teaching us those things which were profitable for us to know, as to the past. If we look at the history of man as given in Genesis, we have at first, after the flood, the general statement in outline of all nations in their ancestry and first formation, and then afterwards a narrower scene is brought before us—one family from which springs one nation—and with this we principally have to do in the remainder of the Old Testament. Just so in the prophetic visions of Daniel; we have Gentile power in its committal, course, and crisis, also in its wideness of extent, its moral relations to God, and its actings with regard to those who belong to God; and besides an account of *who* it is that succeeds to the dominion which has been forfeited by the last of the Gentile powers: and then comes the narrower scene, in which we see these things set before us in their connection with that same one nation which had been so early taken up in history.

With this chapter the Hebrew portion of the book recommences and this continues to be the language of all the remainder, the whole of these visions relating distinctly to the Jews and Jerusalem.

This vision was seen in the third year of king Belshazzar, the last king of the first monarchy, just when the

Medo-Persian kingdom had so risen into power as to be ready to subvert the Babylonian.

The *place* where the prophet sees the vision is at one of the capitals of the Medo-Persian kingdom, "Shushan, in the province of Elam, by the river of Ulai". It may be doubted whether Daniel were actually there personally or whether it was only in vision. The words are, "I saw in a vision; and it came to pass, when I saw, that I was at Shushan in the palace, which is in the province of Elam; and I saw in a vision, and I was by the river of Ulai." This is wholly different from the manner in which he speaks in chap. x. 4, of his being actually by the river Tigris: "I was by the side of the great river, which is Hiddekel." Here it seems as though in vision the prophetic scene were selected within the territory of the power, the pre-eminence of which first comes into view: "there stood before the river a ram".

The vision is given us from verses 3 to 14, the interpretation from verses 19 to 26. Daniel first sees "a ram which had two\* horns, and the two horns were high; but one was higher than the other, and the higher came up last". The ram is then described as to the exercise of its power, etc.: "I saw the ram pushing eastward, and northward, and southward, so that no beasts might stand before him, neither was there any that could deliver out of his hand, but he did according to his will, and became great."

The interpretation of this, as given in verse 20, is— "The ram which thou sawest having two horns, are the kings of Media and Persia."

---

\* The word "two" in our modern English Bibles is in italics, as though it were supplied in translation. This, however, is one of the needless changes introduced by Dr. Blayney in 1769. "Two horns" is the rendering of the Hebrew *dual*, as our translators well knew. In verse 7 the numeral is expressed.

The next object in the vision is thus stated: "As I was considering, behold, an he goat came from the west, on the face of the whole earth, and touched not the ground; and the goat had a notable horn between his eyes." The following verses, 6, 7, describe the manner in which the prophet saw the ram destroyed by the he goat. The interpretation of the goat and its great horn is given in verse 21: "The rough goat is the king of Grecia: and the great horn that is between his eyes is the first king."

We have thus a point of connection between this vision and those of the second and seventh chapters; we first of all have the power which was about to succeed to that of Babylon brought before us in a defined form; the "reign of the kingdom of Persia" (2 Chron. xxxvi. 20) is that which we have seen as springing into power, that is the breast and arms of silver of chapter ii, or the second beast like to a bear of chapter vii. The power of this second monarchy, detailed just prior to its taking its place of supremacy, and its overthrow by that of Grecia, next come before us, and then the rest of the vision has some relation to a form of things which results from the divided power of the third monarchy.

Is the general subject of the remainder of this vision past or future? If past, our only concern with it would be to learn those lessons which the Spirit of God may have seen fit to record therein, but if future, it assumes, of course, a yet deeper interest, for in that case it would be one of those portions of revealed truth in which our God vouchsafes to call us to fellowship of mind and thoughts with Himself, opening to us those things which will come to pass in the development of His holy counsels.

Some may say, If the vision belongs (as seems clearly

to be the case) to the third monarchy, and if that monarchy was superseded (as we know was the fact) long ages ago by the Roman, then, of course, this vision is a thing entirely accomplished and exhausted, as much so as the vision of the third chapter, which related personally to Nebuchadnezzar.

Now, in reply to the question as to the past or future aspect of this vision, we must mark as carefully the period on to which it reaches as we do that at which it commences. In the beginning of the explanation given by Gabriel to the prophet he says (verse 17), "At the time of the end shall be the vision," and again (verse 19), "Behold, I will make thee know what shall be in the last end of the indignation: for at the time appointed the end shall be." This is certainly an intimation that the distinguishing features of the vision belong to the time when God's indignation against Daniel's people shall reach its completion, when all the circumstances of their rejection and chastisement shall arrive at their end. We know from many scriptures (such as Jer. xxx. 7) that the time which immediately precedes Israel's forgiveness and deliverance will be that of their extremest trouble and suffering: in other words, it will be thus in "the last end of the indignation".

Thus we have a point to which the vision reaches, as well as a starting point, and we have therefore to see what portions belong respectively to the past and to the future.

After the rise of the empire of Alexander and his personal rule have been spoken of in the vision (verses 5-8), we find, "The great horn was broken: and for it came up four notable ones toward the four winds of heaven."

In the interpretation this is stated (verse 22), "Now

## DIVISION INTO FOUR KINGDOMS 79

that being broken, whereas four stood up for it, four kingdoms shall stand up out of the nation, but not in his power." This we know to be a past thing, not merely historically, but as a simple matter of revelation; for these things were to spring out of the breaking off of the first king. This fourfold division had been intimated in chap. vii by the four heads of the third beast, and it is also mentioned in chap xi.

We know simply as a matter of historical fact that after the death of Alexander his dominions were parcelled out amongst his generals, and that after a few years (subsequently to the battle of Ipsus, 301 B.C.) four kingdoms were formed.

Ptolemy possessed Egypt, Cyrene, Cœle-Syria, and some of the southern parts of Asia Minor.

Cassander, Macedon and Greece.

Lysimachus, Thrace, Western Bithynia, Lesser Phrygia, Mysia, and Lydia (the Meander being the boundary) —and

Seleucus all the rest.*

These historical facts enable us to give names, etc., to the four kingdoms here mentioned, and this is a convenience; but it cannot be too fully borne in mind that for the real understanding and use of the truths revealed in Scripture history possesses no authority whatever; the Scripture itself supplies us with all that is *needful*.

The vision, after speaking of the formation of the

* Some of the districts included in the fourfold division became subordinate states. The kingdom of Lysimachus included the territory in which his lieutenant founded the more durable kingdom of Pergamus; this may, perhaps, be regarded as a continuation of his kingdom.

four horns, proceeds thus: "And out of one of them came forth a little horn, which waxed exceedingly great toward the south, and toward the east, and toward the pleasant land." This is stated thus in the interpretation: "And in the latter time of their kingdom, when the transgressors are come to the full, a king of fierce countenance, and understanding dark sentences, shall stand up", etc. The history of this horn or king is then given, and it reaches to the end of the vision; everything concerning this person and his actings must therefore belong to the period called "the last end of the indignation".

The point then at which the vision divides itself between that which is past to us and that which is future is at the statement of the fourfold division of the kingdom of the he goat (verses 8 and 22); all that follows, "the latter time of their kingdom," and the springing up of the persecuting power, must be future.

The dealings of God in the latter day with the Jews and Jerusalem possess an exceeding interest to all those who see the importance which God attaches to that place and people. A degree of prominence, which might at first seem strange, is given in the prophetic word to those scenes; but it is our place to sit as learners, having our ears open to receive the instruction of God, even when we are most at a loss to perceive the bearing of that instruction. Whatever is important in God's eyes ought to be so in ours, as being made the children of God; He has said of Jerusalem, "My eyes and my heart shall be there perpetually." He has said of Israel that if His covenant with the day and night cannot be broken, then He will not cast off His ancient people. Jesus died for that *nation*; they are still "beloved for the fathers' sakes". No marvel then that our eyes are directed again and again to the closing scenes of the period of God's indignation, and the dawn of that day in which God has said, "In those days and at that time, saith the Lord, the iniquity of Israel shall be sought for, and there shall be none; and the sins of Judah, and they shall not be found: for I will pardon them whom I reserve." What soul is there that has tasted the mercy of God and rejoices in the grace which has been shown in the precious blood of Christ, that does not feel joy in the contemplation of this great and surpassing display of the same grace? It is indeed a privilege to be allowed to know what God is going to perform; and, knowing what the result is, we cannot judge any of the details to be unimportant.

To this period, then, the issue of this vision belongs: a king rises from one of the four parts of that dominion which once was in the power of Alexander; his power extends in various directions, amongst others "towards the pleasant land"; this, of course, means the land of Israel, and this is the first direct intimation in the chapter of its connection with Daniel's people. Violent oppression and blasphemy appear to characterise this king both from the vision and the explanation given by Gabriel. "He shall destroy wonderfully, and shall prosper and practise, and shall destroy the mighty, and the holy people [people or nation of the holy ones or saints]. And through his policy, also, he shall cause craft to prosper in his hand, and he shall magnify himself in his heart, and by peace shall he destroy many." General as these terms are, they very clearly show the persecuting and oppressive power of this king; it is also clear, from the mention of the nation of the holy ones or saints, that these oppressions are especially inflicted on the Jews.

What the condition of the Jews may be at this time, how divided into classes as regards their recognised standing before God, etc., we can learn from other scriptures; but however these things will be, one thing is clear, that this horn is present in persecuting power at the last end of the indignation.

Another of his prominent characteristics is blasphemy: "He shall stand up against the Prince of princes" (verse 25). "He magnified himself even to the Prince of the host" (verse 11), so that he is found not merely as the opposer of God's ancient people, but also of the Lord Himself.

It is scarcely possible for us to have examined this chapter thus far without being struck with many points of resemblance between this horn and that which has been spoken of in the seventh chapter: that in the seventh chapter continues to act till Christ takes the kingdom, the one before us acts up to "the last end of the indignation." These two periods are synchronous, for the deliverance of Israel belongs to that point of time which is the epiphany of our blessed Lord: when He appears, then they will look upon Him whom they pierced, they will mourn for Him, and the fountain for sin and for uncleanness will be known by them as opened to their souls. Thus the horn in this chapter and that in chapter vii coincide as to period of time.

Further, the four divided kingdoms which formed themselves out of the empire of Alexander were one by one incorporated with the Roman empire, but it is out of one of these kingdoms that the horn in this chapter springs, hence it is clear that he belongs to the Roman earth. Thus the persons spoken of in the two chapters are found within the same territorial limits.

The moral features which are alike in the two have been already noticed. But it may be added that both the one and the other coincide remarkably in this respect with a king mentioned in the eleventh chapter of this book: the origin of this king is altogether similar to the

## IDENTIFICATION OF THE "LITTLE HORN" 83

horn of chapter viii, that is, from one of the four parts of Alexander's empire.

Compare the following passages:

| | |
|---|---|
| Chap. vii. 25. "He shall speak great words against the most High." | Chap. xi. 36. "He shall speak marvellous things against the God of gods." |
| vii. 25. He shall "think to change times and laws". | xi. 37. "Neither shall he regard the God of his father", etc. |
| vii. 21, 22. "The same horn prevailed until the time came that the saints possessed the kingdom." | xi. 36. "He shall prosper till the indignation be accomplished." |
| viii. 9. He waxed great "towards the pleasant land". | xi. 41. "He shall enter also into the glorious land." |
| viii. 17. "At the time of the end shall be the vision." | xi. 40. "And at the time of the end", etc. |
| viii. 19. "In the last end of the indignation." | xi. 36. "He shall prosper till the indignation be accomplished." |

The conclusion from all this appears to be inevitable, that the horn of chapter vii and that of chapter viii are one and the same person. If this be not the case, we have at the same time, within the same territorial limits and similarly described, two kings, alike in blasphemy and persecution, alike in claiming divine honours, alike in their almost unhindered course of evil. The non-identity of the two would involve difficulties of the greatest magnitude—so great that the supposition may be regarded as a moral impossibility. I believe that those who have considered that they are not one and the same have supposed that they were not marked as belonging to the same period: this, however, is utterly contradicted by the express statement of "the last end of the indignation" in this chapter, and by events which are detailed as following immediately on the destruction of the king in chapter xi.

But it has been sometimes asked (rather, I believe, in the way of difficulty than of objection), How can these powers be identical, for that in chapter vii springs out of one of the ten parts of the Roman earth, that before us from one of the four parts of the third empire? The answer to this is simple and, I believe, satisfactory: In chap. vii we see that the whole of the Roman earth is to be divided into *ten* kingdoms, these ten being found in its whole extent, the East as well as the West. The four parts of Alexander's empire formed a considerable portion of the eastern half of the Roman territory, and as we see here these four existent as kingdoms at the time of the end, it only follows that four kingdoms out of the ten will be identical with the parts into which the third empire was long ago divided. A horn springs out of one of these parts: it may be described in a general manner, as in chapter vii, as rising from one of the ten kingdoms, or else in a much more definite way, as in this chapter, in which we see even what part or direction of the Roman earth will give him his origin.

There appears to be a peculiar fitness in the way in which these things are presented in this chapter: the Medo-Persian power is first seen, and then the ground is cleared (so to speak) by the Grecian he goat; then that distributive form of the countries bordering upon the Holy Land, which came into existence after the death of Alexander, is mentioned. "The pleasant land" being the central object, there was no occasion for going beyond the countries with which that was *locally* connected; for here we have no statement about wideness of extent of dominion; it does not come at all into consideration; but it is the power as exercised in one place and over one people. The consideration that this is in the Hebrew portion of the book, and that chapter vii is in the Chaldee, tends to make the whole matter simple.

No one need find any difficulty in the idea of his being spoken of as springing from one of the ten parts of the

Roman earth, and here from one of the parts of Alexander's empire: every one would see how Simeon (for instance) might be described as one the twelve sons of Jacob, or as one of the six sons of Leah; the latter designation would be the more definite, but the sons of Leah would be all comprehended under the more general expression "sons of Jacob".

We may now consider particular statements which this chapter presents, both in the vision and the interpretation. In verse 23 the description of the condition of the kingdoms when this power arises is worthy of particular attention: "in the latter time of their kingdom *when the transgressors are come to the full*": these are solemn words—the line of demarcation between what is long past and what is yet future is found in the vision between verses 8 and 9, and in the interpretation between verses 22 and 23. The fullness of transgression belongs to a yet future period. These words do not state to what people, whether Jews or Gentiles, this description applies, but it surely must be regarded as a solemn, general statement of the condition of things which will immediately precede the advent of the Lord Jesus.

If we were to look backward at the history of past ages we should see scarcely a parallel to the wickedness found among Alexander's successors, and this whether they were looked at in themselves, or in their treatment of God's people, the Jews. But evil as these things have been, here is something yet more dreadful. God has given further light, and after this light has been received for awhile, it has been rejected. The countries once subject to Alexander have been used as the scene on which God has especially acted; those were the lands in the midst of which Israel was set as a witness for God; there it was that Christ, God's blessed Son, in due time appeared, was rejected and suffered: there by his command the gospel was first preached, and fruit was gathered from among Jews and Gentiles. Indeed, the record of the book of Acts (with the exception of the very end) simply narrates the preaching of the gospel within those limits.

We can compare the statements in 2 Tim. iii and similar passages with this expression, and thus we shall see how the fullness of transgression will come in amongst those, wherever they may be, who have in former times heard the gospel, but who have departed from the holy commandment delivered to them. As to Israel, we know that the closing scenes of their blindness will be the darkest scenes, "If another shall come in his own name, him ye will receive." They will not only be found as the rejectors of the Messiah, but also as the receivers of him who thus stands as the enemy of God, and blasphemer of His holy name. Thus on every side there will be the full accomplishment of transgression.

Verse 24: "His power shall be mighty, but not by his own power." Light is thrown, I judge, on this statement by Rev. xiii. 2: "The dragon gave him his power and his seat, and great authority." He acts by the power of Satan, and all the greatness that he displays is from this source. God at length shall send on men who have wilfully rejected this truth, "strong delusion that they should believe a lie". Satan's energies will be freed from many of those restraints which God now imposes; and then Gentile power will be found with this additional characteristic in the person of this king.

Verse 10: "It waxed great, even to the host of heaven; and it cast down some of the host and of the stars to the ground, and stamped upon them." This, we must remember, was a symbolic scene in vision: "the host of heaven" and "the stars" appear to me to be descriptive symbols of those whose portion from God is heavenly glory. Here they seem destroyed by the horn, but they bear a symbolic name, taken from what they are in God's purpose: we may compare chapter xii. 3, "They that be wise shall shine as the brightness of the firmament; and they that turn many to righteousness as the stars for ever and ever." If this refers simply to those who are Jews by nation (and this seems to be the case from the mention of "the pleasant land" immediately before), then it must apply to that portion of them who are not under that blindness which has *"in part* happened to Israel": it must belong to those whose calling is heavenly, as being believers in Him who is above at God's right hand.

Verse 11: "Yea, he magnified himself also to the prince of the host." Verse 25: "He shall also stand up against the Prince of princes." These statements may be well compared with what we read in Isa. xiv of the king of Babylon and his blasphemy; he takes the place which belongs to Christ and to Christ alone, and says in his heart, "I will ascend into heaven, I will exalt my throne above the stars of God: I will sit also upon the mount of the congregation, in the sides of the north: I will ascend above the heights of the clouds; I will be like the most High" (Isa. xiv. 13, 14).

The things stated about the connection of this horn with the daily sacrifice, in the eleventh and following verses, are obscure; but there are some points on which remark may be made, rather in the way of suggestion than in that of teaching.

From the mention of "the daily sacrifice" and the "sanctuary" it is plain that at part of the actings of the horn these things will be found in existence—a portion of the Jews will have returned in unbelief to their own land, and the worship of God will be attempted to be carried on according to the Mosaic ritual. This horn takes away the daily sacrifice and casts down the place of the sanctuary; this apparently implies that he desecrates it to other purposes. From verse 12 it appears as if God gave up these things into his hand as not owning or acknowledging the worship so rendered, "by reason of transgression", and then the opposition of the horn to the truth, and its practising and prospering, are especially mentioned.

It appears that in the history of this horn there are various points or stages of narration to be observed; the particular point to be noticed is the difference between what *precedes* and what follows the taking away of the daily sacrifice; when that is done his blasphemous position becomes the more marked, as well as his acting in persecution.

In verses 13 and 14 we find the prophet listening to certain inquiries: one holy one speaks and asks, "How long shall be the vision concerning the daily sacrifice and the transgression of desolation, to give both the sanctuary and the host to be trodden under foot?" And he said *unto me* [this is remarkable, the answer is made *to Daniel* and not the inquirer], "Unto two thousand and three hundred days, [evenings, mornings,] and then shall the sanctuary be cleansed" [justified or vindicated]. This term of 2,300*

---

* Some writers on prophecy have, in their explanations or interpretations of this vision, adopted the reading "two thousand and *four* hundred days", and in vindication of it they have referred to the common printed copies of the LXX version. In this book, however, the translation of Theodotion has been long substituted for the real LXX: and further, although "two thousand *four* hundred" is found in the common printed Greek copies, that is merely an erratum made in printing the Vatican edition of 1586, which has been habitually perpetuated. I looked [in 1845] at the passage in *the* Vatican MS, which the Roman edition professedly followed, and it reads exactly the same as the Hebrew text; so also does the *real* LXX of Daniel. [So too Cardinal Mai's edition from the Vatican MS which appeared in 1857.]

recurrences of the morning and evening sacrifice appears to me to relate to the whole period of this horn's connection with it; during, first of all, the time in which, as found in other Scriptures (see in "Remarks on the Seventy Heptads, Daniel ix"), it is carried on as upheld and sanctioned by him, and also during the "time, times and a half" (three years and a half) in which he will directly and avowedly oppose God and all worship rendered to Him.

The expression "transgression of desolation" is not to be passed over without notice, for it is the first of the varied mentions made in the book of Daniel of that "abomination of desolation" to which our Lord refers us in Matthew xxiv.

In the explanation in verse 26 all the further light given to Daniel about this latter part of the vision is a confirmation of its truth and certainty: "and the vision of the evening and the morning which was told is true: wherefore shut thou up the vision: for it shall be for many days".

The conclusion of the history of the "king of fierce countenance" is briefly this—"he shall stand up also against the Prince of princes, *but he shall be broken without hand*" (verse 25). These latter words appear to be intended to call back our minds to the description which we had given us in chap. ii of the destruction of the fabric of Gentile power by a stone cut out of a mountain without hands. That stone is "the Prince of the kings of the earth, the first born from the dead", the Lord of all glory; although the power of the enemy in blasphemy goes on long, it reaches its highest point, and the personal interference of the Lord Christ in judgment closes the scene and new things are introduced. "When the wicked spring as the grass, and when all the workers of iniquity do flourish, it is that they shall be destroyed for ever" (Ps. xcii. 7).

We find then in this chapter—

First, the rise of the Grecian power on the ruins of the Medo-Persian. This gives us the territorial platform of the vision.

Second, the Grecian kingdom in a state of fourfold division.

Third, this fourfold division existing as a thing yet future, at the time of the last end of the indignation, and then another king rises from one of the divided parts.

Fourth, this king acts in blasphemy against God, in persecution against His saints, in tyranny and destructive power over Israel.

Fifth, he stands up against the Prince of princes, and is destroyed by the direct action of God's power.

We must not leave unnoticed the effect which this vision had upon the mind of the prophet: "And I Daniel fainted, and was sick certain days; afterwards I rose up, and did the king's business; and I was astonished at the vision, but none understood it."

The vision appeared as one which held forth a sad prospect for Daniel's people: here were these sorrows to be endured in future ages. It is true that, inferentially, a point of bright hope might be discovered, for these things belonged to "the *last end* of the indignation". Beyond, then, all that other prophets had spoken of, blessing and grace must lie in a bright perspective. But Daniel was confounded at the intervening sorrows; his soul had not been as yet sustained (as we know that it afterwards was) to look through and beyond the sorrow and thus to see the exceeding brightness of the the distant glories.

The place in which we are set is indeed one of many privileges: God looks on His whole redeemed people as one body, "the heir". While in a state of nonage, i.e. before Christ came, the Spirit was not given as He now is, as the Spirit of sonship, and as the leader of God's children into the apprehension of all the truth which is revealed to us in the word. It is our place to enter into God's revealed counsels and to see that He is making everything tend onward to the glory of Christ: every portion of truth will have unction for our souls, if we can see it as connected with Him.

In a vision like the present it is true that we have mostly a narrative of evil; but it is our place to see it where it is set in God's counsels. We have not to faint or be astonished like Daniel, but to have our souls so filled with the knowledge of Christ, and what God's purposes of grace are, as to know assuredly that every intervening hindrance will only tend to its more full and glorious display. Opposition to Christ, and the working of Satan, will reach to a head, and then the Lord, taking the power into His own hand, will be manifested as the King of Israel, as well as being our Head; then will the indignation be accomplished, and the remnant of Jacob will return to "the mighty God", and Jerusalem, the holy city of the great King, will indeed be made "a praise in the earth".*

---

\* I may refer the reader who wishes for further examination into Scripture testimonies concerning the person denoted by the horn in this chapter to a tract of mine entitled *The Man of Sin*, and also to *Prospects of the Ten Kingdoms of the Roman Empire*, by B. W. Newton, and to *Aids to Prophetic Inquiry*, by B. W. Newton (Sovereign Grace Advent Testimony).

# THE SEVENTY HEPTADS (DANIEL IX)

THE soul of a saint always finds establishment when it can truly repose upon the revealed will of God, when, amid the conflict of human thoughts and human actions, it can be brought simply to "God and the word of his grace". Those who are not so reposing may only look at the storm, but those who, like Paul in the tossed vessel, have had the word of God brought home to their ear can take courage themselves and rely upon the promise of safety even for the guidance of others.

This gives prophecy a peculiar value to the soul of the instructed Christian—he thus is warned of the coming events; but though he sees them he is not cast down, for he knows the issue beforehand. Our present calling is to walk in the midst of human things in the full practical recognition of the glories which have been made known to us as belonging to us in Christ our head, above at God's right hand. Prophecy has been bestowed on us in order that we may know how, in the midst of confusion and the varied forms of Satan's working, we may stand and act as those who belong to Christ. We know as a simple fact how the Church has greatly overlooked this important portion of God's revealed truth. We know also how the enemy has sought to cast a kind of discredit upon every effort which is made either for any to understand and use prophecy themselves, or to give instruction to others therein. But this, instead of leading us to overlook this precious deposit of God's truth, ought to make us the more earnest in not neglecting that which is so important.

If discredit be cast upon such investigation it ought to cause us to look the more to the God of all grace, that He may vouchsafe to us the teaching of His Spirit that so we may use it aright.

In considering the ninth chapter of Daniel we see at once the value which previous prophecy possessed in his soul. He had been favoured with many direct communications from God, but here we find him using the prophecy which had been given through Jeremiah as the ground of his confession and prayer. "In the first year of Darius, I Daniel understood by books the number of the years, whereof the word of the Lord came to Jeremiah the prophet, that he would accomplish seventy years in the desolations of Jerusalem." The "books" to which Daniel refers were apparently the letters which Jeremiah had written to the captives in Babylon (Jer. xxix. 10), as well as his other mention of "seventy years" (xxv. 11). The date does not commence from the destruction in the reign of Zedekiah, but from the former part of the captivity, when those persons to whom Jeremiah's letter was addressed were carried away to Babylon.\*

It is interesting to see how Daniel connected hope resting upon promise with prophecy: the hope was that the captives should return from Babylon; but instead of this being vaguely held he used the intelligence which God had given him through prophecy, so that he hoped confidently, while waiting for God's time before appointed, for the hope to be accomplished. The knowledge of the detail connected with these things brought his soul into a healthy condition before God as to the exercise of his conscience about these matters.

---

\* "Thus saith the Lord, that after seventy years be accomplished at Babylon, I will visit you, and perform my good word toward you, in causing you to return to this place" (Jer. xxix. 10).

And so, surely, the Spirit always teaches: we may either follow our speculations about the things which God has revealed, or else have our ears open to hear all His instruction: the latter is our only safeguard against speculation. Happy is that believer who holds what God has revealed, in dependence upon His grace, and the power of His Spirit, to enable him to use it aright.

But the mind of Daniel did not merely lay hold of the fact of the restoration of his people; this was, indeed, an object of hope, but he saw God, and the working of God in the matter: he saw God as the one who had laid on them this punishment of captivity, as the one who had promised to bring them back, and as the one who had a mind concerning the whole.

And very solemn were the thoughts of the prophet when his heart was thus brought before God: he saw the faithfulness of God in those things which told of judgment, for here was the proof—that they were in Babylon; and thus he was led to what God had said about restoration from captivity in the very places which in the Law of Moses denounced that punishment, Lev. xxvi. 40, etc.: "If they shall *confess* their iniquity, and the iniquity of their fathers, with their trespass which they have trespassed against me, and that also they have walked contrary unto me; and that I also have walked contrary unto them, and have brought them into the land of their enemies; if then their uncircumcised hearts be humbled, and they then accept the punishment of their iniquity: then will I remember my covenant with Jacob, and also my covenant with Isaac, and also my covenant with Abraham will I remember; and I will remember the land." So too in Deut. xxx repentance is spoken of as that which God calls for as the prerequisite to His bringing back His people to their land. These promises of course belong, in their full application, to the future and final deliverance and restoration of Israel; but we find the principle of them taken up and used by Daniel. With regard to the return after the seventy years, God had distinctly said that the fulfilment of His absolute promise should be preceded by prayer: "Then shall ye call upon me, and ye shall go and pray unto me, and I will hearken unto you. . . . And I will be found of you, saith the Lord; and I will turn away your captivity", etc. (Jer. xxix. 12–14). God had promised to end the Babylonish captivity in seventy years; God had also said that repentance and the confession of their sin, and the sin of their fathers, were prerequisites. Daniel, instead of seeing these things in opposition to each other, looked at the seeming condition, not as taking away from the certainty of the promise, but rather as stating what God Himself would work and provide. He relies upon the promise of God, and doing this he takes himself the place of confession and humiliation; he makes confession of the sin of all Israel, their fathers, their kings, and all; he consents to the righteous judgment of God in all that He had wrought, and thus, as it were, on behalf of all Israel "accepts the punishment of their iniquity". He pleads with God to work on behalf of his people, and his land, and Jerusalem the holy city, for His own name's sake— that he would *now* show his faithfulness at the close of the seventy years, in ending the captivity: "O Lord, hear; O Lord, forgive; O Lord, hearken and do; defer not, for thine own sake, O my God; for thy city and thy people are called by thy name."

Full of blessed instruction as all the former portion of this chapter is, I am only now regarding it as introductory to the response on God's part to the prayer of the prophet. In verses 20, 21, we find that the angel Gabriel was forthwith sent forth to the prophet—"O Daniel, I am now come to give thee skill and understanding" (verse 22). We find at the end of chapter viii that the vision had not been understood; but now the teaching from God assumes a different form. God gives the instruction by direct statement, and not by symbol which required interpretation. It is also well to observe that the symbolic visions in this book and their interpretations do not run exactly parallel to each other; each presents certain features which are omitted in the other, and each helps to give definiteness and consistency to the truth taught.

Verse 23: "At the beginning of thy supplication the commandment came forth; and I am come to show thee; for thou art greatly beloved": the margin has here "a man *of desires*", whence some have questioned whether it refers to the desire on Daniel's part to know the things, or to the desires being on God's part towards him: it is clear from the form of the word that the latter is correct. "Therefore understand the matter and consider the vision."

The following verses of the chapter contain the prophetic part of the vision: much is comprised in them, but the things spoken of are stated so concisely that they require very particular attention.

Daniel had made inquiry about seventy *years* of the captivity in Babylon; the answer speaks also of seventy periods, which in our English translation are called "weeks"; the word, however, does not necessarily mean seven *days*, but a period of seven parts: of course it is much more often used in speaking of a week than of anything else, because nothing is so often mentioned as a week which is similarly divided. The Hebrews, however, used a septenary scale as to time, just as habitually as we should reckon by tens; the sabbatical years, the jubilees, all tended to give this thought a permanent place in their minds. The denomination here is to be taken from the subject of Daniel's prayer; he prayed about years, he is answered about periods of seven years, i.e. the recurrence of sabbatical years.

His prayer had related to the deliverance of Israel from their then captivity, the reply goes much farther: for it sets out, not from the release of the people, but from the edict to restore and to build Jerusalem, and it reaches through events of varied kinds, until the absolute and established blessing on the ground of righteousness and forgiveness is brought in.

I will now give the verses from the 24th to the end, departing in some places from our English translation, together with remarks interspersed; and the whole prophecy may be considered in detail. I retain the word "week" for convenience' sake, and not as implying seven days to be the import of the Hebrew word.*

Verse 24: "Seventy weeks have been determined (more strictly, 'divided') upon thy people and upon thy holy city, to finish the transgression, and to make an end of sins, and to make reconciliation for iniquity, and to bring in everlasting righteousness, and to seal vision and prophet, and to anoint the holy of holies." (This expression is used in no other place as signifying a person, nor ought it, I believe, to be so taken here.)

Verse 25: "Know then and understand, from the issuing of the decree to restore and to build Jerusalem unto Messiah the Prince (shall be) seven weeks, and threescore and two weeks: the street shall be again built, and the trench (or scarped rampart), even in pressure of times" (i.e. in times of straitness or pressure).

Verse 26: "And after the threescore and two weeks

* See the Note on the "Year-day System", below, p. 111.

shall Messiah be cut off, and there shall be nothing for Him; and the city and the sanctuary shall the people destroy of a prince who shall come; and his end shall be in the overflowing; and until the end (there is) war (even) that which is determined for desolations."

Verse 27: "And he (the prince who shall come) shall confirm a covenant with the many (or with the multitude) for one week; and at half the week he shall cause sacrifice and offering to cease; and upon the wing (or pinnacle) of abominations (shall be) that which causeth desolation, even until the consummation, and that determined shall be poured upon the causer of desolation."

Here, then, we have the objects of hope placed first, just as we find in the Psalms and so many other portions of prophetic Scripture: the soul is first set in the place of strength by the apprehension of the blessings which are to be brought about; and then the intermediate trials become subjects of prophetic instruction.

In verse 24 the expression "are determined" is more strictly "are divided"; this may relate to the seventy weeks being a period of time divided out, as it were, from the whole course of ages, for God to deal in a particular manner with the Jews and Jerusalem; or it may refer to the period being itself divided into parts, as we see in the verses which follow.

Daniel in his prayer, in addressing God, had constantly spoken of Israel as "thy people", "thy holy city", etc.; but the angel Gabriel in the reply takes them up simply as Daniel's people—"thy people, thy holy city", etc.—as though God would intimate that until the everlasting righteousness should be brought in, He could not in the full sense own them as His.

The various things spoken of "to finish the transgression, to make an end of sins, to make reconciliation for iniquity, and to bring in everlasting righteousness", are all, I believe, future. I do not regard any of them as referring strictly to the work of Christ upon the cross (although we, as believers in Him, know that many of these things have a blessed application to us), but it rather appears to me that they all belong to the time of Israel's blessing, when the preciousness of the blood of Christ shall be *applied* to those "who are spared of them": when "thou shalt call me my Father; and shalt not turn away from me" (Jer. iii. 19).

I believe that "to seal vision and prophet" means this —to give the seal of confirmation to the vision by the issue of events as predicted; and in the same manner to confirm the prophet by the fulfilment of those things which God has spoken through him.

The expression "to anoint the most holy" (or rather "holy of holies") has often been taken, as I am well aware, as referring to our blessed Lord; this I believe to be an erroneous application of the words: the expression does not in a single case in any other passage apply to any person, but always to the most holy place of the tabernacle or temple, or else to things such as sacrifices which were "most holy". Here I believe that it simply refers to the most holy place, the sanctuary of God, which in the days of Israel's blessing will be set apart and owned by God as peculiarly His. "My tabernacle also shall be with them; yea, I will be their God, and they shall be my people. And the heathen shall know that I the Lord do sanctify Israel, when my sanctuary shall be in the midst of them for evermore" (Ezek. xxxvii. 27, 28).

These, then, are the objects of hope—circumstances which will be brought to pass when the seventy weeks have run to their termination. The point from which they commence is next stated: "from the issuing of the decree to restore and to build Jerusalem". This is not the decree of Cyrus (Ezra i. 1), for that was simply to build the house of the Lord God of Israel in Jerusalem; neither was it the decree given to Ezra by Artaxerxes in the seventh year of his reign (Ezra vii), for that related to the worship of God, etc.; but it evidently must be the decree given to Nehemiah in the twentieth year of the same Artaxerxes in the month Nisan. This last is the only decree which we find recorded in Scripture which relates to the restoring and building of the city. It must be borne in mind that the very existence of a place *as a city* depended upon such a decree, for before that, any who returned from the land of captivity were only in the condition of sojourners; it was the decree that gave them a recognised and distinct political existence.*

\* *On the 20th of Artaxerxes.*—Some have found a difficulty in making out the chronology of the seventy weeks, because they have thought that the time from the 20th of Artaxerxes to the crucifixion of our Lord would not fully accord with that marked out in the prophecy. If it had been so, it need have surprised no one; whatever be the result of chronological calculations, the word of God is the same; we know that it is certain, and everything else must bend to it.

But here I believe the difficulty to be wholly imaginary. It is true that we may find some from the date pointed in the margin of our Bibles; but the history of this date, as it there stands, is rather curious. Archbishop Ussher drew up a scheme of Chronology which is commonly followed, rather from convenience than from its absolute correctness being supposed. About a hundred and fifty years ago Bishop Lloyd undertook to affix Archbishop Ussher's dates to our English Bibles; but, *in this instance*, he made a considerable alteration and substituted another date of his own, so as to adapt the reign of Artaxerxes to his own theory.

The date which stands in our Bibles for the 20th of Artaxerxes is 446 B.C.—this makes the commencement of his reign 465 B.C.; but the authority of the best and most nearly contemporary historian will put the matter in a very different light. Thucydides mentions that the accession of Artaxerxes had taken place before the flight of Themistocles; this authorises us to adopt Ussher's date and to place the commencement of the reign 473 or 474 B.C. This would give the date of 454 or 455 B.C. If we add to this the date of the crucifixion it will just give us the exact period of the sixty-nine weeks. In doing this we must remember that the birth of our Lord was about four years before the common era, so that the thirty-third year of His life, when He is supposed to have suffered, would correspond with the year twenty-nine of our reckoning. I believe this to

The twentieth of Artaxerxes gives us a starting point from which the reckoning of the seventy weeks begins; we have next to pay attention to the manner in which this period is divided into distinct parts. Two portions of the time are first spoken of—"From the issuing of the decree to restore and to build Jerusalem unto Messiah the Prince, shall be seven weeks, and threescore and two weeks": i.e. two periods, the one forty-nine years, the other four hundred and thirty-four years; the whole period of the four hundred and ninety years being included, except seven years.

---

have been the true date; first because of the day of the week on which the passover commenced in that year; and also, because of the consuls of that year (the two Gemini) having been mentioned by several writers as those of the year when our Lord was put to death.

This remark does not affect the instruction given us by God in this chapter; it is a point which I only notice for the removal of difficulties.

It is great pity that Archbishop Ussher's date should in this particular have been misrepresented: it was a point to which he had paid particular attention. About the year 1613 he lectured on the subject at Trinity College, Dublin, resting on the testimony of Thucydides. He then discussed difficulties connected with the supposed length of the reigns of Darius and Xerxes so as to adapt other events to this certain date. From October 1615 he corresponded at various times on the point with Thomas Lydiat (the scholar most familiar with such subjects of any in England), until 1643; and in 1650, after thirty-seven years of minute consideration, he published the result in his *Annales Veteris Testamenti*, where the date is 3531. This answers in Ussher's *Collatio Annorum* to 474 B.C., or the third year of the seventy-*sixth* Olympiad. His judgment in 1613 seems to have been doubtful; but in 1617 he says, "These things being laid together do show, that the expulsion of Themistocles from Athens fell no later than the beginning of the fourth year of the seventy-sixth Olympiad; to which time you (i.e. Lydiat) doubtfully refer the beginning of his troubles; how much sooner soever, my opinion is, that at that time Themistocles fled into Persia, as Eusebius noteth, whose testimony I have no reason to discredit, unless I have some better testimony or reason to oppose against it. The year before that, which is the third of the seventy-sixth Olympiad, I suppose Artaxerxes Longimanus to have begun his reign: to whom, as yet νεωστὶ βασιλεύοντα, Themistocles fled, as Thucydides sufficiently proveth" (*Works*, xv, p. 111).

Ussher in thus laying down this date had no motive for bringing the space of 483 years from the 20th of Artaxerxes to A.D. 29; for his division of the seventy Heptads differs from mine, and he did not regard A.D. 29 as the date of the crucifixion of our Lord.

There is next added, "the street shall be built again, and the scarped rampart, even in pressure of times"; then follows, "and after the threescore and two weeks", etc. Hence it is clear that the whole period from the decree to Messiah the Prince is four hundred and eighty-three years, and that forty-nine of these years are appropriated to something peculiar; the only thing so mentioned has been the building of the street, rampart, etc.—these things are, I judge, to be allotted to the first division of the time, namely, forty-nine years.

Some have thought that this same interpretation was supported by the expression "in pressure of times", which they would render "in the shorter space of time"—a rendering wholly destitute of ground, only supported indeed by its supposed fitness in this place. I quite agree with the explanation which allots the first forty-nine years to these events, but I could not support it by any such supposed rendering.

But it may be asked, What is the evidence that forty-nine years were spent in the restoration of the city? I answer, I believe it to have been so, simply on the authority of this passage; no other portion of Scripture says anything about the length of time, and here forty-nine years are mentioned, and also the restoration of the city is so placed in juxtaposition that they appear clearly to belong together.

Verse 26: "And after the threescore and two weeks, shall Messiah be cut off"; this period is marked by the definite article as identical with the threescore and two weeks of the preceding verse. The four hundred and eighty-three years from the issuing of the decree run on "to Messiah the Prince"; it becomes then important to inquire to what part of our Lord's earthly path the reference is made. He was "born King of the Jews", but this appears to be something more than the mere title: now, the only time in which we find the Lord Jesus taking this title in the presence of Jerusalem was six days before He suffered, when He came thither on the ass's colt; He was then presented as King, and six days afterwards was put to death as the King of the Jews. I should regard the limit "unto Messiah the *Prince*" as reaching on to His having been thus presented to Jerusalem. It is worthy of remark that the decree of Artaxerxes was issued in the month Nisan, the very month in which the passover was kept, and in which our Lord both rode into Jerusalem and was crucified.

I should not thus consider the expression "*After* the threescore and two weeks" as implying an interval; but rather as being just the same as "at the end of the sixty-two weeks", "when they are accomplished".

The words which stand in our English version, "but not for Himself", have often been taken as if they spoke of the vicarious character of our Saviour's suffering; this would however be, I believe, placing a most true and important doctrine upon an insufficient basis. I believe that the words simply imply, "and there shall be nothing for Him"—He will be rejected, and His earthly kingdom will be a thing on which He will not then enter.

The series of years has run on unhinderedly from the issuing of the edict to the cutting off of Messiah; but at this part of the vision there are various events spoken of before the one remaining week comes into notice at all. "And the city and the sanctuary shall the people destroy of a prince who shall come." This refers, I have no doubt, to the destruction of Jerusalem by the Romans; as was also foretold by our Lord in Luke xxi, "When ye see Jerusalem compassed about with armies, then know that the desolation thereof is nigh." This destruction is here said to be wrought by a certain people; not by the prince who shall come, but by his people. This refers us, I believe, to the Romans as the last holders of undivided Gentile power: they wrought the destruction long ages ago. The prince who shall come is the last head of the Roman power, the person concerning whom Daniel had received so much previous instruction. It is most important to attend to the exact words of the passage; it is thus that we avoid the mistake of confounding the people and the prince who afterwards springs up.

"And his end shall be in the overflowing": I suppose that this speaks of the end of the prince who shall come; in the expression "the overflowing" allusion seems to be made to some known event in prophecy; I suppose that it is the same overflowing as that which is alluded to in Isa. x. 22 and xxviii. 18. This would identify the time of this prince with the crisis of Israel's history; this identification is (as we shall see) yet more decidedly brought out in the subsequent part of the vision.

The interval up to "the end" is only characterised by war and desolations; just so our Lord teaches us in Matt. xxiv, "Nation shall rise against nation, and kingdom against kingdom." The expression "that which is determined" appears to be taken up from Isa. x. 23.

The vision gives us no intimation about the times of events which belong to the interval—we only find at the cutting off of Messiah, one seven years is unaccomplished; this "reserved week", as some have aptly called it, belongs to the time of the prince who shall come.

Verse 27: "And he (the prince who shall come) shall confirm a covenant with the many for one week." In "Remarks on Chapter viii" (pp. 75-76) I sought to show that the horn spoken of in the two chapters is identical, and here he again appears to come before us; in fact, the allusion seems to be made to known circumstances about him. He makes a covenant with the multitude; that of course means the multitude of Daniel's people, they are leagued with him and he with them. This takes place three years and a half before he causes sacrifice and oblation to cease, hence it is clear that they go on as under his patronage for some time. This will, I believe, throw some light upon the two thousand three hundred days mentioned in chapter viii. 14. We find him here making a covenant for one seven years, then breaking it at the end of three years and a half; and the removal of sacrifice, etc, is so spoken of as to connect it with the breaking of the covenant. This tends, I think, to show that one thing done in pursuance of this covenant had been the establishment of the temple worship. The period of two thousand three hundred days is a few months short of the whole term of the seven years, enough being not included, it may be, to be allotted for those preparations which will be needful for the worship to be set up; then follows the time during which it is carried on under his auspices, and then follow three years and a half of distinct persecuting and blasphemous power.

The character of this period of three years and a half is to be specially gathered from chapter vii, in which mention is made of "a time, times, and a half", and also from the forty and two months, 1,260 days, etc., which are spoken of in the book of Revelation.

The identity of the time, times, and a half, of chapter vii, with the last half week of this chapter, might almost be taken for granted; the proof, however, is simple: the horn in chapter vii acts in blasphemy and persecution until the Lord Jesus and His people take the kingdom;

the three years and a half run on to that point; here in this chapter the whole period of seventy weeks issues in the absolute and established blessing of Israel, Daniel's people—the week of this covenant is the last portion of the seventy weeks, and the half week after the sacrifice is taken away is the latter portion of that week. Thus the period in chapter vii and the concluding period before us run on to the same point, they are also equal in duration; hence they begin at the same time and are altogether identical. If we would form a just estimate of the events of the last half week we must gather it from chapter vii.: here we have the same power in its local connection with Jerusalem.

The seventy weeks when distributed into portions will then stand thus:

I. From the edict to the building of the wall, etc. . . 49 years
II. From the building to Messiah the Prince, and his cutting off . . . . . . . . . 434 ,,
[Then an interval of unmarked length.]
III. The period of the covenant of "the prince that shall come" . . . . . . . . 7 ,,

One of the blessings spoken of in verse 24 had been "to finish the transgression"; this may be suitably compared with the expression in chapter viii, "when the transgressors are come to the full".

"And upon the wing of abominations [shall be] that which causeth desolation." The phraseology of this passage is rather obscure, but I believe that this is the meaning of the words. "The transgression of desolation" had been mentioned in the previous vision. This appears to be a reference to what had been there said —there is further elucidation to be obtained from what we find in the subsequent vision—but all these passages have a solemn interest and importance for us, when we remember what our Saviour said in Matt. xxiv, "When ye see the abomination of desolation, spoken of by Daniel the prophet, stand in the Holy place; whoso readeth, let him understand", then do so and so.

"The Holy place" is that in which this abomination will be set; this of course means the temple of God at Jerusalem. This place was once honoured by His manifested presence; and, little as God can own or recognise the worship which the Jews may offer there in unbelief, whether in times past or future, yet the place is that which He looks upon as one with which His own honour is greatly connected: it is the Holy place still. An abomination, in Scripture language, signifies an idol—that on account of which God brings in desolation. This idol appears to be set in some most conspicuous place, the wing or pinnacle, which is thence called "the wing of abominations". Our Lord speaks of "the Holy place" as that in which the abomination of desolation is set—the place is here termed "the wing of abominations"—in the one case, the place is regarded according to the thoughts of God; in the other, according to the actings of man, in matured evil against God.

These things—the cessation of sacrifice, and that which causeth desolation standing on the pinnacle—continue "even until the consummation and that determined shall be poured upon the causer of desolation". The expression "the consummation and that determined" is quoted from Isa. x. 22, 23. This connection is one of great interest; for on the one hand the return of the remnant of Jacob to the mighty God is spoken of, and on the other, faith is encouraged not to be afraid of the terrible power of Asshur.

In rendering the concluding word by "the causer of desolation" I believe that I follow the true sense of the original. I am quite aware that the verb, the participle of which is here employed, is used sometimes in a neuter, and at other times in an active, sense; sometimes implying that which is made desolate, at others that which occasions the desolation. I believe that the former of these is the more common, but the latter is proved, I think, to be its sense in this connection, by chapter xii. 11, where it is clear that the abomination that *maketh* desolate is spoken of, and not anything which has been *made* desolate.

It is indeed remarkable to see how Daniel was confided with the counsels of God in these things; the response to his prayer gave him instruction as to far deeper truths. *He* only thought of the past iniquity of his people, *God* thought of a deeper iniquity when they will receive one who comes in His own name, after Messiah has been rejected; when He makes a covenant with them, and it issues in awful idolatry. Grace and faithfulness would have been displayed in bringing the people back from Babylon, but how much more would God manifest these things when they stand in contrast to the ripened iniquity of man as found in Jerusalem! It was Daniel's place to look at all these things and to learn God in them, to see Him as above the whole, and to apprehend something of what the full manifestation of this grace will be, and what the blessings in store for Jerusalem and for Israel are, when the seventy weeks have run their course. This might in some measure enable Daniel to enter into God's mind; and we must remember that Gabriel was expressly sent to give him skill and understanding.

These seventy weeks appear to me to relate to the period of God's defined dealings with the city of Jerusalem and the people there, from the time when it should be reconstituted *as a city*, and onward. At the cutting off of Messiah the recognition ends; then comes the interval, and the time is again taken up for one week at the close. There is one thing relative to this subject which it appears to me to be desirable to notice, though not exactly connected with the chapter. Some have thought from such an interval being found here, and from the Church having become a constituted body upon earth just at the end of the sixty-ninth week, that it was no longer found on earth when the interval is past and the seventieth begins. Nothing about the matter can be found from the vision, the Church not being mentioned in it.

But other parts of Daniel throw abundant light upon the matter; the horn of chapter vii wears out the saints of the most high places, until the coming of the Son of Man and the taking of the kingdom; in fact, the time of their being persecuted is the same three years and a half as the last portion of time before us here.

But the whole question is rendered perfectly simple by such statements of the New Testament as "Let both grow together until the harvest" (Matt. xiii. 30). Thus there will be both tares and wheat upon this earth till then; true believers in Christ, and others who put on the semblance or profession, until the end of the age.

Also, "blindness in part hath happened unto Israel until the fulness of the Gentiles be come in; and so all Israel shall be saved" (Rom. xi. 25, 26). The issue stated in this passage is the same as that of the vision before us, namely, the established blessing of Daniel's people. That blindness in part which was upon them when the Apostle Paul wrote, and which is upon them still, will remain until the fullness of the Gentiles, those whom God by His grace converts from among the Gentiles, shall have been brought in. And then what follows?

The salvation of all Israel. If we suppose the Church to be taken away before the time of "the prince who shall come" of this chapter, then we must say that Israel's deepest and most awful blindness, instead of being until the coming in of the fullness of the Gentiles, is after it is completed altogether.

I do not go into more elaborate evidence as to this point: I merely suggest a few simple facts. I only add that our Lord, in His use of the prophecy of Daniel and His whole teaching in Matt. xxiv, assumes that some of His beloved Church will continue to be cared for as His sheep upon earth, until He comes in manifested glory, until He destroys *"that* wicked" with the breath of his mouth.

Some may think these observations on this point to be mere digression—I think so myself, and I only add them because of statements having been not only connected with the ninth of Daniel, but even based upon it, statements which have no relation whatever to the contents of the chapter.

It is remarkable to observe the difference between the manner in which God reveals truth, and that in which man would seek to gain knowledge. Those things which God reveals are not only profitable themselves, but the manner also in which they are presented is for profit. This we shall do well to bear in mind in reading God's word: it is easy for us to get out minds informed about truth and to hold it apart from God; but what we have to seek is that our hearts and consciences may be so exercised by all we read of God's revealed counsels that we may have deeper apprehensions of grace and learn more of the glories of Jesus our Lord.

# NOTE ON THE "YEAR-DAY SYSTEM"

MANY have adopted a principle of interpretation with regard to designations of time, when they are found in prophecy, to which they have given the name of "the year-day system". This principle is that in such prophetic designations of time the literal meaning must not be held, but that in all expressions of periods of time in future events a *day* stands as the representative of a *year*, and all other spaces of time in similar proportion.

There are not a few who hold this as an opinion so established in their minds that they regard it as an undoubted truth, without knowing definitely on what grounds it was adopted; they speak of a *prophetic* day or a *prophetic* year as if it were an axiom that these expressions denote the one a literal *year*, and the other a term of three hundred and sixty literal *years*.

On this principle they would interpret the designations of time in the book of Daniel and in the Revelation; they thus speak of the 1,260 *years* and the 2,300 *years*. Of course, if we find distinct Scripture warrant for this assumed canon we must bow to it, and interpret accordingly. But if this canon is supposed to be a deduction from Scripture, let us examine whether the inference be legitimate, and let the reception or the rejection depend on the grounds of proof.

It is not, I believe, stated by any that this canon is a subject of direct teaching in Scripture, at least none of the points advanced seem to be relied on as showing this; some of the maintainers of the system expressly repudiate such a thought, for instance Mr. Conder says:

"The application of the year-day principle to the prophecy would, *a priori*, have been incapable of proof, and might seem scarcely compatible with probability" (*Literary History of the New Testament*, p. 585). And to this he subjoins the following note:

"It is admitted that, for the first four centuries, the days mentioned in the prophecies of Daniel and in the Apocalypse were interpreted literally by the Fathers of the Church; but from the fifth to the twelfth century, a mystical meaning came to be attached to the period of 1,260 days, though not the true one. At the close of the fourteenth century, Walter Brute first suggested the *year-day* interpretation, which was fully espoused by the Magdeburg Centuriators, and applied to the Papacy (Elliott, vol. ii, pp. 965-972). That the true solution of the enigma should not have occurred to the earlier writers, is not surprising. It was not intended, and was scarcely possible, that it should be shown, *a priori*, that such was the principle of interpretation. As Mr. Elliott remarks, while the period was yet distant, a moral purpose was answered by a temporary veil of mystery being thrown over the prophetic period; for the Church was not to know the times and seasons, that she might be kept from the earliest age in the attitude of watchful expectation. It was accordingly, not till the time drew near, that the solution of the chronological enigma began to be perceived. Nor does it form any objection to its truth, that the *a priori* evidence scarcely amounts to a probability, when the *a posteriori* demonstration is all but irresistible. It seems to be the divine intention that the discovery of the prophetic mystery should wait upon the facts, not anticipate them."

Some, who have received the year-day principle without inquiry, will be surprised at these admissions of the weakness of the *a priori* evidence by which it is upheld; others may think that too much is surrendered. At all events, however, it must be owned that this canon of interpretation is not known as an intuitive truth; the early Church knew no such axiom; and therefore I hold that it should be shown to be either laid down in Scripture or else that it should be *proved thereby*, before any one can be expected to receive it, and before it is applied to the interpretation of prophetic statements.

In the quotation just given I do not suppose that anything irreverent was *intended* in saying that "a moral purpose was answered by a temporary veil of mystery being thrown over the prophetic period"; but surely such ideas and expressions should be avoided. It is by *truth* that God teaches His people, and thus we can never attribute to Him the accomplishment of a moral purpose by that which would be a virtual deception. He may produce a moral effect by leaving us uninformed as to many things; but this is wholly different from such an effect being wrought by positively false conclusions and opinions occupying the mind. Where Scripture is silent, we know nothing as to God's truth, and this silence may accomplish a moral purpose; but where the Scripture speaks to us, how can it be according to God's mind and appointment that a moral purpose should be answered by our thoroughly misunderstanding it, by its being for ages a delusive light? Scripture may mislead the *rejecters* of truth, but God can never have designed that it should direct His people wrongly: had He done this, He would have made the reverse of truth profitable to their souls. If it is right that we should *now* understand the designations of time in prophecy, it was equally right from the earliest period of the gathering of the Church. Unless the Scripture taught, as a fact, that God had drawn such a veil, I would not believe it; and if I thus learned that a veil existed, I would not believe that it had been withdrawn, unless I had distinct proof to that effect. To do otherwise would be to assume the existence of some other depository of God's truth beside the treasury of holy Scripture. Observe, I do not say that Scripture truth on various points may not have been misunderstood, and that for long ages; this is wholly different from maintaining that God laid *over His Scripture*, from the first, a veil of mystery. *Our* hearts are dull of apprehension, so that they constantly need the teaching of the Spirit of God; the Scripture itself is the recorded testimony of that same Spirit.

God has taught us in His word what is our object of hope; He also teaches us the intermediate scenes as to some of their more important features. A *right* apprehension of any of the details set before us can never deaden in our minds the moral "attitude of watchful expectation". Nay, it is only so far as we are *truthfully* instructed that we can watch and expect aright.

What, then, are the Scripture proofs which are advanced in favour of the year-day system?

It is true that some expositors show that this principle is needful in *their* explanations of the prophecies themselves; this really is only a *petitio principii*: a certain exposition cannot stand, unless this canon is *assumed*, therefore (it is concluded) the canon *must* be true. The right mode of treating the question would be this: if a certain exposition stands or falls together with a canon of interpretation on which it is based, then the exposition in question must be held or not according as that canon is proved or supported by God's word. I am quite aware that dogmatic arguments are sometimes employed: such a doctrinal system depends on such a mode of interpretation, therefore that mode of interpretation must be maintained; and then when a great deal has been said on the *doctrinal importance* of the points involved, it *seems* to some minds as if strong *a posteriori* grounds, at least, had been assigned for the mode of interpretation. This, however, is not a legitimate mode of drawing deductions from Scripture. We can never judge of the *truth* of any part of Revelation by our notions of its importance.

If, then, the prophecies containing designations of time do not state anything on the face of them which supports such a mode of interpretation, we must look elsewhere for the *a priori* grounds of this opinion; I have then to consider certain passages which are commonly referred to in support of this hypothesis.

I. Numbers xiv. 34: "After the number of the days in which ye searched the land, even forty days, each day for a year, shall ye bear your iniquities, even forty years."

This passage speaks of a denounced fact, but in it there is nothing that implies a principle of interpretation. The spies had searched the land of promise forty *days*, and God sentences the murmuring and rebellious Israelites to wander in the wilderness the same number of *years*. In the prophetic part of the verse *years* are literal *years* and not the symbol of anything else. Apply the year-day system to this passage, and then "forty years" will expand into a vast period of *fourteen thousand four hundred years*. All that can be deduced from this passage, as to the connection of the terms "day" and "year", is that as the search of the land had occupied forty literal days, so the wandering in the wilderness should continue for forty literal years. Literal years answer to literal days.

II. Ezekiel iv. 4–6: "Lie thou also upon thy left side, and lay the iniquity of the house of Israel upon it: according to the number of the days that thou shalt lie upon it, thou shalt bear their iniquity. For I have laid upon thee the years of their iniquity, according to the number of the days, three hundred and ninety days: so shalt thou bear the iniquity of the house of Israel. And when thou hast accomplished them, lie again on thy right side, and thou shalt bear the iniquity of the house of Judah forty days: I have appointed thee each day for a year."

Now this is not a symbolic *prophecy* at all, but simply a symbolic *action*, which was commanded by God; and unless there had been the express statement we never could have known that what Ezekiel did, for so many days, really represented the actions of the same number of years. It is true that this is an instance in which a day *symbolically represents* a year, but the way in which this is done is wholly different from any such ground being taken as though in prophetic language the one were used for the other.

If in this passage *day* meant *year*, or if it were to be interpreted by *year*, what should we find?—that Ezekiel was commanded to lie on his left side *three hundred and ninety years,* and on his right side *forty years.*

III. Another passage which has been used as a basis for this system is the latter part of the ninth of Daniel; some, however, of the strenuous advocates of the year-day principle fairly own that it has no bearing upon the question. Its supposed connection arises from the word שָׁבוּעַ, rendered "week", having been taken as though it must be simply in its literal meaning seven *days*. This might be called wholly a question of lexicography; the word itself is strictly *something divided into* or consisting of *seven parts—a heptad, a hebdomad.* It bears the same grammatical relation to the numeral *seven* as one of the Hebrew words used for ten does to the other of similar meaning. Gesenius simply defines its meaning to be "a septenary number", he then speaks of its use as applied sometimes to days, sometimes to years; the word itself, however, defines nothing as to the denomination to which it belongs, whether the one or the other. In Ezek. xlv. 21 it is used almost entirely like a numeral, standing with a feminine plural termination in connection with a masculine noun, שְׁבֻעוֹה יָמִים (according to the peculiar usage of numerals in Hebrew and the cognate languages); and this passage is important as showing its use. It is not to be denied nor yet to be wondered at that it should be more often used of *week* than anything else, for this obvious reason, that of all things admitting a septenary division there is nothing so often spoken of as a week. In this sense, however, it more commonly takes the feminine plural termination.

In the present passage it takes its denomination from *years*, which had been previously mentioned in Daniel's prayer. Daniel had been praying to God, and making confession on behalf of his people, because he saw that the seventy *years*, which had been denounced as the term of the captivity of Judah, were accomplished; and thus the denomination of *years* connects itself with the answer granted to him. He had made inquiry about the accomplishment of *seventy years*; he receives an answer relative to seventy *heptads of years*. The word has here the masculine plural termination, which *may* arise from *year* being *feminine*; but this could not be absoluely stated as the reason, for it is once used (Dan. x. 2) with the masculine plural joined to *days*.*

* In this case, the addition of the word יָמִים *days*, is important, as it

I am well aware that strong assertions have been made to this effect: that if we follow the conventional reading (i.e. with points) it is simply "seventy weeks" (i.e. of seven *days*), but that if we reject the points, it must mean "seventy seventies"; this statement is very incorrect. I do read with the points, but the argument does not rest upon them. I do not admit that periods of seven days are necessarily indicated by the word itself. But if we paid no attention to the points, we are not left to any such meaningless rendering as "seventy seventies"; the fact must have been overlooked that in verse 27, where the word occurs in the singular, it is twice written *full* (i.e. with the letter Vav inserted), and this, without any points to help us, decides the matter.

In translating we may use the word "week" not at all as conceding the point of the meaning of the Hebrew word, but simply for convenience' sake, and as requiring less explanation and circumlocution than any other in common use. I believe that I need say no more to prove that this ninth of Daniel in no way upholds the year-day scheme.

IV. Luke xiii. 31, 32: "The same day there came certain of the Pharisees, saying unto him, Get thee out and depart hence, for Herod will kill thee. And he said unto them, Go ye, and tell that fox, Behold, I cast out devils, and I do cures to-day and to-morrow, and the third day I shall be perfected."

In transcribing this passage, I feel such astonishment at its ever having been used as the basis of an argument on the subject that I think that some readers may be incredulous as to the fact; I must inform such, that the

---

shows that the term *might* else be understood differently: it is therefore a natural addition, especially as it comes just after the prophecy of the seventy heptads of *years*.

passage was used a century and a half ago by *Fleming* (whose speculations as to the *weakening* of the Papacy were deemed by many, in 1848, so *wonderfully convincing*), and recently by Mr. Birks. But what use *can* they make of the passage? Mr. Birks says that the incident occurred several weeks before our Lord's sufferings. He therefore interprets it thus, "our Lord's ministry commencing with a passover, closed at the passover, after an exact interval of three years. The words of this passage would therefore exactly describe the continuance of that ministry: the three days importing the three years." On this I remark, *first*, that *if* our Lord's ministry did continue exactly three years, it is what no one has distinctly proved, and if true, it is not what is commonly held;* and, *secondly*, that if in this instance our Lord meant *years* by days, there must at this very time have been at least *two years* ("to-morrow and the third day") of His ministry yet to come. Most readers will, I should think, consider that the three days here are as literal as the three days during which our Lord lay in the grave, and that the term "third day" is here as simply third *day* as in the passage which speaks of the marriage at Cana in Galilee. I am not now concerned to expound the passage in Luke, but it seems to me to relate to our Lord's arrival at Jerusalem, three days, I should think, after this conversation.

V. Mr. Elliott has recently brought forward Heb. vii.

* Three years and six months is the term ordinarily assigned to our Lord's ministry, while others would limit it to a year and a few months, and others (such as Dr. Chr. Benson) think that the Gospels supply evidence that it continued for about two years and a half. In the face of this uncertainty of opinion I was surprised to see the direct assertion that it lasted exactly three years. I do not remember any writer who had held this. I do not think that it could be proved from Scripture that it began at the passover; at least it had commenced before the passover in John ii, and that is the first spoken of in connection with our Lord's ministry.

27 as another passage to support the *year-day* system: "Who needed not *daily* as those high-priests, to offer up sacrifice, first for his own sins, and then for the people's". Mr. Elliott supposes (following Macknight) that the high-priest offered sacrifice but once in a year and therefore *daily* must mean *yearly*. On this *mistake* (for a simple mistake it is) the supposed argument drawn from this passage entirely rests. On this point I need only refer to Mr. Newton's *Aids to Prophetic Inquiry* (First Series, 2nd ed.), pp. 176, 177.

In all these passages the days when mentioned are simply *days* and the years simply *years*: there is not a single phrase in which it is said that the word *days* must mean years, except the very places the meaning of which is the point under discussion. One supposition cannot be brought forward as proof of another.

A distinction has indeed been drawn between *symbolic* and *literal* prophecies: it is said that in the former we are not to understand *days* literally, but as the symbols of something else. If this distinction be good, no *literal* prophecies ought to be brought forward amongst the supposed proofs: the sentence of forty years of wandering was a literal, not a symbolic, denunciation; Ezekiel, indeed, lay on his side symbolically; but there was no prophecy in the case at all. The *use* which has been made of this distinction has been to seek thus to avoid the force of literal periods of time mentioned in prophecy which have been literally fulfilled.

And now, to consider the principal statements of time to which this supposed canon is applied:—they are—

I. The time, times, and a half, Dan. vii. 25 and xii. 7.

II. The two thousand three hundred days, Dan. viii. 14.

III. The twelve hundred and ninety days, Dan. xii. 11.

IV. The thirteen hundred and five and thirty days, Dan. xii. 12.

V. The five months, Rev. ix. 5, 10.

VI. The hour, and day, and month, and year, Rev. ix. 15.

VII. The three days and a half, Rev. xi. 9, 11.

The *first* of these periods is mentioned in the same manner in the book of Revelation xii. 14; in that book we also find a similar period spoken of as forty and two months, xi. 2, xiii. 5; and twelve hundred and sixty days, xi. 3, xii. 6. In neither of the passages in Daniel does this designation of time occur in the midst of a symbolic prophecy at all; for in chapter vii the period is spoken of in the plain literal interpretation of the symbolic horn, which is said to mean a literal king, who shall subdue three literal kings (not described as horns in *this part* of the chapter), into whose hand the saints shall be given for a time, times, and half a time—three years and a half. If we make these words *symbolic*, may we not arbitrarily explain away any other expression of Scripture? In chapter xii there is no symbol at all; the communicator of truth to Daniel "held up his right hand and his left hand unto heaven, and sware by Him that liveth for ever, that it shall be for a time, times, and a half". It seems to me as if the solemnity of this oath, "by Him that liveth for ever", would exclude the thought of mere metaphor and symbol: at least I know of no words in Scripture on which emphatic exactitude is more impressed.

But when we turn to the book of Revelation and see how variously this period is expressed, 1,260 days, forty and two months, a time times and half, it seems as if care had been taken to prevent all possibility of misconception; whether occurring in symbolic description or in literal explanation, the same isochronous expressions are repeated.* As to "*time, times, and a half*", we have the period stated in three languages, Chaldee, Hebrew, and Greek.

The *second* passage (Dan. viii. 14) is literally "unto two thousand three hundred evenings mornings", referring to the offering of the daily sacrifice each morning and evening. This also occurs in an explanation, so that the symbolic theory (even if it had any true foundation, instead of being, as it is, a gratuitous assumption) would avail nothing. The expression seems such as intentionally to exclude all thought of other than real days.

The *third* and *fourth* passages (in Dan. xii) have nothing whatever to connect them with symbols, or with anything other than literal statement. In fact there is nothing to bring these under the year-day theory, except it be an assumed interpretation.

The fifth of the passages has nothing whatever in it to

* I may mention that when first my attention was directed to the prophetic parts of Scripture it was by this threefold mode of speaking of the same term in the book of Revelation that I was led to inquire into the grounds of the year-day theory—a thing of which everyone who knows anything about Scripture has heard traditionally, whether interested in prophecy or not. As a Hebraist I was already aware that the passage in Daniel ix had no bearing in favour of the theory; and the varied mode of statement in the Revelation showed me that unless it possessed *distinct proof* it was not to be received.

The maintainers of the year-day theory accuse those who reject it with repeating the same arguments over and over again: perhaps they do this, but what of that? If we seek *truth*, not originality, we shall often act thus. How can we set forth the foundation doctrines of Christianity—the redemption of Christ, and the testimony borne by the Holy Ghost to the efficacy of His blood for the salvation of every believing sinner—without repeating what has been spoken reiteratedly from the Day of Pentecost and onward? And do not the upholders of this theory repeat the same arguments? Although I care but little whether I say the same things as others have said before me (so long as the things are *true*), I may inform the reader that my views on the year-day system were published in 1836; so that at least I did not copy from subsequent writers. Let, however, *truth* be maintained, as set forth in Scripture, irrespective of such points as *who* those may be who have previously held the same.

call for this theory as needful. There is nothing to hint any meaning except five literal months.

The sixth passage has been supposed by some to intimate a very precisely defined period of three hundred and ninety-one years, fifteen days. This would require proof. I cannot see that it speaks of a period of time at all; the passage only says that the four angels were loosed that "had been prepared for the hour, and day, and month, and year"—a solemn designation (as it seems to me) of the *point of time* spoken of; just so our Lord says, "of that day and hour knoweth no man".

The seventh passage, "three days and a half", Rev. xi, has nothing in it to require any other than the literal interpretation. Some advocates of the year-day system have been fond of laying stress on this passage, because, they say, that it was early perceived by the Church that the period meant *three years and a half*. Had this been the *fact* it would have proved nothing to any who does not feel bound to follow a supposed *consensus patrum* in the understanding of Scripture. The fact has, however, been *over*-stated. Prosper, in the fifth century, says that the three days and a half of the slain witnesses *answer* to the three years and a half of antichrist. Others repeated the expression a little more strongly; but such passing remarks do not invalidate the correctness of the statement of Mr. Conder that "at the close of the fourteenth century" "the year-day interpretation" was "first suggested".*

* As far as I know, the first who spoke of a period of *twelve hundred and sixty years* was the celebrated Abbot Joachim of Calabria at the close of the twelfth century. But he did not excogitate this as a prophetic period by using any year-day theory, but he formed it from the designation of "a time, times, and the dividing of time", *thus*: he assumed *a time* to be the largest measure of time in use amongst men, *a thousand years*; *times* to be two of the next smaller measures of time, *two hundred years*: the *dividing of time* he assumed to be *part* of the last-named measure; he

But still, even if we have no exact *proof* of the theory, may we not apply it to the interpretation of Scripture? Is every word in the Bible to be taken literally?

There is nothing relative to Scripture which can be pressed as a matter of teaching, unless it can be proved from Scripture, or from the force of the words, or from the facts of the case: and thus no one can be condemned for rejecting a theory not so proved. No doubt that in the Bible, as well as in other books, figurative terms and expressions are used. Thus, when our Lord called Herod "a fox" He used a figure which none could mistake; when He said "Destroy this temple" he used a figure of deep meaning, which was misunderstood. But where there is no figure at all, we have no authority to go out of our way to invent one; especially when it is both inapt and inapplicable. This mode of procedure will never aid us in understanding Scripture, for thus we should only be bending it to our own minds, instead of taking the place of learners and inquiring, What has the Spirit of God written for our instruction?

Thus the *meaning* of the words *day* and *year* may be considered a simple matter of lexicographical investigation, just as is the import of the word rendered *week* in Dan. ix; and then the responsibility of proving that they may signify something else rests upon those who so understand them. But with regard to *Scripture terms*, we need not always treat them as mere matters of lexicography, and in the case before us we possess ample and absolute evidence *against* that theory, the supposed proofs of which have been discussed.

---

probably adopted *sixty* precisely (instead of fifty which he should have done as it is properly "half a time") from the analogy of the 1,260 days. I ought to inform the reader that Abbot Joachim considered himself to be inspired. The year-day theory of two centuries later seems to be only a carrying out of the supposed revelation to Abbot Joachim.

I. In Dan. iv. 16, 23, and 32, king Nebuchadnezzar was told that he should be driven from men, etc., "till *seven times* should pass over him". This on the year-day theory would be a period of *two thousand five hundred and twenty years*—longer than from the time of Nebuchadnezzar to the present day. And the term "seven times" occurs both in the symbolic part of the chapter and in the literal, so that the force of words cannot be avoided by any such distinction. Nebuchadnezzar, however, says (verse 28), "All this *came upon* the king Nebuchadnezzar." The prophecy related to literal years, and in literal years was it accomplished. If then, in chapter iv, seven times are seven actual years, of course the period in chapter vii is half that number. Thus king Nebuchadnezzar is an unexceptional witness that prophetic Scripture does not admit the year-day theory.

II. The next witness is Daniel the prophet himself. In chapter ix. 2 he tells us that he understood by books the prophecy of Jeremiah that the Lord would accomplish *seventy years* in the desolations of Jerusalem. Daniel did not understand the period spoken of by Jeremiah, according to the arbitrary canon which some would now apply to his own prophecies. He understood seventy years to mean seventy years and not *twenty-five thousand two hundred years*. Thus this very chapter of Daniel, from which some (even though it is a prophecy free from all symbol) would draw a proof of their theory, supplies *decisive* evidence against it.

III. The prediction of our Lord as to his own resurrection on the third day is also of importance. It is useless to evade the application of this and similar passages by saying that they do not occur in symbolic prophecies; the answer is simply, "Neither do some of the passages to which you apply the year-day theory;

they, too, are in simple statements." Thus, if, in the case of our Lord's burial, the third *day* meant *day* and not *year*, then we may plainly see that the canon which assigns the meaning of year to the word day, when it is used in prophecy, utterly fails in its application.

Instances might be multiplied—such for example as the four hundred years in Genesis xv foretold to Abraham as the limit of the bondage of his descendants in Egypt—but it is needless to accumulate proofs when the point is established, according to the Scripture rule, at the mouth of two or three witnesses.

This, then, is a case in which the Scripture *has* spoken; we are not, therefore, at liberty to form any conclusions of our own (as if it had been silent) whether day *might not* mean or symbolise year; we are bound in subjection to the word of God to say that it *does not* and *cannot* so mean, and that thus every interpretation which depends on that theory is *necessarily* incorrect.

If we were to admit a *non-scriptural* canon of interpretation we should do much injury to truth, and we should adopt that to which we could not authoritatively direct the attention of any one; but the injury to truth is far greater when we admit a canon which is positively *anti-scriptural*—in the former case we should be adding to the word of God, but in the latter we should be even contradicting it.

It is by *truth* that God works on the hearts of His people; to *this* we must then adhere, however it may run counter to conventional ideas. The prophecies of Scripture can never be used for their legitimate purposes if they are explained by the aid of a primary canon, which is in itself not only unsupported by Scripture but is actually in contradiction to it.

# THE PROPHECY CONCERNING THE JEWS IN THE LATTER DAYS (DANIEL X, XI, XII)

THESE three chapters contain one vision, the last of those communications from God through His angel to the prophet, of which the record is given us in this book. The time when it took place is stated to have been "in the third year of Cyrus, king of Persia". Daniel had then already witnessed the faithfulness of God in causing the desolation of Jerusalem to cease; the decree of Cyrus for the rebuilding of the temple, and the permission for the people to go back to their land, had gone forth in the first year of his reign. The aged prophet had thus seen an answer to his prayer in chapter ix; and although the instruction then vouchsafed him had taught him that the interval would be great, before his people were established in unchanging blessing in their own land, yet every proof of the faithfulness of God to any promise He had made was an earnest of the greater things yet in store.

Daniel was now occupying a remarkable position: he had been one of the original captives "in the third year of Jehoiakim, king of Judah"; he had now continued for the whole of the seventy years' captivity as a faithful witness for God, and as the one employed to testify concerning Gentile power, in its varied aspects and its issue, up to the time when "one like the Son of Man" should take the kingdom, and his people should be securely set in their own land. A portion of the Jews had gone back to their land, as they had been permitted by the decree of Cyrus, but the aged prophet was still in the land of

Gentiles; he sees this vision "by the side of the great river, which is Hiddekel" (the Tigris), verse 4. And here —in the midst of the Medo-Persian kingdom, and on the eastern limit of what was afterwards to be the Roman earth—he receives a vision in which minute and definite instruction was given as to many of those things, the outline of which had been previously communicated.

The mode of teaching which God now used was not symbol and explanation, as had been the case in the general outlines of chapters ii and vii and in the more limited picture of chapter viii, nor yet general statement such as the prophetic part of chapter ix, but here we have minute and definite detail; it is in fact anticipative history of the most explicit kind. The object of this is evidently to fill in the statements which had before been made, and to give them a yet further definiteness in application to the events to which they belong.

The vision is thus introduced: "In the third year of Cyrus, king of Persia, a thing was revealed unto Daniel, whose name was called Belteshazzar; and the thing was true, but the time appointed was long; and he *understood* the thing, and had understanding of the vision." In this there is a marked contrast to what had occurred in the symbolic visions which the prophet had seen. Chapter vii concludes thus: "As for me Daniel, my cogitations much troubled me, and my countenance changed in me; but I kept the matter in my heart." And at the end of chapter viii we find, "And I Daniel fainted, and was sick certain days: afterward I rose up, and did the king's business, and I was astonished at the vision, but none understood it." Here however it is different; Daniel did understand; the messenger was sent for that purpose (verses 11 and 14), just as he had been in chapter ix, verse 22. It is remarkable that this vision is mostly parallel to that of chapter viii, which Daniel had *not understood*.

The prophet had been mourning and humbling himself for three weeks (verses 2, 3): the object of this had been (as we learn from what the angel says to him in verse 12) that he had set his heart to understand; his words had been heard and the angel had come on account of his words; what his prayer had been we only find from the communications made to him. From verses 5-11 we have the account of the appearance to him of the messenger that had been sent, and of the effect which his appearance had upon the men who were with Daniel, and upon Daniel himself. In verses 11 and 12 he thus addresses the prophet: "O Daniel, a man greatly beloved, understand the words that I speak unto thee, and stand upright: for unto thee am I now sent. And when he had spoken this word unto me, I stood trembling. Then said he unto me, Fear not, Daniel; for from the first day that thou didst set thine heart to understand, and to chasten thyself before thy God, thy words were heard, and I am come for thy words."

After speaking of how he had been withstood by the prince of Persia for the one and twenty days of Daniel's mourning, an indication of the mysterious agency of both evil angels and good, he states the distinct object for which he had come: "Now I am come to make thee understand *what shall befall thy people* IN THE LATTER DAYS: for yet the vision is for many days." This, then, tells us the subject of this concluding prophetic vision—*what should befall Daniel's people in the latter days*. This, I believe, is an intimation to us that we are not to expect in the vision the detail of events occupying a long series of years, and running on from the time of the vision; but that it simply belongs to the concluding scenes of the history of Daniel's people prior to the Lord's coming and their restored blessing.

In a similar manner, in chapter viii, the vision had been given to let Daniel know "what shall be in the last end of the indignation" (verse 19): Daniel had not understood what the vision had taught, but now I believe that we shall find the same ground gone over with much minuteness of detail in order that Daniel might understand. We may take as a preliminary point that the purport of the two visions is identical.

In chapter viii the prophecy is given concerning Persia and Greece before the Persian power had arisen into pre-eminence; in this vision the prophetic detail is given after this had taken place, so that here there is no occasion for the Medo-Persian power to arise into view (as it had in chapter viii) for the prophetic detail to commence. Both of these visions have to do territorially with those countries which are geographically connected with Jerusalem, and not with the whole of the Roman earth in its wide extent. It is important to bear this in mind in reading them, lest we should expect to see such references to extent of power and territory as those which are given in chapter vii. The Hebrew parts of this book take up in application to the Jews the last forms of power in the hand of mere man, which had been spoken of in the Chaldee parts in connection with Gentiles.

It is important, in reading a prophecy of this kind, to take hold of any parts which we know from other Scriptures to be definite points. There are certain portions of God's history of the Jews and Gentiles which we may call definite and (as it were) chronological points; and thus, although we cannot count statements of prophecy by centuries and years, so as to say *when* such and such events will occur, yet on many subjects the relation of events has been revealed to us, so that we know them to be synchronous, or else standing in a particular order and consecution.

Now, the beginning of chapter xii furnishes us with one of these points; it is said, "There shall be [rather, *it* shall be] a time of trouble such as never was since there was a nation, even to that same time: and at that time thy people shall be delivered." Here then we have the final suffering and deliverance of God's ancient people, just as in Jer. xxx. 7: "Alas! for that day is great, so that none is like it; it is even the time of Jacob's trouble, but he shall be saved out of it." This we may take as a date, and from this we may, in a certain sense, count backwards, and look on the preceding part of the vision as reaching up to it and introducing it.

In the last verse of chapter xi we have a similar date, which we may in the same manner connect with other Scriptures: we have the destruction of an oppressor in a peculiar manner—a statement which is most manifestly parallel to that of chapter viii, for the oppressor in this vision was to "prosper till the indignation be accomplished" (verse 36).

As to the starting point in these two visions there can be no difficulty, it is the time when they were respectively seen by the prophet. The outline of chapter viii, in symbol and interpretation, is here filled in with direct statement communicated in simple language.

The prophetic part of the vision before us commences with chapter xi, verse 2, "Behold, there shall stand up yet three kings in Persia; and the fourth shall be far richer than they all, and by his strength, through his riches, he shall stir up all against the realm of Grecia." We know as simple matters of history that the three successors of Cyrus on the Persian throne were his son

Cambyses, the imposter Smerdis the Magian, and Darius the son of Hystaspes. But we find them all three mentioned in Scripture also, though partly under different names. In Ezra iv. 6, 7, the successor of Cyrus is called Ahasuerus and his successor is called Artaxerxes; and then in verse 24 the next king is mentioned by the same name that he bears in profane history, namely, Darius.

No one need be surprised that Scripture should give to kings and princes names which are different from those which they bear in profane history written in after ages. We find a similar thing with regard to several of the Roman emperors; Caligula, for instance, and Caracalla, whom we know by names or rather appellations which have been since appended to them—the latter of these is called in his inscriptions Marcus Aurelius Antoninus, a name by which he is now scarcely known.\* This will serve to illustrate the variation in names between Scripture and profane history. It is interesting, however, to find that three kings thus incidentally mentioned in a prophecy are also recorded historically in Scripture.

The conduct of the fourth king (Xerxes) in stirring up all his power against Greece sets these two states (the second and third monarchies) in a position of contention, ending only in the conquest of the former by the latter, so soon as it also became a monarchy.

The next verse describes the first king: "And a mighty king shall stand up, that shall rule with great dominion, and do according to his will." The divisions of this third monarchy next appear: "And when he shall stand up his kingdom shall be broken, and shall be divided toward

---

\* Thus the decree of *Antoninus* for conferring Roman citizenship on the whole empire was supposed by some to emanate from the *benevolent* feelings of *Antoninus Pius*, instead of proceeding from the cupidity of Bassianus, who called himself *Antoninus* but who is known by posterity as *Caracalla*, from the hooded cloak of that name which he wore.

the four winds of heaven; and not to his posterity, nor according to his dominion which he ruled: for his kingdom shall be plucked up, even for others besides those." It is impossible for us to avoid seeing how parallel this portion of the vision is to chapter viii—there, in verses 7 and 8 in the vision, and in verses 21 and 22 in the interpretation, exactly the same ground has been gone over.

In chapter viii, immediately that the fourfold division of Alexander's empire has been mentioned there is a transfer of the time of the vision from continuous history to "the latter time of their kingdom, when the transgressors are come to the full" (verse 23); and the object of this is to instruct Daniel as to "what shall be in the last end of the indignation: for at the time appointed the end shall be". Just so do I believe that we have in this concluding vision an interval which commences at the fourfold division of the monarchy and which ends by the events being mentioned which introduce the concluding period of Israel's blindness, at which time the four divided parts of Alexander's empire are found existing as kingdoms. (See remarks on chapter viii, p. 79.)

It is certain that this last vision extends to the time when Daniel's "people shall be delivered, every one that shall be found written in the book" (xii. 1); it is also plainly said that the messenger had come "to make thee understand what shall befall thy people *in the latter days*" (x. 14). This expression seems at least to intimate that a long detail of the successors of Alexander is not to be expected here, that the object of the vision is quite different. Also, as the point to which it leads us on is certain, and as it is clear that a break or interval must exist somewhere, this must be its place, unless any other can be found in another part of the chapter. Also, if any possible place be found where such an interval can be *supposed*, and if any event mentioned *previous* to such a place belongs to Israel's crisis, then any such supposed place for a break must be incorrect.

Now, this is the actual place of the interval in the parallel vision; it will, I believe, be found that in no other place is such an interval admissible in this, and if so it will follow that between verses 4 and 5 is the line of demarcation between that which is long past and that which is future, as introducing the events which befall Daniel's people in the latter days.

Before considering the former part of the chapter, sentence by sentence, it will be well to state that I believe that from verse 21 to the end we have the continuous history of one king. Some have supposed that in this part of the chapter there is a break about verse 33; this I regard as impossible for several reasons: in verse 31 "the abomination that maketh desolate" is mentioned, and as this vision is the only one in Daniel in which it is *expressly mentioned in these terms*, it must be to this vision that our Lord refers in Matt. xxiv when speaking of events yet future; also, in verse 29, three invasions of Egypt are spoken of—the one mentioned in the verse itself, "the former" of which the account is given in verse 25, and "the latter" which is not mentioned at all till verses 42 and 43. Some of these things will call for further observation, but thus much stated preliminarily will clear the way.*

I now take the former part of the chapter, in order to follow closely the persons and events brought before us; this requires attention, but I believe it will be found that this anticipative history is just as definite (with the single

---

* See a subsequent section of this volume, on "The Interpretation of the Former Part of Daniel xi by Past History".

exception of the *names* not being mentioned) as is God's record of the past. I take the words of the chapter, introducing what I consider suitable explanation, and affixing, for distinction's sake, *numbers* to the kings of the north and south who are spoken of; by these numbers I simply mean the first, second, etc., who are *here* mentioned.

Verse 5: "And the [first] king of the south [i.e. Egypt, see verses 7, 8] shall be strong, and one of his princes [shall also be strong]; and he [the prince] shall be strong above him [the first king of the south], and have dominion; his dominion shall be a great dominion." Thus, a great dominion is possessed by a prince who had previously belonged to the first king of Egypt here mentioned; the prince is spoken of immediately after as "king of the north". This seems to occasion a rupture between them, and an attempt to accommodate this appears to be the purport of the beginning of the next verse.

Verse 6: "And in the end of years they [i.e. the first king of the south, and the prince] shall join themselves together; for the [first] king's daughter of the south shall come to the [prince now become the first] king of the north to make an agreement: but she shall not retain the power of the arm: neither shall he [i.e. the first king of the south] stand, nor his arm: but she shall be given up, and they that brought her, and he that begat her, and he that strengthened her in these times."

Thus, this attempt to form an alliance by marriage becomes wholly fruitless, and only ends in the destruction of the first king of the south.

Verse 7: "But out of a branch of her roots [i.e. out of the same family from which she sprang] shall one stand up in his estate" [this means, I believe, rather, *on his own basis,* and not, *in his stead,* which would here be inapplicable, as a woman had been spoken of], "which shall come with an army, and shall enter into the fortress of the [first] king of the north, and shall deal against them and shall prevail: (verse 8) and shall also carry captives into Egypt their gods, with their princes, and with their precious vessels of silver and gold; and he" [i.e. the branch out of her roots, now become the *second* king of the south] "shall continue more years than the [first] king of the north. So the [second] king of the south shall come into his kingdom" [i.e. Egypt, as shown in the preceding verse] "and shall return into his own land."

In order to understand to whom the pronouns in the next sentence refer the whole passage must be read, and then it becomes clear that they relate to the king of the north. Verse 10: "But his sons" [those of the first king of the north] "shall be stirred up, and shall assemble a multitude of great forces: and one shall certainly come, and overflow, and pass through; then shall he" [i.e. this one of the sons of the first king of the north, who is himself presently spoken of as becoming king] "return and be stirred up even to his fortress.

Verse 11: "And the [second] king of the south shall be moved with choler, and shall come forth and fight with him, even with the [second] king of the north: and he [the second king of the north] shall set forth a great multitude: but the multitude shall be given into his [the second king of the south's] hand.

Verse 12: "And when he [the second king of the south] hath taken away the multitude, his heart shall be lifted up; and he shall cast down many ten thousands: but he shall not be strengthened by it.

Verse 13: "For the [second] king of the north shall return, and shall set forth a multitude greater than the former, and shall certainly come after certain years with a great army and with much riches.

Verse 14: "And in those times there shall many stand up against the [second] king of the south; also the children of the robbers [see margin] of thy people shall exalt themselves to establish the vision, but they shall fall."

The Egyptian and Syrian kingdoms are thus, then, found in continued dissension, under their second kings here mentioned. At this point of time the *children* of the robbers of Daniel's people exalt themselves to establish the vision, but in this attempt they are wholly unsuccessful. The Gentiles have been, age after age, the oppressors of Israel; they have fulfilled, it is true, the denounced doom of God, but they have done this, not as desiring to perform the will of God, but as gratifying their own self-will; but here the *children* of these robbers adopt a different course of policy: does not this appear like an intimation of efforts on the part of Gentiles for setting the Jews in their own land as a people? The issue of the vision is that settlement—what is here called the establishment of the vision is what they will seek, but the endeavour will be fruitless. This certainly appears to me like some attempt of the nations to check the continued wars between Syria and Egypt, by interposing Israel as an independent nation. There are many who have thought that this would be acting in conformity with the will of God: because they have seen in His word that He will gather and replant His people, therefore they have thought that human effort could be rightly directed to that end; they have overlooked a most important part of prophetic statement, namely, that which refers to the closing scenes of Israel's history, previous to the coming of the Lord, the period of their peculiar darkness, blasphemy, and suffering. It is indeed strange how it has been supposed by many, with the scripture in their hands, that human and Christian effort was to be the instrument of the accomplishment of God's purposes with regard to His ancient people. He Himself will set them in security after the coming of the Lord Jesus and the purging out of the rebels; their repentance and conversion will be wrought by their looking upon Him whom they pierced, and mourning for Him when He appears in the clouds of heaven.

It is true that we are not to look on Christian effort on behalf of Israelites now as a *hopeless* thing—"blindness *in part* hath happened to Israel"—but the conversion of any of them now makes such individuals a part of the Church and has no relation to God's general dealings with the nation. Paul, and tens of thousands of other Jews, believed in Christ before the destruction of Jerusalem, but this did not alter the aspect in which the nation stood before God, as having stumbled upon the stone of stumbling.

Verse 15: "So the [second] king of the north shall come, and cast up a mount, and take the most fenced cities; and the arms of the south shall not withstand, neither his chosen people, neither shall there be any strength to withstand." Verse 16: "But he [the second king of the north] that cometh against him [the second king of the south] shall do according to his own will, and none shall stand before him: and he shall stand in the glorious land" [i.e. the land of Israel] "which by his hand shall be consumed." Thus frustrating the efforts spoken of in verse 14, and making the Holy Land the particular scene of his military operations.

Verse 17: "He shall also set his face to enter with the strength of his whole kingdom, and upright ones with him" [some apparently who are ignorantly aiding his designs]; "thus shall he do: and shall give him [the second king of the south] the daughter of women, corrupting her: but she shall not stand on his side, neither be for him." Verse 18: "After this he shall turn his face unto the isles, and shall take many; but a prince for his own behalf shall cause the reproach offered by him to cease; without his own reproach shall he cause it to turn upon him." This verse appears to describe certain actings of this second king of the north in a western direction towards Europe, until he meets with an unexpected check from a prince whom he thought to have easily overcome. Verse 19: "Then shall he turn his face toward the fort of his own land; and shall stumble and fall, and not be found."

It is evident from the entire omission of all mention of the kings of the south in this part of the chapter that the affairs of that kingdom are only treated of here incidentally: the two kingdoms of Syria and Egypt have an importance which the other two parts of Alexander's empire have not, because of their bounding the Holy Land on two sides, and the only communication by land between them passing through that country. The names of north and south appear to be taken not from their position amongst the four parts of the third empire, but from their relative situation with regard to Jerusalem.

In this history we have had, from verse 5, the account of the manner in which Syria becomes the kingdom of an Egyptian prince, and the actings of himself and his successor: Syria has, I believe, this prominence to this chapter, because of its being the part of the divided empire out of which "the vile person" springs who is mentioned in verse 21. In verse 20 the short interval is described between the destruction of the powerful second king of the north and the rising of this vile person: "Then shall stand up in his estate" [*on his own basis,* see verse 7] "a raiser of taxes in the glory of the kingdom: but within few days shall he be destroyed, neither in anger nor in battle." The expression, "in the glory of the kingdom", marks this person to be the *third* king of the north: his destruction appears to leave the kingdom in utter anarchy; and then within the Syrian kingdom there arises "a vile person" whose history appears to me to be given continuously to the end of the chapter. He is presented in the same abrupt manner as Alexander the Great is introduced in verse 4. *There*, did we not know that he was the Grecian monarch, we could hardly have proved it from *this* vision: that in chapter viii is assumed in each case to be known truth, both as to the rise of Alexander and as to the king who shall spring out of one of the parts of his empire.

I need hardly make the remark how entirely this is parallel to both the vision and the interpretation of chapter viii. There we had a little horn growing out of one of the four others; this is interpreted as being "a king of fierce countenance" who shall stand up. I do not regard this person, who is introduced in verse 21, as being a fourth successional king of the north: first, because it is said expressly of him, "to whom they shall not give the honour of the kingdom" (in direct contrast to the raiser of taxes in verse 20), "but he shall come in peaceably, and obtain the kingdom [or rather *a* kingdom] by flatteries"; second, because in verse 40 a king of the north comes against him; if, as I believe it will be manifest, this person's history runs on through the chapter; third, because of the parallelism of the history in this vision with that of chapter viii, in which the little horn is distinguished from that out of which it springs, and in chapter vii, the little horn rises as one in addition to the ten.

The object of the detail of the chapter, from verse 5 to this place, has been, I believe, to give a definite statement of the condition and relations to each other of those countries which are locally connected with the land, at the time which introduces the rise of the antichrist out of one of them, whose reign is in fact "the last end of the indignation" against Jerusalem. It is clear from chapter viii that the tenfold division of the Roman empire exists at that time; it is also clear from chapter viii that the four divisions of Alexander's empire are four out of the ten so existing; and this detail shows us, I believe, how the Syrian kingdom is formed, as introducing the events here spoken of. I do not say that it shows us that Syria will not become a kingdom in any other way—as to that, this vision is wholly silent; but that which introduces the putting of the kingdoms in the relative positions here spoken of is, Syria being a kingdom in the hands of one who had been a prince of the king of Egypt.

In the history of the "vile person" we have apparently to observe three portions: first, his rise, by which he obtains his kingdom, verses 21, 22: second, the time which elapses from his making a covenant with the people, to the taking away of the daily sacrifice, and the setting of the abomination of desolation, verses 23-31; and third, the time of his peculiar career of blasphemy reaching on to his destruction, verses 32-45. These two latter periods appear to be the heptad for which he makes a covenant with many, chapter ix. 27, and the last of them is identical with the last half-week of chapter ix and also with the time, times, and a half of chapter vii. He obtains his "kingdom by flatteries", then he is seen exerting military power to establish himself—"with the arms of a flood shall they be overflown from before him, and shall be broken; yea, also the prince of the covenant". That is apparently a prince who had made a covenant with him, by which his power had been originally established: "And after the league made with him shall he work deceitfully"; this appears to refer to the covenant made with many for one week, of which Daniel had been told by the angel in chapter ix. 27. From this time he stands connected with Israel, and we do not find in this chapter his wideness of dominion contemplated as in chapter vii, but simply what he does with regard to the people and the land. He works deceitfully; he uses the league for his own aggrandisement and for subjecting the land to himself—"for he shall come up, and shall become strong with a small people. He shall enter peaceably even upon the fattest places of the province; and he shall do that which his fathers have not done, nor his fathers' fathers; he shall scatter among them the prey, and spoil, and riches; yea, and he shall forecast his devices against the strongholds, even for a time."

Thus he shall obtain popularity by a show of most profuse liberality, but his real object shall be to get the fortified places of the land into his own power. His next acting which is mentioned is an invasion of Egypt, the first of the three attacks which he makes upon that country; verse 25, "And he shall stir up his power and his courage against the king of the south with a great army; and the king of the south shall be stirred up to battle with a very great and mighty army; but he shall not stand, for they shall forecast devices against him." Whether this king of the south be the same as the one who was last mentioned we have no evidence in the chapter: he is not only met by external force, but by internal treachery likewise; verse 26, "Yea, they that feed of the portion of his meat shall destroy him, and his army shall overflow; and many shall fall down slain." His power is thus broken, but some treaty appears to be made with him, although there is secret treachery on both sides: "and both these kings' hearts shall be to do mischief; and they shall speak lies at one table, but it shall not prosper". The manner in which they are acting in mutual treachery is shown in the account in verses 29 and 30 of the second expedition against Egypt.

The expression at the close of the verse, "for yet the end shall be at the time appointed", appears to intimate that these transactions belong to the closing scenes; see verses 35 and 40.

After this first successful invasion of Egypt the king returns to his own land "with great riches; and his heart shall be against the holy covenant; and he shall do exploits [rather 'shall work'], and return to his own land". The second invasion of Egypt is the next point in his history: "At the time appointed he shall return and come toward the south." The mention of a time appointed for the second invasion shows his secret treachery: "but it shall not be as the former" [the successful invasion spoken of in verses 25 and 26], "nor as the latter" [that mentioned in verses 42 and 43]. Just as his treachery had been shown by the mention of an appointed time, so does the next verse indicate a treacherous league formed against him by the Egyptian king with some other power: "For the ships of Chittim shall come against him, therefore he shall be grieved and return." It may be uncertain what country is intended by Chittim, probably some maritime European power; the Jews appear to have understood it to mean Macedon or Greece, for in the beginning of the first book of the

Maccabees, Alexander the Great is said to have come out of the land of Chittim against Persia.

The position of affairs at which we have arrived in the vision is this: the "vile person," who has become a king, has been at first successful in his invasion of Egypt; a treaty has been made between the two kings; the "vile person" presently breaks the treaty (as he had with secret treachery intended to do), but he finds the king of Egypt acting with equal treachery against him, and thus he relinquishes for the present his scheme of conquest.

A new feature in the character and history of this king at once shows itself: "He shall be grieved and return, *and have indignation against the holy covenant*"; his heart had been against it before (verse 28); this appears to intimate that the Jews are found in their own land (which is locally interposed between Egypt and Syria), and in his return his hatred is stirred up against the worship of God, which has been restored in Jerusalem, and of which at first he may have been, as it were, the protector (see Remarks on chapter viii, p. 75, and also on chapter ix, p. 93). His overt actings are against the holy covenant and in violation of his own league of seven years, which had been mentioned in chapter ix and also alluded to in this chapter (verse 23). His course of wickedness proceeds step by step from the time that "his heart shall be against the holy covenant". "So shall he do; he shall even return and have intelligence with them that forsake the holy covenant." Here there is the commencement of a party of apostates—of those who turn aside from God, not merely from Christ whom the Jews have never owned nationally, but from God as God, the one who as such is entitled to praise and worship. The consequences of this apostate league formed round this "vile person" next appear: "And arms" [arms of the body, i.e. human power, apparently, not *weapons*] "shall stand on his part, and they shall pollute the sanctuary of strength, and shall take away the daily sacrifice, *and they shall place the abomination that maketh desolate*." At this point the closing period of three years and a half commences, the latter half of the concluding heptad of the vision of chapter ix, so that although we cannot arrange the remaining events of the chapter as to the length of time that each of them will occupy (and several of them are evidently general), yet from this point to the destruction of this oppressor we find to be a period of specified duration.

Our attention is directed to the prophecy of the Lord Jesus on the Mount of Olives, by the use which He there makes of the 31st verse of this chapter; it will therefore be necessary to turn to Matt. xxiv and Luke xxi in order to lay hold of the instructions in their full value which are here brought before us. In Matt. xxiv. 3 there are three questions proposed to our Lord by some of His disciples, relative to what He had told them as to the destruction of the temple: "Tell us when shall these things be? and what shall be the sign of thy coming? and of the end of the world [rather *age*]?" In His reply He brings before them moral truth which bears on the conscience: from verses 4–14 He gives an outline of what would be the characteristics of the dispensation; He shows how the hopes which the ancient prophets of Israel had set before the people must be deferred as to their accomplishment until this dispensational period should have closed. Wars, rumours of wars, evil increasing, the people of Christ hated and persecuted for His name's sake by all nations, and the gospel preached for a witness to the same nations—such is the general picture, putting the child of faith into a position of waiting for a deferred, although secure, blessing, and therefore, in that respect, resembling much that we find in the testimony of Daniel. All that is found in Luke xxi, from verses 20 to 24, would belong to the time which commences, or nearly so, the dispensational period, the past destruction of Jerusalem being introduced, and the consequent dispersion and captivity of the people, which only ends with the closing dispensation. Then follows the important warning, "When ye therefore shall see *the abomination of desolation*, spoken of by Daniel the prophet, stand in the holy place (whoso readeth let him understand); then let them which be in Judea flee unto the mountains", etc. The Lord thus contemplates Jerusalem with the people dwelling there again after the Roman destruction, and amongst them those whom He can instruct with regard to His own coming, and also the condition of things at that time. Whatever testimony of the gospel may have been given in Jerusalem up to this time, the servants of Christ now receive another direction; they have to flee forthwith when a certain sign is manifest before them, namely, the setting of "the abomination of desolation" in the sanctuary of God. It is most evident that those who give heed to this warning cannot be Jews in their unbelief, for no one could use this prophecy unless he owned Jesus to be the Christ (see verse 5); but they must be believers in His name, who are accepted through His blood: these are instructed how to act and how to use the prophecy of Daniel. But how (it may be asked) can this personally concern us? We are Christians living in countries far distant from Jerusalem, how then can the warning affect us at all? To this I answer that the persons addressed are assuredly of a particular place and period, but if they are a part of the Church of God (which cannot be denied unless we put the Four Gospels away from us), then, as members of the same body, we have as deep an interest in the Church's future history as we have in that which is past, as that, for instance, which is recorded in the book of Acts. And further, just as the Spirit of God instructs by principles drawn from what we know as past, so ought we to have our hearts opened to receive the lessons which He would set before us out of the revealed future; but how can that be the case, unless we regard these future events as things which concern us? The more a soul sees to what this present dispensational period is tending, the more will it (if rightly submitting to the guidance of God's Spirit) find its own proper place in the midst of present things, seeing what it can have fellowship with, and what it cannot.

The point of evil at which we can look definitely is, then, the setting of the abomination that maketh desolate: so soon as this is done we must regard this king, not as one of those who has been led on by the mere motives of ambition, which are so common amongst the great ones of the earth, but as directly energised by Satan. At this point of time belongs, I believe, the description contained in the 32nd and three following verses of Dan. xi. On the one hand, there is this king corrupting by flatteries such as do wickedly against the covenant, while on the other hand there is the activity of the people that do know their God. I should not regard these verses as being in order of time subsequent to the setting of the abomination of desolation, but as describing the condition of things at that time. Before the onward course of this king's iniquity is dwelt on, the prophetic statement rests for a moment upon "the people that do know their God".

This expression is remarkable; it surely cannot mean merely those who have the external knowledge that

Jehovah is the God of Israel, and who do not turn aside to the blasphemy and idolatry and evil which are coming in; it must surely imply more than this, even those who, through the working of God's grace, possess the real saving knowledge of Him as revealed in Jesus Christ. In the midst of all this evil they "are strong and do exploits" [or rather "work"]; they have their work assigned them of God, and they perform it, as we are told in the next verse—"and they that understand among the people shall instruct many; yet they [namely, the people] shall fall by the sword and by flame, by captivity, and by spoil, many days." On this verse I make three remarks: First, "they that understand" are a class of persons definitely set before us in this vision; they are again spoken of in verse 35, "them of understanding" "they that be wise" in chapter xii. 3, and "the wise" of xii. 10. To avoid all ambiguity which might be caused by the variation in the rendering, it will be convenient to use the Hebrew word "*Maskilim*", the *Maskilim* of the people—these then are Israelites by nation, but though, in Jerusalem, when wickedness is coming to a head, they are found separate from it and intelligent witnesses against it. They must be a part of "the remnant according to the election of grace" of Rom. xi, for that designation comprehends all of Israel who believe in the Lord Jesus during the blindness of the nation at large. Second, that it is *the people* who fall, as is here described, and not the *Maskilim*, is shown by comparison with verse 35. Third, the expression "many days" does not necessarily imply a long period of time; it may or may not, according to the nature of the case; see Dan. viii. 27, where the same expression is rendered "certain days"; compare also 1 Kings ii. 38; 1 Chron. vii. 22; Neh. i. 4; Esther i. 4. There is nothing which would make it necessary to suppose a period of time for which the last half week of Dan. ix would not be amply sufficient.

Verse 34: "Now, when they [the people] shall fall, they shall be holpen with a little help; but many shall cleave to them with flatteries." The power of this king is now felt by the Jews as being against them, and treatment of this kind is what we find here (as well as in many other Scriptures) as being their portion, up to the time when the Lord works His own deliverance for them. Some seek to aid them, but all is fallacious, and this they are made to feel.

"And some of them of understanding [the *Maskilim*] shall fall"; these words show that the falling by the sword, etc., in verse 33 applies to the people and not to the Maskilim. It might be asked, if they know their God and are doing His will, will they not be upheld by Him, as standing in power in their place of testimony? This verse simply tells us, No! testimony in the midst of felt and manifest weakness (like those in Heb. xi. 35-38) has been the common position to which Christian faithfulness has led while encountering opposition, and this is here the case with at least some of these Maskilim; "they shall fall [by the power of persecution, etc.], to try them and to purge, and to make them white, even to the time of the end; because it is yet for a time appointed." Here these Maskilim disappear from our sight for a while; the persecuting power of this king cuts off those of them who fall into his hands, and this is continuously done, "even to the time of the end". Their testimony also ceases for another reason—the Lord Jesus has taught His people, "When ye see the abomination of desolation, spoken of by Daniel the prophet, stand in the holy place (whoso readeth let him understand); *then let those that are in Judea flee unto the moun-*

*tains*," etc.—this shows us how every obedient-hearted servant of Christ would know that the time for testimony in Jerusalem, and even in the land of Judah, was past; they are called on to flee, for He has commanded it.

Thus, when the abomination of desolation is actually set up, the course of this king is simply evil: men are given over to strong delusion, that they should believe a lie; and those who had previously given testimony are withdrawn, either in obedience to the command of Christ or else by the power of persecution.

From this place (verse 36) to the end of the chapter we have the king in all his unhindered course; he takes a place of blasphemy, even assuming divine honours. "The king shall do according to his will; and he shall exalt himself, and magnify himself above every god, and shall speak marvellous things against the God of gods"; the connection of this is most obvious with 2 Thess. ii. 3, 4—"that man of sin . . . the son of perdition, who opposeth and exalteth himself above all that is called God, or that is worshipped; so that he sitteth in the temple of God, showing himself that he is God". The connection of this description with the horn of blasphemy in chapters vii and viii is very marked: "He shall speak great words against the Most High," chapter vii. 23; "because of the voice of the great words which the horn spake, etc. (verse 11); "He magnified himself even to the Prince of the host" (viii. 11); "He shall also stand up against the Prince of princes" (verse 25).

God has a purpose and definite design in allowing evil thus to reach its height: "When the wicked spring as the grass, and when all the workers of iniquity do flourish; it is that they shall be destroyed for ever" (Ps. xcii. 7). He "shall prosper till the indignation be accomplished (see viii. 19), for that that is determined shall be done".

Verse 37: "Neither shall he regard the God of his fathers, nor the desire of women [some idol, apparently], nor regard any God; for he shall magnify himself above all."

And yet in secret he is found to be the slave of abject superstition (verses 38, 39): "But in his estate shall he honour the god of forces; and a god whom his fathers knew not shall he honour with gold, and silver, and precious stones, and pleasant things. Thus shall he do in the most strong holds with a strange god, whom he shall acknowledge and increase with glory: and he shall cause them to rule over many, and shall divide the land for gain." What this object of his worship may be is not, I think, apparent: it shows, however, the twofold acting of this king, who takes before men the place of the supreme God, and yet is himself a secret idolater; he is a successful conqueror, and he honours the god of forces in strong holds.

The last six verses of the chapter bring before us the crisis of his history: "And at the time of the end shall the king of the south push at him: and the king of the north [now again mentioned as a kingdom] shall come against him like a whirlwind, with chariots, and with horsemen, and many ships; and *he*" [namely the king who is *the subject* of this part of the chapter] "shall enter into the countries, and shall overflow and pass over."

He next turns his arms towards Egypt, passing through the Holy Land: "He shall enter also into the glorious land, and many countries shall be overthrown; but these shall escape out of his hand, even Edom, and Moab, and the chief of the children of Ammon." It is interesting to observe how these three districts, of which at this time he does not take possession, are specified in Isa. xi as falling into the hands of restored Israel: "they shall lay their hand upon Edom and Moab; and the children of Ammon shall obey them".

Verse 42: "He shall stretch forth his hand also upon the countries; and the land of Egypt shall not escape" [the latter invasion referred to in verse 29]. "But he shall have power over the treasures of gold and of silver, and over all the precious things of Egypt; and the Libyans and Ethiopians shall be at his steps." He thus appears to be going on in an unhindered career of conquest; but the "time of the end" is approaching. "But tidings out of the east and out of the north shall trouble him: therefore he shall go forth with great fury to destroy, and utterly to make away many. And he shall plant the tabernacles of his palace between the seas" [the Dead Sea and the Mediterranean] "in the glorious holy mountain; yet he shall come to his end, and none shall help him." Thus, when he has come in his pride and rage again to Jerusalem, the hand of God stops his career, just as we are told in 2 Thess. ii. 8, "that wicked whom the Lord shall consume with the spirit of his mouth, and shall destroy with the brightness of his coming" (compare Isa. xi. 4). Just so do we learn in Zech. xii and xiv that the future and final deliverance of the Jews and Jerusalem from their foes is when the Lord comes forth and fights against them, when his feet stand upon the Mount of Olives; and it is when He thus delivers them that they shall look upon Him whom they pierced, they shall mourn and be in bitterness for Him.

The place in which he is said in verse 45 to plant the tabernacles of his palaces (as well as the blasphemy of his assumptions) brings before us the description of a certain king of Babylon who is spoken of in Isa. xiv: the Jew there, using the song of reproach after the future and final deliverance of his people, speaks thus: "How art

## DOOM OF ANTICHRIST

thou fallen from heaven, O Lucifer, son of the morning! how art thou cut down to the ground, which didst weaken the nations! For thou hast said in thine heart, I will ascend into heaven, I will exalt my throne above the stars of God: I will sit also upon the mount of the congregation, in the sides of the north: I will ascend above the heights of the clouds: I will be like the Most High. Yet thou shalt be brought down to hell, to the sides of the pit", etc. An objection has been made to the application of Isa. xiv to the antichrist on the following grounds: The beast in the Revelation is said expressly to be cast "alive into the lake of fire" (Rev. xix. 20). This beast has been identified (most truly, I have no doubt) with that power of blasphemy and evil who is spoken of so much in the book of Daniel: then the difficulty is raised from Isa. xiv. 18, 19, as though they spoke of something absolutely incompatible with his being cast alive into the lake of fire. The expressions "those that are slain, thrust through with a sword", and "a carcase trodden under feet", have been taken up, as though this person there called "the king of Babylon" were actually slain and his dead body were thus treated; but observe that this is simply a comparison: "But thou art cast out of thy grave LIKE an abominable branch,—the raiment of those that are slain, thrust through [plural] with a sword; that go down to the stones of the pit; AS a carcase trodden under feet." The grave does not receive this king; other monarchs have been buried, but he shall not be; the lake of fire receives him alive;\* he is too polluted even for the grave; he is loathed by it, even as men would loathe the disgusting blood-stained raiment of a confused mass of the dead, or a carcase trampled under feet.

\* Slain indeed by the breath of Christ's lips, but alive in resuscitated being.

But it is remarkable to observe how carefully the Scripture guards us, in many points, from applying to past things and persons those statements which it is of importance for us to know as future. To what king of Babylon could these things have applied? Did any of them set himself as God in the mount of the congregation? Scripture mentions but three who *could* have done it; but Nebuchadnezzar, though the destroyer of the temple and city, was brought at length, through the discipline of God's hand, to own Him and give Him glory. We do not find the other two, Evil-merodach and Belshazzar, as personally connected with Jerusalem at all; the scene of the impiety of the latter was simply Babylon: and further, the deliverance of Israel which is here celebrated is utterly different from the return of the Jews from the Babylonish captivity (see verses 1 and 2). So carefully is the prophecy guarded against application to things past.

With the eleventh of Daniel that part of the vision concludes which refers to this king; all the latter part of it, which relates to his actings after the setting of the abomination of desolation, is of solemn interest. Whatever be thought of the early part of the chapter, I feel that it is of special importance not to overlook the bearing of the latter portion. It is clear from the first verse of the next chapter that the deliverance of Daniel's people and the destruction of this king belong to the same time; this alone shows us the future bearing of the latter part at least of this prophecy. He persecutes the people of God up to the time of his destruction, for we find in chapter vii that the saints of the most high places are given into his hand, and he wears them out until the Ancient of Days takes his judicial place; hence we see that, although we find the saints not kept in view in the latter part of this chapter, there will be those who during his reign of blasphemy will witness in the midst of suffering, not loving their lives even unto the death, and overcoming by the blood of the Lamb, and the word of their testimony.

His reign is a time of grievous and grinding oppression to Israel; his abominable idol (the image of the beast, that the false prophet causes both to speak and breathe, Rev. xiii.) being set in the holy place, all who refuse to worship are the objects of his wrath; death is the doom which their disobedience receives. But God preserves some in His own sovereign power, each one whose name has been written from before the foundation of the world in the book of life of the slain Lamb. This is proved by a remnant being spared, when the Lord Jesus comes with power of destroying judgment: for none can be spared who have joined in the Antichristian blasphemy: "If any man worship the beast and his image, and receive his mark in his forehead or in his hand—the same shall drink of the wine of the wrath of God", etc. (Rev. xiv. 9, 10). This remnant must not be confounded with those who have confessed Christ previous to His coming; they as being an integral part of the Church of the firstborn will share His millennial reign in glorified bodies; this remnant, on the contrary (however previously acted on by testimony), will not know the Lord Jesus until they see Him, and the Spirit of grace and supplications is poured out upon them.

We never can apprehend clearly the teaching of Scripture as to these things unless we see distinctly what these two remnants are; the one may be called a Christian remnant, the other a Jewish remnant. The former are of "the remnant according to the election of grace" in Rom. xi (for that includes all the believing Israelites of this dispensation); of the latter it is written, "the remnant shall return, even the remnant of Jacob, unto the *Mighty God*," Isa. x (the "child born" whose name should be so called): this return is when the Lord Jesus shall have come, and not before.

Dan. xii. 1 speaks of three of the circumstances of the time when these things are accomplished: "And at that time shall Michael stand up, the great prince which standeth for the children of thy people; and there shall be [rather, *it* shall be] a time of trouble, such as never was since there was a nation even to that same time; and at that time thy people shall be delivered, every one that shall be found written in the book." The standing up of Michael is of course an event which is secret from the eye of man; he is called in the New Testament the archangel, and some have supposed that he is the same person as the Lord Jesus: there appears to me to be no evidence to support this thought, and a good deal to contradict it: for instance, could Jude have used such language of our Lord as he does of Michael?—"Yet Michael the archangel, when contending with the devil, he disputed about the body of Moses, *durst* not bring against him a railing accusation, but said, The Lord rebuke thee." This seems to show that Michael cannot be himself the Lord. I should, therefore, not identify the standing up of Michael either with the Son of Man coming to the Ancient of Days to receive a kingdom, or yet (according to the language of Psalm cx) the Lord leaving the right hand of Jehovah because His enemies are made His footstool. It is something which in the economy of God's dealings closely concerns Israel.

This time is one of trouble, such as has never been equalled: our Lord, in Matt. xxiv, predicts a time of tribulation also unequalled, and that without the like ever having been before, or to be after. This, then, in Daniel cannot be subsequent to that in Matt. xxiv, for our Lord's words would then be contradicted; Daniel's people are delivered at the time here spoken of, so that there is no place for the tribulation in Matthew as a subsequent thing, hence it follows inevitably that the same period is spoken of in both places, the time of which it is said in Jer. xxx, "It is the time of Jacob's trouble; but he shall be delivered out of it." This tribulation is during the reign and blasphemy of the antichrist, whose fearful power will be thus permitted of God. Past history will afford no parallel, and the energy of Satan will then have an unhindered character, which God at present does not permit.

Daniel's people shall then be delivered, every one that shall be found written in the book. This was a point of hope to his soul; to this the vision had tended, to what should befall his people in the latter days. We know from other Scriptures that the spared will be but a portion of the Jews: "And it shall come to pass, that in all the land, saith the Lord, two parts therein shall be cut off, and die; but the third part shall be left therein. And I will bring the third part through the fire, and will refine them as silver is refined, and will try them as gold is tried: they shall call on my name, and I will hear them: I will say, It is my people; and they shall say, The Lord is my God" (Zech. xiii. 8, 9). This speaks of those who are spared in the land, and in Ezek. xx we learn concerning the spared of those who have been scattered among the nations; these shall unitedly form "the remnant that shall return", who will be blessed upon earth, according to all that had been promised of earthly blessing under the reign of Messiah. They will know His redemption; the fountain prepared for sin and uncleanness will be opened to them, and of them it will then be said, "Their sins and iniquities will I remember no more." It is a happy thought to us to look on and see these blessings yet in store: Jesus saw of the travail of His soul and was satisfied; He was the captain of salvation bringing *many* sons (God's children, given into his hand for redemption) unto glory: and surely as belonging to the redeemed we may rejoice in seeing any truth which tells us of the wide numbers of those "many brethren" (younger, it is true, than the "Church of the first-born") of the same household of God to which we belong.

But was Daniel told merely of earthly blessing? Was there no intimation of higher and better things to be bestowed at this very time upon some? (Verse 2:) "And many from among the sleepers of the dust of the earth shall awake; these shall be unto everlasting life; but those [the rest of the sleepers] shall be unto shame and everlasting contempt." I have given, I believe, the most literal rendering of this verse;* it speaks of a resurrection, not the general, when all shall be called forth, but one of an eclectic character, "many from amongst the sleepers". Just so in Rev. xx, after "the first resurrection" has been mentioned, we are told, "the rest of the dead lived not again until the thousand years were finished." It is at the coming of the Lord Jesus that Israel is delivered; it is then that the first resurrection also takes place. Just in the same manner do we read of a resurrection in Isa. xxvi. 19, in connection with the Lord coming out of His place to punish the inhabitants of the earth for their iniquity: "Thy dead men shall live; they shall arise my dead body." [Such are the words literally. Identified with Christ as being His members.]

* See "Note on The Rendering and Connection of Daniel xii. 2", below, page 164.

"Awake and sing ye that dwell in dust: for thy dew is as the dew of herbs, and the earth shall cast out the dead." To that day belongs the statement of the same continuous prophecy: "He shall cause them that come of Jacob to take root: Israel shall blossom and bud, and fill the face of the world with fruit" (chapter xxvii. 6).

Is anything stated as the result of this resurrection to eternal life? Verse 3: "And they that be wise [the Maskilim] shall shine as the brightness of the firmament; and they that turn many to righteousness as the stars for ever and ever." Here then they are described by symbols of heavenly glory. And here are again the understanding ones, the Maskilim of chapter xi. 33, 35; we last saw them worn out by the power of the antichrist, but now they have their portion in the day of blessing. The same vision tells us thus how they at length are vindicated of God.

After a word addressed to Daniel as to the use to be made of this vision at "the time of the end", the direct statement made to him ceases; he then sees two others besides the angel, and hears the communication which passes between them: "How long shall it be to the end of these wonders?" "And I heard the man clothed in linen, which was upon the waters of the river, when he held up his right hand and his left hand unto heaven, and sware by him that liveth for ever, that it shall be for a time, times, and a half; and when he shall have accomplished to scatter the power of the holy people, all these things shall be finished." Here there is the same period spoken of as in chapter vii—the three years and a half of the blasphemous rule of antichrist as Satan's vicegerent; when all God's purposes of chastening Israel shall have been accomplished, this period ends: "It shall come to pass that when the Lord hath performed his whole work upon Mount Zion and on Jerusalem, I will punish the stout heart of the king of Assyria, and the glory of his high looks" (Isa. x. 12).

There was doubt upon the mind of Daniel as to what he now heard: his mind was intent upon what should come after—upon what had been spoken of in the end of verse 1, and verses 2 and 3: "And I heard, but I understood not; then said I, O my Lord, what shall be in the *end* of these things? And he said, Go thy way, Daniel; for the words are closed up and sealed till the time of the end". This is to be taken in connection with verse 4: "But thou, Daniel, shut up the words, and seal the book, even to the time of the end: many shall run to and fro [perhaps, 'scrutinise (the book) from end to end'], and THE knowledge (thereof) shall be increased." In order rightly to apprehend these two statements, we must go on with another portion of the last declaration to the prophet, verse 10, "Many shall be purified, and made white, and tried [as had been said in chapter xi. 35]; but the wicked shall do wickedly; and none of the wicked shall understand; *but the wise* [the Maskilim] *shall understand*." Thus we see that the shutting and sealing do not imply that none shall understand or use this prophecy, for, on the contrary, *the Maskilim shall understand*: we have seen them in their place of testimony (chapter xi. 33), of suffering (verse 35), received into their celestial glory (chapter xii. 3), and now we find them mentioned as those who are to understand and to use this book. Let this be taken in connection with what our Lord says in Matt. xxiv, "When ye see the abomination of desolation, spoken of by Daniel the prophet, stand in the holy place, *whoso readeth let him understand*"—let him be one of these Maskilim, who know the truth of God, and are allowed to stand in the closing scenes in such an honoured place. If sealing means in these places a withholding of the knowledge of what these things are, then it is well to observe that with such a seal the Church is not concerned, for the word of Christ has authoritatively taken it away: "Whoso readeth let him understand." The truth of God is in the hands of men, written in His holy word, and yet without the heart possessed of that spiritual understanding which is according to God, what does it avail them? —"none of the wicked shall understand". There is such a thing as the detail of truth being held apart from God —it is, therefore, powerless: this is not understanding. But the wise-hearted have to know the truth of God to hold it as the truth of God, and He will make it their safeguard in the hour of need. These prophecies of Daniel, and the predictions of Christ in Matt. xxiv, will be used in the day of the setting of the abomination of desolation in the holy place. The Church ought therefore to know what these things are in order to stand prepared and not find these things taking her by surprise.

Verse 11: "And from the time that the daily sacrifice shall be taken away, and the abomination that maketh desolate set up [see chapter xi. 31], there shall be a thousand two hundred and ninety days." Verse 12: "Blessed is he that waiteth, and cometh to the thousand three hundred and five and thirty days." Here are two periods which have not been previously mentioned. One thousand two hundred and ninety days run on a month beyond the time, times, and a half; the other period with the conclusion of which a blessing is connected is yet forty-five days more. With regard to these periods a few considerations only can be suggested: we must bear in mind that the deliverance of the Jews from their oppressors is effected by the Lord at His coming, but after that their being set in blessing as His people is not an instantaneous result; He deals first with their consciences:

they see Him whom they pierced; they mourn for Him and this appears to be not a very brief time of humiliation and sorrow; it issues, however, in their knowing the value of the vicarious sufferings of Messiah. But there are other things also to be done; the outcasts of Israel must be gathered, and not till then can the united blessing take place. It is not improbable that these two periods may relate to the stages of the Lord's actings, the one thousand three hundred and thirty-five days bringing in the united blessing.

Verse 13: "But go thou thy way till the end be; for thou shalt rest, and stand in thy lot at the end of the days." These words close the book; the communication of God to the prophet is completed, and whatever further inquiries he might have made, they are thus prevented. But his soul is pointed onward as regards himself, even as he had been before with regard to his people. To know of the full blessing of his people had been the desire of his heart, in those things which introduce the vision in chapter ix, as well as this; and these desires had been responded to by God in that way which He saw to be the most profitable: "the end" was a point of time to be waited for, both as to THEIR blessing and the fullness of *his* personally. Daniel was to rest, to lie in his grave amidst the other sleepers of the dust of the earth; but in the end of the days he should stand in his lot, even that lot of which he had been before instructed, in the heavenly glory of those who rise to eternal life.

The saints of old died after having obtained a good report through faith, not having received the promise. In this consummation they are to be associated with others, even us, saved by the same grace, and made members of one body. They received not the promise, that they without us should not be made perfect: God has provided better *for us* than if the consummation had been otherwise.

Thus was he instructed as to "patience of hope" with regard to his people and himself; this is a lesson which we too have to learn; we have to wait for the coming day, and we are warned of intervening darkness, but this is not to cause hope to wax dim in our souls. We have far more instruction as to these things vouchsafed to us than Daniel had, and the hopes are presented to us more vividly. Well then may we wait till the end be, knowing that whether among the dead in Christ, or those who are alive and remain till His coming, we shall stand in our lot at the end of the days; till then Jesus is with His people, though unseen, according to his word, "Lo, I am with you all the days, even to the end of the age." Then we shall see Him as He is, we shall bear His image, our vile body being fashioned like unto His glorious body, and instead of His guidance through the wilderness we shall ever be with Him and all His departed saints in the heavenly city.

## NOTE ON THE RENDERING AND CONNECTION OF DANIEL XII. 2

I DO not doubt that the right translation of this verse is what has been given above: "And many from among the sleepers of the dust of the earth shall awake; these shall be unto everlasting life; but those [the rest of the sleepers, those who do not awake at this time] shall be unto shame and everlasting contempt." The word which in our Authorised version is twice rendered "some" is never repeated in any other passage in the Hebrew Bible, in the sense of taking up distributively any general class which had been previously mentioned; this is enough, I believe, to warrant our applying its first occurrence here to the whole of the many who awake, and the second to the mass of the sleepers, those who do not awake at this time. It is clearly not a general resurrection; it is "many *from among*"; and it is only by taking the words in this sense that we gain any information as to what becomes of those who continue to sleep in the dust of the earth.\*

This passage has been understood by the Jewish commentators in the sense that I have stated. Of course these men with the vail on their hearts are no guides as to the use of the Old Testament; but they are helps as to the grammatical and lexicographical value of sentences and words. Two of the rabbis who commented on this prophet were Saadiah Haggaon (in the tenth century

---

\* This translation is given as undoubtedly correct in Gerard Kerkherdere's *Prodromus Danielicus.*

of our era) and Aben Ezra (in the twelfth); the latter of these was a writer of peculiar abilities and accuracy of mind. He explains the verse in the following manner:

"*And many*:] The Gaon [i.e. R. Saadiah, whom he often quotes] says, that its interpretation is, *those who shall awake shall be unto everlasting life, and those who shall not awake shall be unto shame unto everlasting contempt*; just like, '*and they shall be a contempt*' [Isa. lxvi. 26, where the English version has *an abhorring*], and the word is the same, and its interpretation is *shame* [the word which, in the plural, preceded in Dan. xii. 2]. And the Gaon says that '*many*' are [here] the few [or the lesser number]; just like 'and many brought gifts' (2 Chron. xxxii. 23); and 'many of the people of the land became Jews' (Esther viii. 17); and 'many will entreat the favour of a prince' (Prov. xix. 6). And the sense, according to my judgment, is that the righteous, who died in the captivities, shall live at the coming of the Redeemer, because of them it is written, 'as the days of a tree are the days of my people' (Isa. lxv. 22). And then shall they feast on Leviathan, and on Ziz [a fabulous bird], and on Behemoth. And they shall die a second time, and they shall live in the resurrection of the dead, when they are in the world to come, where they shall enither eat nor drink, but shall be lightened with the brightness of the Shechinah; and he said that thus is the interpretation of 'and thou shalt rest, and stand in thy lot at the end of the days', with which the book concludes."

These, then, are the sentiments of Aben Ezra, in which he connects his own opinions with those of R. Saadiah. As to the rendering of the words, he is an authority in favour of the translation which I have given: his grammatical explanation of the force of words is by no means affected by his Jewish exposition. Although he applies the first resurrection to Israel only, and gives it a thoroughly *carnal* character, yet he distinctly recognises a first and second resurrection, although his doctrine as to this is directly contradictory to that of our Lord and His apostles—so much so, as to make it probable that the same notions had been current among the Pharisees even in our Lord's days. Aben Ezra says that the dead of Israel who shall rise shall die again, and rise again at the general resurrection. Our Lord says, "They which shall be accounted worthy to obtain that world and the resurrection from the dead, neither marry nor are given in marriage; *neither can they die any more*; for they are equal unto the angels; and are the children of God, being the children of the resurrection" (Luke xx. 35, 36). "It is raised in incorruption." "It is raised a spiritual body." "This corruptible must put on incorruption, and this mortal must put on immortality" (1 Cor. xv). "Blessed and holy is he that hath part in the first resurrection; on such the second death shall have no power" (Rev. xx). These are the truths which God has vouchsafed that we should know; but still in all their ignorance the Jewish teachers did hold two resurrections, one of the just, whom they confined to Israel, and the other, the only one in which the unjust should rise at all. To suppose that "everlasting life" was as limited as the "days of a tree" was a proof of but little apprehension of the exactitude of Scripture. It is marvellous, with the words of Scripture before them, mentioning "everlasting life", they could have thought that the participants in the first resurrection could die again: had they known Christ's resurrection they *could* not have thus erred.

It may seem hardly needful to make a remark on the opinion that passages such as this relate only to temporal deliverance, or something of the kind. "Sleepers in the dust of the earth" is a fitting designation of those who sleep the sleep of death, whose bodies are returned to dust of the ground. If such words were used to denote persons suffering from oppression, and thoroughly degraded, it could only be by a figure taken from the appearance and condition of the dead. But if such a figure were supposed, what would be the import of the "everlasting life" to which the sleepers awake? Could there be such a thing as earthly, temporal, deliverance to *everlasting* life? This alone shows the impossibility of thus limiting the meaning of the passage. But, besides this distinct point, it may well be asked, if the language of this verse be not declaratory of a resurrection of the dead, actual and literal, is there any passage of Scripture at all which speaks of such a thing as a resurrection? Where, at least, can it be found in the Old Testament? And yet we *know* that it is taught there; else how could our Lord have reproved the Sadducees for their ignorance of *the Scriptures*?* That the Old

---

* "We know from other parts of Scripture, that all the righteous dead will then awake to life—'LIFE' and not '*awake*' being the word which implies the possession and exercise of the power of resurrection-being. The souls of the departed saints, whilst in a disembodied state, although in Paradise, and perfectly conscious of their blessing, are not in the exercise of the *functions* of life—those functions requiring the presence of the body. Hence, our Lord in his reply to the Sadducees, who denied the resurrection of the body, proves it by saying, that, if there were no resurrection, God would not be called the God of Abraham; for that He is not the God of the dead, but of the living. The *soul* of Abraham is now consciously receiving blessings *from* God—but Abraham will not be able to live *unto* God, until he again receives his body, and in this sense is still regarded as dead, not as living. So, also, the departed wicked are not represented in Scripture as living, although their souls exist in torment. Hence, it is said, 'the rest of the dead lived not' (οὐκ ἔζησαν) until the thousand years were finished,—'live' being here used, not in the sense of '*exist*', but as denoting the exercise of the functions of life. Man, therefore, is not said to live, i.e. in the sense of exercising the functions of life, either when he is dispossessed of his body, or when, having his body he is placed in the second death."—*Prospects of the Ten Kingdoms*, Third Ed, by B. W. Newton, p. 194.

Testament, as well as the New, does teach the resurrection of the dead is evident to every one who simply receives the words of Scripture according to their force. Had not the Jews learned this doctrine from God's written Revelation, how could they have known it at all? Even the Samaritans, who have only the Pentateuch as of divine authority, believe in the resurrection, and they prove it from Deut. xxxii. 39, "I kill, and I *make alive*"; this is to them a sufficient warrant for believing that God will raise the dead.

But when we proceed further, and examine the writings of the prophets, we find statements sufficiently explicit, in which, however, it seems as if a well-known truth were mentioned. And this doctrine of resurrection presents to us a point of connection between *our* hopes and those of Daniel's people. Just as their restoration and blessing shall tell of the grace and redemption of Jesus their Messiah, so shall *our* resurrection and heavenly glory speak of the efficacy of all that has been wrought by the same Saviour. They will see "the Church of the first-born" entering into *heavenly* blessing, while they receive that which is *earthly*; but even then the heavenly things will tell them of the hopes before them. If it is as "children of God" that the Church receives its higher blessings, it shall then be true of Israel that they too are *children*; they shall call God *Father*, and no more turn away from Him: to them pertaineth the *adoption*. If the sharers in the first resurrection receive their heavenly portion as *heirs*, then the same inheritance is that which redeemed Israel may expect, for they are then made children, and the revealed statement is ever true in divine things—"if children, then *heirs*".

The Spirit of God leads our minds, in Scripture, to connect our resurrection with Israel's blessing. Thus,

PROOFS FROM SCRIPTURE 169

in the chapter of resurrection, we read, "when this corruptible shall have put on incorruption, and this mortal shall have put on immortality, then shall be brought to pass the saying that is written, Death is swallowed up in victory". Thus the resurrection of those who are "Christ's at his *coming*" is authoritatively declared to be at the same epoch as the fulfilment of an Old Testament promise. If we turn to Isa. xxv, the place where this "saying" is "written", we find that it is in the midst of a description of the restored blessing of Israel in earthly things, that the promise is introduced which is a point of hope to *our* souls.

The first resurrection *only* is spoken of in 1 Cor. xv; the *saved*, and no others, are mentioned. The *order* of the resurrection is told us in verses 23, 24: first, "Christ the first-fruits"; second, "afterwards they that are Christ's at his coming" (all the family of faith); third, "Then cometh the end", the time of the general resurrection. "Then" is not here, as in verse 54, equivalent to "at that time", but wholly a different word, indicating *successional order*; the rest of the dead live not till the *close* of Christ's millennial reign.

# NOTE ON THE INTERPRETATION OF THE FORMER PART OF DANIEL XI BY PAST HISTORY

THERE are *four* schemes of interpretation of Daniel xi.

*First*: That which regards the whole chapter as belonging to the successors of Alexander, in Syria and Egypt, on to the end of the reign of Antiochus Epiphanes.

*Second*: That which applies the predictions on to verse 20 to the Seleucidæ and Ptolemies, and which there supposes a trajection to be made to the closing events of Israel's history, and the reign of the personal antichrist.

*Third*: An interpretation which looks at the history of Alexander's successors as being here given, up to and *including* the reign of Antiochus, to whom it applies verses 21–32. It then supposes a break to exist in verse 33, and then in verse 36 brings in the antichrist.

*Fourth*: The explanation which I have given in the preceding pages, supposing that from verse 21 to the end is the history of one person, and that verses 5–20 relate to the condition of the kingdoms of Syria and Egypt prior to his rise; so that there would be the long break or interval between verses 4 and 5.

I need not speak further in explanation of this view than I have already done in the preceding pages, except in connection with the other schemes of interpretation. If the chapter be so joined together as I have sought to show, then no alleged past accomplishment need detain our minds from looking onwards, and no testimony of past history ought to hinder us from so doing.

I have already remarked on the especial importance of seeing the application of the *latter part* of the vision; and this the reader will observe is similarly maintained in all except the first of the four schemes of interpretation to which I have referred. In maintaining this, however, we ought not to overlook what the Scripture makes the application of all the parts of the vision.

The *third* of the schemes of interpretation to which I have referred above is stated in Mr. Newton's *Prospects of the Ten Kingdoms*,\* 3rd edition, ch. XI. In the *general* application of the prophecies of Daniel he agrees with the explanations which I have given, and so, too, as to the *issue* of this vision our conclusions accord; he, however, applies verses 21–32 to the actings of Antiochus Epiphanes against the Jews and Jerusalem, and of course he considers the previous part of this chapter as accomplished in the early Syrian and Egyptian monarchs. He considers it to be impossible to suppose that prophecy does not mention Antiochus Epiphanes, who so wonderfully *foreshadowed* the antichrist. Farther than this I do not go: I believe that Antiochus *prefigured* the antichrist, and that this alone leads to terms and expressions being used in this chapter which are capable of application to the former. Mr. Newton considers that in this chapter it cannot be the antichrist who sets this abomination of desolation, because it is here set by a king who returns from an unsuccessful expedition against Egypt, instead of being the work of one who stands in plenitude of power. I do not think that this objection is conclusive; indeed, I should apply the remark in another way; it shows, I think, that the early actings of the antichrist are *not* characterised by that resistless power which they

\* *Prospects of the Ten Kingdoms of the Roman Empire considered*; 3rd edition, by B. W. Newton.

afterwards display. It is unquestioned that, from 1805 to 1812, Napoleon was paramount amongst the sovereigns of continental Europe; and yet this same man had been checked in his career of conquest in Syria before the walls of Acre. But in Daniel xi the king described seems only to recoil in order to strike a more destructive blow. As to the objection that this "vile person" is king of the north, and therefore not the king who in the lattter part of the chapter fights against the king of the north (verse 40), it does not appear to me to be valid; he rises *in* the northern kingdom, but I should use verse 40 as showing that he is not the successional monarch of Syria.* Whether the events from verses 31 to 45 are too many to be included in the 1,260 days of antichrist's *unhindered* power may best be judged, I believe, from the other accounts which Scripture gives of that time; I cannot see that these verses would occasion greater difficulty than many other descriptions of that period. The special hindrance to my regarding this scheme as tenable is found in the mention of the abomination of desolation to which, *in the same vision*, reference is made in chapter xii. I cannot suppose the one to be past and the other to be future.

The *second* scheme of interpretation is that which was approved by some of the writers of the early Church, and by many, I believe, of those in later times who retained the early opinion of a personal antichrist. It will

* However I do not accord with the hypothesis that the *fulfilment* of the former part of Daniel xi is to be sought in the history of the Ptolemies and Seleucidæ, yet we may rightly, I believe, see in the history of those kings the same *kind* of a condition of things as is here foretold. We know that in the Syrian kingdom there were *repeatedly* found new monarchs who arose, who might be spoken of just in the same manner as the king who rises in verse 21. There was again and again a reigning king of the north in possession of Antioch, and another king obtaining and exercising sovereign power at Ptolemais (Acre), or elsewhere, within the limits of the northern kingdom.

THE FOUR KINGDOMS 173

be worth while to enter into the detail of this interpretation, which to the end of verse 20 belongs equally to the third scheme also.

In opposing the Revelation of God in the Scripture, Porphyry attacked the authenticity of the book of Daniel, which was (he said) written after the events of the Maccabean period. He was therefore anxious to show that from verse 21 to the end was a *history* of Antiochus Epiphanes, and that the preceding verses were equally *a history* of his predecessors. The former part of the chapter was admitted by Jerome to be a *prophecy* of the predecessors of Antiochus; the latter part (verse 21 to end) he denied to relate to Antiochus (however in parts it might resemble him), believing it to belong to the antichrist. It will be well to go through the former part of the chapter, following Jerome's remarks on Porphyry, and adding the dates as they stand in the tables of Petavius and Dean Prideaux. This will show the *selected* portions of history to which the prophecy has been applied.

After the four kings which should rise in Persia (verse 2) there is an interval of 146 years, from the expedition of Xerxes, 480 B.C., to the invasion of Persia by Alexander, 334 B.C.; this interval or break is clear and manifest on *any* of the schemes of interpretation.*

Jerome understands the four parts of Alexander's empire to be those which existed for a short period *before* the battle of Ipsus, in 301 B.C.,† when Antigonus pos-

* It is scarcely needful to mention that some early writers, in utter ignorance of chronology and history, interpreted the fourth king to be Darius, the son of Hystaspes, whom they identified with the last Darius, a century and a half later. This impossible scheme, of course, excludes a break in this part of the chapter.
† I regard the division which resulted from that battle as being clearly the fourfold distribution of territory intended; for then, and not till then, was there a precise division into *four* parts, all of which were ruled

sessed a large portion of Alexander's dominions, which he *here* explains to be the kingdom of the north: farther on in the chapter he interprets the kingdom of the north to be that of Seleucus.

In verse 5 Jerome understands the strong king of the south to be Ptolemy, the son of Lagus, the first of Alexander's successors who ruled over Egypt. The strong one of his princes he explains to be, not a sovereign of another country, but his son and successor, Ptolemy Philadelphus, who reigned from 285 to 247 B.C. In verse 6 he regards the vision to relate to the endeavour made to form a federation confirmed by marriage between this king Ptolemy Philadelphus and Antiochus Theos, the third king of Syria, to whom the former gave his daughter in marriage, requiring him to repudiate his former wife Laodice; these events occurred 248 B.C.*

Verses 7 and 8 were understood by Jerome to apply to Ptolemy Euergetes, who reigned 247 to 221 B.C., and who made a successful expedition against the kingdom of Syria to revenge the murder of his sister Berenice. This therefore supposes the "king of the north" to be a different person from the sovereign so designated in

---

over by some of Alexander's generals—indeed, by the only four then surviving.

* There is a difficulty in this interpretation as to the words "and he that begat her", for we cannot apply the prediction historically to her father. The word, as it stands in the present Hebrew text וְהַיֹּלְדָהּ (the article placed usually before a noun with suffix), clearly admits of no other rendering. The margin of our English translation has "he whom she brought forth"—a rendering which seems to have been adopted to fit the prophecy to the history, as if the Hebrew had been וְהַיְלָדָהּ. In Theodotion's translation of Daniel (commonly printed as the LXX) καὶ ἡ νεάνις is the rendering given: in the *real* LXX of Daniel nothing can be defined as to this word. The Vulgate has *adolescentes ejus*; and in Jerome's Commentary the rendering is *juvenes ejus*; the rendering of the Syriac is *adolescentulæ ejus*. All this seems to show that some difficulty was felt as to this word, while at the same time we find no *united* testimony to uphold any different reading from that of the present Hebrew text.

verse 6,* for Antiochus Theos was poisoned by Laodice after a reign of fifteen years, 247 B.C. He therefore makes the king of the north in these verses to be Seleucus Callinicus (the successor of Antiochus Theos), who reigned till 227 B.C., and against whom the victorious war of Ptolemy Euergetes was directed.

Jerome applies verse 10 to the actings of Seleucus Ceraunus and Antiochus the Great, the sons of Seleucus Callinicus; the former of these reigned from 227 to 224 B.C., when the latter succeeded him for thirty-six years. He says that "after the flight and death of Seleucus Callinicus, his two sons, . . . stirred up with the hope of victory, and of avenging their father, waged war with Ptolemy Philopator".† This Egyptian king, however, did not reign at the same time as Seleucus Callinicus; for his rule (221 to 204 B.C.) began in the second year of his successor Antiochus the Great. The following verses are of course applied to the actings of the same Antiochus, and to his wars with the kings of Egypt, Ptolemy Philopator, and his successor Ptolemy Epiphanes (204–180), to whom he gave his daughter Cleopatra in marriage, an event which Jerome considered to be foretold in verse 17. This interpretation makes the check which this king of the north received (verse 18) to be the rout of Antiochus by the

* This is a conclusion to which I should have thought the words of the prophecy would not have led; I should have considered the identity as very obvious.

† This application of the prophecy appears to blend together events which were twenty years apart. The *flight* of Seleucus Callinicus refers apparently to his defeat by Ptolemy Euergetes, while his *death* took place in captivity amongst the Parthians: his two sons had no occasion to carry on a war of revenge against Egypt, with which their father had long been at peace. In fact, the expedition of Seleucus Ceraunus was against the king of Pergamus, during which he was treasonably poisoned. On the accession of Ptolemy Philopator, Antiochus the Great set himself to recover all the parts of Syria which were in the hands of the Egyptian kings, who had held some places (as Seleucia near the mouth of the Orontes) for twenty-seven years.

N

Roman forces, 190 B.C., an event which brought the Romans into connection with Asia and which permanently placed the Syrian kingdom in a subordinate condition.

Verse 20 is applied by Jerome to Seleucus Philopator, who reigned 187 to 176 B.C., "who did nothing worthy of the empire of Syria and of his father, and died ingloriously without any wars". He adds that Porphyry will not admit that Seleucus is intended in this place, but Ptolemy Epiphanes, who formed designs against Seleucus, and was cut off by poison.\* He asks how this Ptolemy could be here introduced after Antiochus the Great. He also says that the Jews applied this verse to a certain Trypho.†

Verse 21 brings us to the point at which Jerome's scheme of interpretation diverges from the *first* and the *third* of those which I have mentioned. He considers that from this point to the end of the chapter we have the prophetic history of *one person*, who was then future, and is so yet. Here, then, he supposes the great break or interval of the vision; for he rightly saw that in the beginning of the next chapter a resurrection is plainly spoken of as contemporaneous with the destruction of a king whom he considered to be the same as the "vile person" introduced in this verse. He says, "Thus far the order of history is followed, and there is no contention between Porphyry and us.‡ As to the other things

---

\* The difficulties which lie in the way of applying this prophecy concerning "a raiser of taxes" to Seleucus Philopator are considerable: he is destroyed, it is said, "within few days", and yet his reign continued for *eleven years*, as long a time as that of Antiochus Epiphanes himself. To make this suit, resort has been had by some to the "year-day system", and thus "within few *days*" has been taken as equivalent to "within few *years*". The authors of the *Universal History* had their minds so imbued with the idea, as though it were a plain and simple fact, that they *quote* this verse "within few *years*".

† Who lived, however, *after* the time of Antiochus Epiphanes.

‡ This statement goes rather too far: Porphyry and Jerome are not in accordance as to the meaning of verse 20.

## THEORY OF JEROME

to the end of the book, *he* interprets them of the person of Antiochus surnamed Epiphanes, the brother of Seleucus, the son of Antiochus the Great, who reigned eleven years in Syria after Seleucus, and took possession of Judæa, under whose reign took place the persecution of the Law of God and the wars of the Maccabees. But *we* consider that all these things are prophesied of antichrist, who is to come in the last time. And when it is objected, why the prophetic discourse should omit so many persons from Seleucus to the end of the world, the answer is, that also in the former history, which spoke of the kings of Persia, four only of the kings after Cyrus are mentioned, and many are passed over; so that Alexander king of the Macedonians is suddenly introduced, and that this is the custom of Holy Scripture, not to narrate everything, but to set forth those things which seem to be of the greater moment." He then speaks of the following part of the chapter as being applicable to Antiochus, merely as a *type* of antichrist. It seems to me that his solution of the difficulty is not very satisfactory; for the deeds of Antiochus were of more consequence to the Jews than the wars of his predecessors. A better answer *on this scheme* would have been to say that the affairs of the Syrian kingdom are treated of until the fourth monarchy appears on the scene, and that *then* there is a trajection to future ages.

It will be observed that, in Jerome's interpretation, events are *selected* at intervals, in the history of Syria and Egypt, to which to apply the predictions: thus the first definite event assumed belongs to the year 248 B.C. or about seventy-five years after Alexander's death;* there are also points of difficulty as to the persons to

* This is just where I believe the interval or hiatus actually to be—immediately after the mention of the fourfold division.

whom the parts of the prediction are applied; so that it is not strictly correct to say that this prophecy gives (on Jerome's scheme) a *continuous* history, nor yet that the succession of kings is *distinctly* denoted in the vision in accordance with the history to which it is applied.

This ought to be borne in mind; for the testimony said to be drawn from past history is a selection of individual events taken from the circumstances of the kingdoms of Syria and Egypt, and put together in the supposition that they meet the terms of the prophecy. The *idea* that this application was correct was probably very ancient, commencing at the time when the Jews thought Antiochus Epiphanes to be the subject of all the latter part of the chapter. I am not, however, aware that any one drew this out into a definite scheme before Porphyry, and he did it for a purpose. Jerome did not object to this, and he seems, up to verse 21, to have accepted Porphyry's statements of the historic facts.*

From verse 21, Jerome compares the statements of Porphyry with the vision and with the facts of history, —vindicating, as he goes on, the application of the prophecy in its strict sense to antichrist solely. "We will follow the order of exposition, and briefly note according to each explanation, what our adversaries think, and what is our opinion." Then, after showing how Porphyry applied verses 22 and 23 to the actings of Antio-

* Although, as previous remarks and notes have shown, there are many discrepancies between the terms of the prophecy and the facts as alleged. Other facts appear to rest solely on Porphyry's *assertion*, grounded on what he found in the prophecy. Just so it is a simple fact that many of the things which Rollin and similar writers bring forward as minute accomplishments of prophecy are points only gathered from the prophecy itself, without their being known from any independent evidence, and therefore all turns on the accuracy with which the prophecies have been understood as to their application and meaning. If this application be *rightly* known, then we may confidently refer to the prophecy for details which it may state, whether *history* has transmitted such particulars or not.

chus against Ptolemy Philometer (180 to 146 B.C.), he says, "But our people interpret both better and more rightly, that in the end of the world antichrist will do these things", etc.

On verse 27 he says, "There is no doubt that Antiochus did make peace with Ptolemy, and that he feasted with him, and that he devised frauds against him, and that he gained nothing by it; because he could not obtain his kingdom, and was driven out by the soldiers of Ptolemy. Since the Scripture now says that there are two kings whose hearts shall be fraudulent, so that they shall devise evil one against another, *this according to the history cannot be demonstrated to be true*; for Ptolemy was of tender age, and was deceived by the fraud of Antiochus;—what evil, then, could he devise against him?" He continues, verse by verse, to show how the terms are *applicable*, in a measure, to Antiochus, but only as a type of antichrist. He also mentions occasionally the opinions of the Jews about the prophecy: thus, in verse 34, "they shall be holpen with a little help", he says that some of the Jews understood the expression of Severus and Antoninus [Caracalla], others of Julian. On verse 36 he says, "From this place the Jews consider that antichrist* is spoken of; that after the little aid of Julian, a king should arise who would do according to his own will", etc. Porphyry, however, still supposed Antiochus to be the subject, on to the end of the chap-

* Some may ask, "But what can *Jews* know about *antichrist*?" Many Jewish writers both in early and in later times speak of Armillus—called also Armillaus, and Armalgus) as one who shall be specially raised up by Satan's power, just before the coming of Messiah, the Son of David. Of this Armillus they say many wonderful things, in part borrowed from their own Scriptures, and in part (as seems evident to me) from the book of Revelation. They ascribe to him miraculous powers, and speak of his blasphemies and persecutions, and they say that his end will be destruction by the breath of the lips of the Messiah, according to Isa. xi. 4 (*vide* Buxtorf, *Lex. Rab. in voc.*).

ter, where Jerome says that he indulges in dreams about this king.

Such is the *second* of the schemes of interpretation, according to Jerome's outline. There are points of historic discrepancy which would prevent my receiving it on to verse 20; where, also, I fail to find that distinct break or interval which *must* exist there on this scheme. This system of explanation, however, so far accords with what I believe to be true, in recognising that from verse 21, to the end, is the history of one person, who makes three invasions of Egypt, and that the abomination of desolation in this chapter is identical with that to which our Lord refers in Matt. xxiv. As to *this* system, I have only to add, that *if* I saw that the earlier portion of this prophecy did really belong to the past period, then all supposed discrepancies of every sort must be charged upon history, and upon that only.*

* We really know very little about the minute points of history, brought forward as the fulfilments, except from Jerome's account of what Porphyry had written. Of the sources from which Porphyry drew, Dean Prideaux says, "He made use of the best Greek historians extant. Such were Callinicus Sutorius, Diodorus Siculus, Hieronymus, Polybius, Posidonius, Claudius Theon, and Andronicus Alypius, and from them made evident proof, that all that is written in the eleventh chapter of Daniel was truly, in every particular, acted and done in the order as there related. . . . Jerome in his comments on Daniel makes use of the same authors that Porphyry did; and what is in these comments are all the remains which we now have of the work of that learned heathen, or of most of those authors which he made use of in it; for this whole work of Porphyry is now lost, *as also are most of the histories above mentioned, which he quotes in it*; and the histories of Callinicus Sutorius, Hieronymus, Posidonius, Claudius Theon, and Andronicus Alypius, are wholly perished, as is also the greatest part of Polybius and Diodorus Siculus. Had we all these extant, we might from them be enabled to make a much clearer and fuller explication of these prophecies, especially from Callinicus Sutorius, who lived in the time of Antoninus Pius. . . . There being at present no other remains of those ancient historians (except Polybius and Diodorus Siculus), but what we have in Jerome's comments on Daniel, and his proem to them" *Connection of the History of the Old and New Testaments*, part ii, book iii, *ad fin.*; vol. ii, pp. 161, 162, ed. 1724, fol.).

Thus we are really limited as to our knowledge of minute points to that which Porphyry gives as the testimony of historians, and which Jerome

The opinion of the Jews (mentioned by Jerome) that verse 36 introduces the antichrist, coincides with the *third* scheme of interpretation which I have named. It appears to have originated with the belief that the actings of Antiochus Epiphanes were the subject of the middle part of the chapter, connected with the distinct apprehension that the vision takes up the destruction of an adversary at the time of the deliverance of the Jews and the resurrection of the just.

The idea that the past history of Alexander's successors is the subject of this chapter first appears, I believe, in the first book of Maccabees (in itself a useful and interesting piece of history). The writer knew what had just befallen his nation in the reign of Antiochus Epiphanes; he knew, too, what Daniel had predicted, and he thought, naturally enough, that the one was the fulfilment of the other. He applied (see 1 Macc. i. 54) the prediction of Daniel, relative to the "abomination of desolation", to the idol which Antiochus had set up. He applied the Psalms, which speak of the Jews in their latter-day trouble, to that time (compare 1 Macc. vii. 17, with Psalm lxxix. 3), and seemed to think that, after the destruction of Antiochus, the promises of blessing would be accomplished. He seems, in chap. ix. 27, to

---

relates as following Porphyry. Dean Prideaux, after stating the point of divergence between Jerome and Porphyry, and the manner in which the former applied from verse 21 to the end to antichrist, gives his own opinion thus:

"The truth of the matter seems to be this, that as much of these porphecies as relate to the wars of the king of the north and the king of the south (that is the king of Syria and the king of Egypt) was wholly and ultimately fulfilled in those wars. But as much of these prophecies as related to the profanation and persecution which Antiochus Epiphanes brought upon the Jewish Church was all typically fulfilled in them; but they were to have their ultimate and thorough completion only in those profanations and persecutions which antichrist was to bring upon the Church of Christ in aftertimes."

take up the words of Dan. xii. 1 as to a time of unequalled tribulation. If it were taken as a fixed point that the pollution of the temple by Antiochus is truly the "abomination of desolation spoken of by Daniel the prophet", then, of course, the former part of the chapter would belong to what immediately preceded his reign.

The *strongest* ground (as I have said) for preventing me from adopting the *third* scheme of interpretation is that which relates to "the abomination of desolation". This form of distinct idolatry is so spoken of by our Lord in Matt. xxiv. that I can only regard it as *one* definite object of prophecy. In *this* vision we have (chapter xi. 31), "they shall place the abomination that maketh desolate." In this *same* vision (chap. xii. 11), mention is made of "the abomination that maketh desolate", which I can only conclude to be one and the same thing, referred to by our Lord as future. The verse just quoted also mentions "the daily sacrifice" as taken away, which connects the statement with Dan. viii. 13, where that event is spoken of together with "the transgression of desolation"—an allusion to the *abomination*, but not under the same name. Dan. ix. 27 tells us of *a causer of desolation on the pinnacle of abominations*, referring, I doubt not, to the same time and event. But it is only in chap. xi. 31 and in chap. xii. 11 (which depends on it) that it is spoken of by the *name* which our Lord uses; to *this* vision, therefore, I believe that he distinctly refers, and this reference I take as a defined point for interpreting the prophecy.

Our Lord, in His discourse on the Mount of Olives, recorded in Matt. xxiv and Luke xxi, foretells events, some long since fulfilled, some yet unaccomplished: it is important to observe this; for if we identify "the abomination of desolation" (Matt. xxiv.) with "Jerusalem compassed about with armies" (Luke xxi), we should be obliged to suppose that all the passages in which Daniel mentions this abomination are long past. Jerusalem was compassed with armies when the days of vengeance on the Jews commenced; the abomination of desolation will be set up three years and a half before that vengeance ends. As to the abomination of desolation having been set up at the siege by Titus (ut verbis utar non meis sed Ambrosii) "*quod ego nec furens dixerim*"—'I could not be so demented as to say it.'

But though I object to the supposition that Antiochus Epiphanes and his pollution of the temple are taught us in this vision, I most freely admit that the deeds of Antiochus form a striking and solemn foreshadowing of what shall be in the days of the antichrist. Antiochus set up on the altar of burnt-offering an idol, and built an altar before it upon which he sacrificed abominations. Fierce and bitter persecution was the treatment of those who abstained from participating in these pollutions. And yet the claims and conduct of the antichrist will go beyond this. In reading the first book of Maccabees\* (simply as a piece of uninspired history) we may form some idea of the more fearful display of evil which is yet to be.

---

\* The providence of God has transmitted to us the books called Apocrypha, comprising the uninspired writings of the Jews from the close of the Old Testament to the time of our Lord. They are of some importance to us, as we learn by their means what were the opinions and feelings on subjects of divine truth in the intermediate times. In thus speaking of the Apocrypha, later forgeries, such as the second book of Esdras, must not be included. Of all these books the first of Maccabees is probably the most important. In John x. 22 we find our Lord at Jerusalem keeping the Feast of Dedication; this was the festival instituted in commemoration of the purging of the temple by Judas Maccabeus, and its observance by our Lord may be considered as a *sanction* of the deliverance which he and his brethren wrought, as being a distinct work of God. Without conceding to the books of the Apocrypha any *authority*, I believe that we may regard their transmission to us as designed in the providential ordering of God for our instruction.

# NOTE ON PROPHETIC INTERPRETATION IN CONNECTION WITH POPERY AND THE CORRUPTION OF CHRISTIANITY

IN the Remarks on the different prophecies of Daniel, I have given reasons for not interpreting the predictions of latter-day evil by the Papacy and the Popish system. Whether the explanation of such prophecies, by applying them to an infidel antichrist, and a system connected with him, be correct or not, must be considered from the terms of the Scripture itself, and not from any preconceived thoughts. It will not do for us to form our opinions on the solemnity and importance of a subject first, and then to go to the Scripture to find something to support it. The primary question must always be, What is it that the Spirit of God speaks of in such or such a passage? If we are sure that the papal system does *not* meet the terms of a prediction, *fully* and *wholly*, then we must not explain away the strict accuracy of prophetic language in the hope of thus making it suit.

What is the worst form of evil which, as we are forewarned in the Scripture, will arise prior to the second advent of Christ, and will then receive *His* destroying judgment? What are its characteristics? What its doom? This is the real question at issue—not whether Romanism is an evil, dangerous to souls, and opposed to the gospel of the grace of God.

Now, the terms of Scripture are plain as to two points: first, the doom of those who own the antichrist; and second, the extent of his influence within his own sphere. As to the doom, we read, "If any man worship the beast and his image, . . . the same shall drink of the wine of the wrath of God" (Rev. xiv. 9, 10)—and thus the adherents of this system (whatever it be) will be certainly *lost*. And as to the extent of the influence, this person or system (or whatever it be) will draw all those within the sphere of its influence (except the elect of God) into its vortex; for "all shall worship him whose names are not written in the Lamb's book of life" (Rev. xiii. 8); that is to say, *all* within the allotted scene of the actions of the beast, except those whose names were written in the Lamb's book of life from before the foundation of the world, will be his worshippers. There will be, therefore, *no* unrenewed hearts except those who own *this* antichrist. Irrespective of all detail of prophetic circumstances, apply *this* to the Papacy: the argument, then as to the countries in which we live, will stand thus: *All who shall reject the claims of antichrist in his time are the elect of God* (this is a truth of Revelation): so that if we assume as an axiom *that Popery is the antichrist*, it follows of necessity that *all who reject the claims of Popery are the elect of God*. Thus, then, all would be saved who are not Roman Catholics; as though there were none wicked outside that pale—a doctrine which no one believes—although many have seemed to pride themselves on being "Protestants" *almost* to this degree. As we *know* that the unrighteous, be they Papists or Protestants, shall not inherit the kingdom of God, *this alone* might lead us to pause before we identified the antichrist of Scripture with a system which does not include all except the elect.

But when we look at the certain doom of the adherents of the antichrist, we find a new difficulty—*they will be all lost*: does any one who values the grace of God, and who knows how the Holy Ghost can savingly apply the blood of Christ to the soul, suppose that *no one* within the pale of the Church of Rome can be saved—that none of them can be quickened by the Spirit of God to trust in that Saviour who takes away the sins of his people? Surely many a one has lived and died in external fellowship with Rome whose heart really rested, through God's sovereign grace, on the blood of atonement and the Saviour's merits.

Take the declarations of Scripture, and then we see that this doom is pronounced on all who own, or have owned, the antichrist: they are looked on as not having "received the love of the truth that they might be saved: and for this cause God shall send them strong delusion, that they should believe a lie: that they all might be damned who believe not the truth, but had pleasure in unrighteousness" (2 Thess. ii. 10–12). Thus they are all contemplated as those who have rejected light, and who therefore have been already given over judicially to darkness. Will this apply to all Romanists? Are all of necessity *lost* who have at any time been within the pale of that body? The Reformers were themselves originally all of them Papists: Luther was not merely a Roman Catholic, but also a priest and an Augustinian monk. Those who hold that the Papacy is the antichrist are hindered by their love of God's truth, and the gracious invitations of the gospel of salvation, from adopting what *might* be legitimately deduced from their applications of prophecy. Happily they do not *act* on any such consequence of their opinions, and thus not a few who maintain the popish system to be antichrist are earnest in preaching the gospel of Christ to Romanists, instead of *actually* applying to them the unqualified and unmitigated sentence of the word of God.* I rejoice that such do not

* The "Appeal" on behalf of "The Edinburgh Irish Mission", recently

*act* on their application of prophecy, but on their own knowledge and apprehension of the gospel message: that all such labours may be blessed in the conversion of souls must be the heart's desire and prayer of those who know the value of the gospel: it may be, however, observed that every Romanist converted is a proof of the fallacy of the mode of interpretation of which I have been speaking.

This searching for Popery in Scriptures which speak of a worse consummation would lead to strange results; and the very declarations of the word of God would have to be *softened*, because the mind feels that such statements *cannot* be *fully* applied to the consequences of Popery. If we admit that a person in the Church of Rome may possibly be saved, in faith on the blood of Christ (not through, but in spite of, his system), and if one who renounces his errors, and leaves that system, accepting the gospel, may be saved, and used as an honoured servant of Christ, then, in fact, the whole matter is conceded —that a worse abomination than Popery is treated of in

---

[1852] put into my hands, signed by Drs. Begg, Cunningham, Candlish, M'Crie, and Duff, speaks of "the true nature of Popery as subversive of the whole Gospel, as *the man of sin, and mystery of iniquity, doomed of God, with* ALL *who take part in its abominations*" (p. 2). If this statement were correct, what benefit could result from bringing Christian effort to bear on Romanists? The Apostle Paul tells us (2 Thess. ii. 7) that "the mystery of iniquity doth *already* work", but that the "man of sin" should "be revealed in his time"; they are thus contrasted and not identical. Hence, nothing but confusion of thought, as to Scripture truth, can result from assuming that *both* of these contrasted forms of evil are the Papacy. Had *either* of the things been asserted to be Romanism, the question would have been *capable* of discussion; but how can this be the case when the very statement involves a contradiction in terms? But this need not cause any surprise, since in close connection with this statement we read of the doom of all who take part in the abominations of this system, and are then told of efforts to deliver souls from this inevitable sentence. May all the efforts be blessed!—for it is not on Romanists that Scripture denounces this irreversible judgment.

the prophetic Scripture, and that it is no palliation of Popery to admit that such is the fact.

But as to palliation of Popery, I say with all confidence that I see such consequences legitimately deducible from the application as such Scriptures as 2 Thess. ii. to the Popedom, that were I to do this I should feel that I were indeed palliating Romanism. What is meant by "the temple of God"? In Scripture this is, first, the elect Church; or, second, the bodies of individual saints—the Holy Ghost dwelling in both; or, third, our Lord's human body; or, fourth, the actual temple of God, at Jerusalem. Has the Pope sat, or could he sit, showing himself that he is God, in any of these four? If it be said that the Pope does this, as taking such a place as he does in the Church, then Popery is indeed palliated, and the line of demarcation between truth and falsehood broken down, by applying to that system a name which belongs to God's elect people. Is the temple of God, St. Peter's? Many have seemed to affirm this, and have talked about the Pope as enthroned on the *high altar* in that building\* (which is itself, in the sense intended, quite a mistake), as the fulfilment of the prophecy. But St. Peter's is not the temple of God, but the temple of an idol, and the Pope may be there seen taking (vidi et ipse) the place of an idolator as much as the meanest in the crowd. Papal claims and doctrines are alike fearful falsehoods: the

---

\* This notion has arisen from a ceremony connected with the creation of a new Pope, in which he receives honours, unchristian indeed, but not as claiming the place of God. The high altar is *on that occasion* stripped of its ornaments, and on it the Pope is set, to receive the recognition of the cardinals, priests, and Roman people. But the altar, *when stripped of its coverings*, loses with Romanists its peculiar character; and I have seen altars at Rome used for meaner purposes than the seat of a Pope. In fact, the whole idea that the Pope sits, or claims to sit, in St. Peter's, "showing himself that he is God", is erroneous. Let Papal claims be stated *accurately*, and let their opposition to God and His gospel be faithfully pointed out. [See a note at the end of this chapter, p. 214.]

word of God supplies the counteracting truths; but an indiscreet zeal may only have the effect of producing the result the very reverse of what had been intended. I utterly reject the charge of palliating the evils of Popery, and I might with truth ask whether this might not result from the acknowledgment of anything in which the Pope sits as being "the temple of God".

But the application of certain prophecies to Popery, or the contrary, does not affect the question whether that system is alike evil in its doctrines and its practices, but only whether there is or is not a greater and worse evil of which we are warned.

But if we do not apply certain predictions to Popery, how can we meet it? How can we show that it is condemned in Scripture?

To this I answer, that it is of the utmost importance for us to see what the real turning-point is between the gospel of Christ and Rome. The question is, "*How* is a sinner justified before God?" To this Rome may reply, Through such obedience to the Church as shall cause a participation in the merit of Christ's passion; through the means of holiness afforded in the Sacraments, etc. Is *this* in accordance with Scripture? Is this in accordance with the gospel that Paul preached? Is not this in direct opposition to all such Scriptures as teach that "it is by faith, that it might be by grace, to the end that the promise might be sure" (Rome. iv. 16): "He that believeth is justified from all things" Acts xiii. 39): "To him that worketh not, but believeth on him that justifieth the ungodly, his faith is counted for righteousness" (Rome. iv. 5)?

Thus, every passage which sets forth the gospel of the grace of God is utterly condemnatory of Romanism, and that not in its mere *details*, but in the foundation and inherent principle of the system. I do not say that the *details* are not condemned in Scripture, for they are: there have often been times when it has been needful to confute and meet these details (*such as idolatrous worship, withholding of the Scriptures, persecuting on principle*); but let it ever be remembered that in every contest a mere *war of posts* seldom is decisive: a petty warfare in details will *sometimes* lead away from the real centre of operations, while, if the deciding point of the war is seen, contended for, *and won*, outposts fall of necessity. Now I believe that Protestants have often treated Romish controversy as if it were a war of posts, so as to forget the real citadel to be attacked. They have looked at the *details* of the claims of Rome so much as not to know that *justification* is the turning-point of the whole matter. The Scripture doctrine of *justification through faith* has been let go by such nominal Protestants as entirely as by those who receive the dogmas of Trent.*

Not so did the Reformers of the sixteenth century think and act. With them arose the word *Protestant*; and if we ask, What did it *then* signify? the Augsburg

---

\* It is important to bear in mind that the canons of Trent are the most binding of all authorities on modern Romanists. Before the Reformation there was much latitude both of opinion and expression on many subjects, although the almost universal *tone* was thoroughly anti-evangelical and Pelagian; at Trent it was thought needful to put Romish dogmas on a very secure basis; and thus, while many statements of doctrine which had passed current in the Church of Rome were tacitly passed by or else repudiated by implication, the general tone of belief was embodied in such a form as to be definitely opposed to the Protestants, while so expressed as not to offend those of the adherents of Rome who had not approved of the phraseology previously used by some. [See in a note at the end of this chapter.]

The doctrinal definitions on *Justification* were especially drawn up to oppose the Reformers, embodying thoughts which Romanists had previously held loosely: the definitions on *Original Sin* were mostly new as dogmatic statements; and the canonisation of most of the books called Apocrypha for the first time by that council seems to have originated in a *mere mistake*.

THE POINT AT ISSUE 191

Confession, in 1530, supplies the definite answer: "The Churches amongst us teach with general consent that men cannot be justified before God by their own powers, merits, or works, but that they are *justified freely for Christ's sake through faith*." This is a true definition of the doctrine of true Protestants against Rome.

Thus, every statement which sets forth the gospel of God's grace is evidence against Rome; but not against Rome merely, but also against everything else in which the doctrines of grace are not fully held and taught. It is needful in opposing Rome not to forget how *negative* a character Protestantism has often had, both formerly and in the present day.

*Details* of false doctrine and evils in practice and requirement have often been argued against by Protestants, who were themselves utterly ignorant of the answer to the vital question—"How can man have peace with God?" On this point (to which for many years I have been accustomed to call the attention of Christians according to any ability which I possess) I will give the sentiments of [the late] Dr. Cunningham, of Edinburgh. He says: "The circumstances in which we have been placed, and the aspects in which Popery has been of late presented to us, have been, perhaps, fitted to give prominence in our minds to Romanism merely as a great system of tyranny and imposture, and to throw into the background the still more important and fundamental views of it as a system of idolatry and heresy, that is, as corrupting the true worship of God, and perverting the right way of salvation. Of course, we cheerfully admit, as all Protestants have done, that man may be, and that some men are, saved, who live and die in the communion of the Church of Rome. But it is not less true that Popery exposes to fearful danger the spiritual welfare of those who embrace it. It would be unnecessary and out of place to attempt to illustrate the truth of this position. I can only remind you of the importance of remembering and applying it, in order that, in exposing the Church of Rome, you may give due prominence to views which are fitted to show that Popery, when fully embraced, leads men to withhold from God the honour and worship which are due to Him, and to rest upon a false foundation for salvation; and that, in dealing with Papists, your bowels of compassion towards them may be stirred, and that you may make it manifest that you are animated by a sincere desire to promote their best interests.

"I am disposed to think that, in the discussions on popery in this country, too little prominence has been given to what may be called the more theological parts of the question—to the guilt of Popery in directly perverting the gospel of the grace of God, and especially by teaching erroneous views on the subject of original sin and justification.

"The cause of all this, no doubt, is, that many of those who have written most ably and learnedly against Popery, had themselves largely departed from the sound theology of the Reformers, and were not more scriptural and evangelical in their views upon these points than the canons of the Council of Trent. When Jeremy Taylor published a work that contained heresy on the subject of original sin, a Papist, who was much sounder in the faith, whose views were much more in accordance with the Bible and the Thirty-nine Articles, published a reply to it. Archbishop Wake, in his *Exposition of the Doctrine of the Church of England*, in reply to Bossuet's *Exposition of the Doctrine of the Catholic Church*, virtually gave up our whole contest with Rome on the subject of justification—Luther's article of a standing or a falling Church."*

Dr. Cunningham then goes on to speak of the similar defect in Bishop Gibson's *Preservative against Popery* and other works, in which, although particular doctrines of Romanism are well and learnedly refuted, yet, as to the vital question of Justification through Faith, there is either an entire silence or what is worse.

Protestantism ought not to be thus negative; it is a name full of meaning and significance; it tells *why* we left the communion of Rome, and *what* is the sole ground of our hope—the Saviour's death and merits applied to the soul by faith. Truly, when *negative* Protestantism arose, there was a condition of things such as was found in Israel after the death of Joshua and the elders who overlived him.

We *know*, in the lamentable inroads of Rationalism, to what negative Protestantism may tend: in *thus* refusing to admit the demands of Rome, the authority of God in His word has been equally cast off: and thus we find a grievous and widespread infidelity—a corrupting gangrene which works its way wherever the real authority of Scripture, as the revelation of God's will and truth, is not rightly maintained. This is a proof that there may be forms of error at least as deadly and soul-destroying as those of Rome itself.

Rationalistic infidelity may not have as yet as concrete a form as the Romish system presents. But all the aspirations of Rationalism tend towards a concrete form, in which there shall be seen the fully developed powers of man's mind triumphing over everything which teaches dependence on God, or the necessity or possibility of a revelation from Him.

* *Evangelical Christendom*, October 1851, pp. 341, 342.

This may be seen in not a little of the popular literature of this country: the same feeling has been distinctly marked in other lands. Dr. Krummacher, of Berlin, after discussing the forms of opposition to belief current in Protestant Germany, thus concludes: "Little more is necessary than that a mighty and talented personality should appear, who should set himself up as the centre of Infidelity, and represent it with energetic pathos and strong decision, and the reign of '*the man of sin*' would be amongst us in more than a state of embryo."*

This is just what I believe to be the fact: a rejection of the truth of God is now gaining ground, and from this will issue at last the system and principles of him who "will deny the Father and the Son". This person will be "*the* antichrist" in contradistinction to the "many antichrists" that have arisen from time to time.†

But is the system of Popery nowhere condemned in the prophetic parts of Scripture? Must we suppose that *the* antichrist is so exclusively a subject of prophecy that the "many antichrists" are overlooked?

To these questions I reply: *First*, that the less is always included in the greater; so that whatever condemns the greater abomination and evil condemns in its measure everything similar in kind or character. Thus, the

---

\* *Evangelical Christendom*, October 1851, p. 334.

† Some, in applying all that is said of the antichrist to the Pope, have given the name a new interpretation: they have said that "Antichrist" is not "opposed to Christ" but "instead of Christ"—that it is in fact one who claims to take the place of Christ as his vicar. Who, then, were the many antichrists of St. John's time? Did they each claim to be Christ's vicar? If not, then no such meaning can be applied to the name, and the argument falls to the ground. Again, How can any one who "denies the Father and the Son" claim to be the vicar of that Son, whose being he thus rejects? The Scripture leaves us in no doubt as to the import of the name antichrist. [Since this note was first published, this point has been well discussed by Abp. Trench, *New Testament Synonyms*, 2nd ed., p. 118.]

*principle* on which anything is condemned as evil in Scripture being once stated, it only remains to *apply* it to all that is similar. The sin of Simon Magus (Acts viii) has rightly been applied to all trafficking in holy things, and so the characteristics of the antichrist are applicable to all that may be similar in kind or degree. But, *Secondly*, the Scripture does give to us statements of the most definite kind as to the corruption of Christianity, such as *has been* and is found in Romanism. Thus we read in 1 Tim. iv, "Now the spirit speaketh expressly, that in the latter times some shall depart [or *shall apostatise*] from the faith [rather *from faith*, that ground on which a sinner is accepted before God through Christ's merits], giving heed to seducing spirits, and doctrines of devils; speaking lies in hypocrisy; having their conscience seared with a hot iron; *forbidding to marry, and commanding to abstain from meats which God hath created to be received with thanksgiving of them which believe and know the truth*." This is a solemn warning: it tells of the footsteps of that apostasy which, according to 2 Thess. ii, will result in the manifestation of "the man of sin".

Of course I do not *limit* this prophetic description to Popery: it includes all that is similar throughout Christendom, whether found in Romanism, in the Greek and Oriental Churches, or in bodies or individuals professedly and nominally Protestant. Wherever faith is departed from, this description will more or less apply. In Romanism, however, we have these things in a more concrete form: and how solemn is the statement that "the Spirit speaketh expressly" that this departure from faith does not result from the ordinary aberrations of man's intellect as estranged from God, but from the direct action of seducing spirits and doctrines of demons; that "speaking lies in hypocrisy", the conscience being cauterised, is the characteristic of the evil system here condemned!

I have already remarked on the fundamental falsehood of this corrupted Christianity—the denial that it is solely through the work of Christ for us, His one sacrifice and perfect righteousness, applied to the soul through faith, that we are accepted of God. Where Satan *obscures* this truth, he can easily lead astray in other things: where he causes it to be *denied*, then he finds men his captives in a twofold bondage.

And thus has it been in the Romish system: IDOLATRY has there established itself—entering in at first in forms hardly perceptible, until (as we now see) the adoration of saints, images, and relics, and the conversion of the Supper of the Lord into an object of worship as the Lord Himself, have taken a place in men's minds and in their religious services which could belong rightly to none but the Father, the Son, and the Holy Ghost, the one God of our salvation.

Solemn, indeed, are the consequences of idol-worship. The Gentiles of old, amongst whom the gospel was preached at first, were thoroughly sunk in this sin; and of them the apostle (1 Cor. x. 20), using the words of Deut. xxxii. 17, thus speaks: "The things which the Gentiles sacrifice, *they sacrifice to devils and not to God*; and I would not that ye should have fellowship with devils." Did the ancient heathens think that they were adoring evil spirits—demons—when they sacrificed to their gods and demi-gods?—when they honoured Jupiter and Hercules? And yet the Scripture thus teaches us that the worship *did actually* go to demons: it was thus directed by Satan. And this put the idolatrous nations under the distinct tutelage of demons, whose power showed itself amongst them in many ways. We should form, I believe, a very inadequate estimate of Romish idolatry if we were to overlook the solemn fact that it is *demon worship* commingling itself with that of the living and true God; so that Romish nations stand under demoniacal tutelage just as did the Gentiles of old.

The worship rendered to saints does not ascend to *them*; the honours paid to the Virgin Mary, to St. Francis, or to St. Philomena,* are not received by them,

---

\* St. Philomena is a saint greatly honoured of late years in the Church of Rome. Her legend sets forth that in the time of Diocletian she was the daughter of the king of Greece, at that time a Christian kingdom, and that for refusing to marry the heathen emperor and sacrifice to the gods, after a wearisome detail of miracles, she suffered martyrdom.

How much of this legend is *believed* by Romanists appears to me very doubtful; but, believed or not, it is publicly offered for sale at Rome on walls and bookstalls—where every book, be it remembered, is subjected to ecclesiastical censorship of the strictest kind, where not a line of Holy Scripture may be read or possessed in the vernacular language, and where not one statement of evangelical truth may be printed or circulated. The history of St. Philomena was said to have been revealed to a holy nun a few years ago, by which she was informed of the name and actions of an individual previously unknown, whose bones were discovered in the Roman catacombs.

Perhaps, however, these legends are not *believed*; if so, what must be the condition of those who render spiritual honours to beings in whom they do not believe? It is not always held needful at Rome to suppose that narrations set forth by ecclesiastical authority are *true*. Of the "holy images" venerated at Rome, none are better known than that of St. Peter in St. Peter's, the Madonna of Sant Agostino, and the *Holy Bambino of Ara Celi*. This last is a figure of the Infant Christ kept in the church of the Franciscans on the Capitol. A history of this Holy Image, by P. G. V. Giannini (printed in 1797), is kept on sale at Rome, with the due *imprimatur* of Passeri, archbishop of Larissa, the then vicegerent, and of Pani, the Master of the Holy Apostolic Palace. In 1845 I bought this little book, and on its being shown to a native of the British Isles, a scholar and a gentleman, then a priest and now a bishop in the Romish Church, who spent several months under the same roof with me at Rome, he said that no one was bound to *believe* the narration as a fact. I asked what then might the "Con licenza de' Superiori" mean: he replied that it was by no means a sanction of the book as authentic, only an approval of it as not unedifying, *just like Æsop's fables*. The misfortune, however, is that this and similar "not unedifying" books *claim* to be true narratives—that they pass current as such with the people at large, and if not true, they are irreverent in the extreme. It would be well if they were half as edifying as Æsop. It is only from such books that thousands learn all their ideas of religion, such as they may be. What a thought it is, that foolish and profane tales are

or by any other saints, whether real, supposed, or non-existent; the worshipper may imagine that he honours the mother of our Lord in the many litanies and prayers in which divine attributes are ascribed to her: the Scripture removes the veil and shows us, not the Virgin Mary as the receiver of the worship, but some potent demon, some especial leader under the banner of Satan This is the source, then, to which we ought to ascribe the system of Rome and the arts by which it is supported: all must be traced to demoniacal power and energy; hence the hold which the system takes on men's minds; hence its adaptation to the thoughts and feelings of man's fallen nature; hence the superhuman skill and wisdom displayed by the followers of Ignatius Loyola and by other Romish advocates. Whenever *God* is honoured in any way, whether in His almighty power or in His works of grace, there He is pleased to acknowledge the recognition of Himself. And thus He has shown Himself the protector of those nations that rejected Romish idolatry, and acknowledged the Father, the Son, and the Holy Ghost, as alone worthy of all worship and praise. A recurrence to Romish connection, a re-commingling in any way with the maintenance of Romish idolatry, would place a Protestant nation again under the sway and influence of those demons to whom idolatrous worship really ascends, whether the name under which they are adored be that of Jupiter or of Simon Peter the Apostle of Christ.

Protestants have often taken pains to disprove every tale or narrative of Romish miracles: no doubt that most of these marvels are mere impostures, finding their

---

approved as "not unedifying", while the *Scriptures* (of which the *Romans* were taught "whatsoever was written aforetime was written for our learning") are utterly proscribed!

origin either in the extreme superstition of minds blinded by demons, in the fraud of deceivers, or in a mixture of both. The character of the alleged miracles is such as almost to lead minds into a condition of scepticism as to all miracles, and this *has been* the case with several. But while the general character of Romish miracles and marvels denotes *weak deception*, we have no occasion, I believe, to attempt to prove that they are *all* void of reality. The Scripture records the miracles wrought by the Egyptian magicians, as well as those performed by Moses: we read of the signs of Simon Magus, as well as of the miracles of Philip and of the apostles. Demoniacal power must be recognised as a *fact*. At the time of the Reformation the servants of Christ did not think it needful to reject all Romish miracles; they only sought to ascribe them to their true source. Thus it was said in England that "God daily permitted miracles to be wrought by the power of the devil, as may be seen at the north door of St. Paul's and elsewhere". The Reformers acknowledged that some of the marvels were real, and yet they rejected the claims of Rome: they held to the truth of God, and denied that miracles could confirm anything, if opposed to that revelation already bestowed.

The Scripture presents a criterion and a safeguard to those who are watchful: "If there arise among you a prophet, or a dreamer of dreams, and giveth thee a sign or a wonder, *and the sign or the wonder come to pass,* whereof he spake unto thee, saying, *Let us go after other gods,* which thou hast not known, and let us serve them; *thou shalt not hearken unto the words of that prophet,* or that dreamer of dreams: *for the Lord your God proveth you,* to know whether ye love the Lord your God with all your heart and with all your soul" (Deut. xiii. 1-3). Thus, if any miracle be wrought in confirmation of any contradiction of a truth previously revealed of God, then such miracle ought not to be received as though it accredited in any way the newly introduced doctrine or opinion. The divine miracles of Scripture were in full accordance and harmony with every previous revelation, and their nature and character were distinctly opposed to Satanic power.

There may be miracles which in themselves give no indication as to their source, whether it be from above or from beneath. Miraculous power, however, in whatever way it may be manifested, should always lead men to examine it with attention, for it would be a proof of supernatural agency—the working either of God or of Satan; unless, then, such power be equally connected with *both truth and holiness*, it cannot be from God: in such a case we must apply the Scripture—"The Lord your God proveth you."

If the alleged miracles of Rome were all realities (instead of being so often obviously the reverse), they could not accredit the Romish system with its denial of the true gospel of Christ—a denial which involves the solemn anathema of God declared against all who preach "another gospel" (Gal. i. 8, 9).

The direct working of Satanic power has been seen from time to time, but it seems manifest that this energy is hindered and restrained in lands where the true worship of God is professed; secret workings of the enemy may there be found, but not the same unhindered might of evil. This might be *expected* to be more fully seen in heathen lands; to be found, but in a less degree, in nations that commingle the worship of God with the honours paid to demons; and to be restrained where God alone is worshipped, and Christ is avowed to be the only Mediator, *until* such nations or their rulers countenance idolatries.

In heathen lands there are many things which are incapable of explanation except on the supposition of direct Satanic power, and Scripture would never lead us to doubt or deny that it *may* be put forth.

In our Lord's days the most remarkable power of Satan over the *bodies* of men was seen in the case of the demoniacs, but we always find that the sphere of our Lord's miracles of mercy in casting them out was in Galilee or Samaria; Jerusalem, "the city of the great king", the place of that worship which Jehovah still recognised, is never then mentioned in connection with unclean spirits. After, however, Christ had been rejected, we do find demoniacs connected with Jerusalem, for in Acts v. 16 those who had unclean spirits are said to have been brought with others in suffering, to be healed in that city by the apostles.

There is a widespread incredulity at present as to Satanic agency and miraculous power—an incredulity which needs to be dispelled, because it leads many to be blind to their danger. The working of the "mystery of iniquity" commenced in the days of the apostles; it has gone on, including Popery and all other forms of corrupted and corrupting Christianity, and at length it will result in the manifestation of "the man of sin", who will arise accredited by Satanic miracles—"with all power, and signs and lying wonders". Surely this is not believed by many; and yet the Spirit of God here speaks of actual miracles and no mere deceptions of men's senses. What some of these miracles are, we read in Rev. xiii, where we are told of fire made to come down from heaven in the sight of men, and an image made to speak and breathe.

If claims to miraculous power be made, let us take heed and hold fast the truth of God; it is nowhere told us in Scripture that God will give us any new revelation confirmed by miracles, but we are warned that Satan will thus introduce the antichrist, and that *in this manner* men will be deceived. *No miracle can invalidate an antecedent fact.* The fact of redemption by the blood of the Son of God will remain as the sure ground-work of all Christian religion, even if ten thousand miracles were wrought to disprove it; this is a truth but little considered, and so little heed *will be paid* to it by men in general that by miracles they will be misled, unless they have received the love of the truth of God into their hearts by the operation of the Holy Ghost.

To some it may seem a dark and discouraging prospect thus to contemplate what the issue will be of professing Christianity within the Roman earth; to see the corruption which goes on as that which will at last increase so as to lead to full antichristian apostasy —the rejection of God and of Christ. But, if it be different from the prospects which many have imagined, we have only to ask whether this is not the truth of Scripture. If this be the case, then it is well for us to know it, for God never instructs us by holding out false expectations. Have not the Apostles Paul (2 Tim. iii), John (in speaking of "many antichrists" as a characteristic of "the last time"), James (v. 1–8), Peter (2 Epistle, chap. iii), and Jude, all taught us that the concluding days of this dispensation will be days of peculiar evil in the Church and in the world, up to the coming of the Lord? But (it may be asked) how are we to understand the Old Testament promises of widespread and universal blessing? Surely these promises shall be thoroughly fulfilled—no word of God is vain; but fulfilled they cannot be in a dispensation in which the many take the broad way and the few find the narrow.

However these things are opposed to the thoughts of

many Christians, the testimony of Christ's apostles is clear; and, further, the Lord Himself, before He laid down His life to redeem His Church, instructed His people as to these things. All the teaching of the Sermon on the Mount, all the instruction of John xiv-xvii, has this character.

In Matt. xii, however, the Lord Jesus gave definite instruction, in a series of seven parables, as to what "the kingdom of heaven" would be in its development on earth; how it would comprehend evil as well as good; and how the evil would be found as continuing to the end of the age or dispensation. How can "the kingdom of heaven" relate to anything evil? is a question often asked. It might suffice to refer to the chapter itself, where the *tares* and the *bad fishes* are quite as much portions of that kingdom as the *wheat* and the *good fishes*. We use as a common expression "Christendom"—the kingdom or dominion of Christ—by which we exclude the world of idolaters and Mahometans, and to which we do not consider the Jews as belonging, although many of them are locally in it. In Christendom there may be and are vast numbers who are not at all subject to the faith and doctrine of Christ, but to Christendom they belong as truly as do spiritual believers. Just so the Scripture phrase "the kingdom of heaven" includes all the individuals and nations that in consequence of the mission of Christ profess His name in any sense: if they are not *heavenly* themselves, it does not alter the fact that they, in the terms of Scripture, belong to the kingdom of heaven.

The kingdom of heaven is now known as developed on earth and subjected to many influences; in the day of Christ it will be known as altogether *heavenly*, all other things having been put out of it and all being conformed to God.

In the first parable of Matt. xiii the Lord shows that the seed sown would in many cases produce no fruit, although in some it would; this might be regarded as a preliminary warning not to suppose that the gospel was to produce universal blessing. Then follow six parables, divided into two groups of three each, as spoken respectively to the multitudes and to the disciples, as similitudes of the kingdom of heaven—that is, as exemplifications of some of its aspects.

In the first, that of "the tares of the field", we have (verses 37-43) our Lord's own interpretation; and we thus learn that in the field especially sown by the Son of Man there would be *evil* mixed with the good, that this evil would continue until the end ("let both *grow together* until the harvest"), and that the evil forms so conspicuous a characteristic that the parable receives its designation (verse 36) from the *tares* and not from the wheat. The last parable (verses 47-50), spoken to the disciples, teaches in some respects the same truths; the net equally enclosed the bad fishes and the good.

Thus any interpretation of these parables which involved the supposition that universal or widespread blessing was predicted must of necessity be incorrect, for it would exclude the possibility of the tares remaining till the harvest among the wheat. The two next parables—that of the grain of mustard-seed and of the leaven —were spoken to the multitudes as that of the tares of the field had been. This seems to direct our thoughts to the ostensible aspects of the kingdom of heaven, as they might be seen by the eye of mere man.

A grain of mustard-seed so grows as to produce not a herb, but a tree, like unto that seen in Nebuchadnezzar's vision (Dan. iv). Few things were more opposed to probabilities than that *this* should have been the issue of

Christianity—that instead of having to do with spiritual and unseen things it should acquire greatness in the earth; a result which the Lord does not explain except by the principles laid down in the interpretation of the preceding parable, by which we see that *while men slept* was carried on *the counter-working of Satan*. Let this be taken into consideration, and then we cannot be surprised that the tree of earthly greatness should thus spring from a seed, from which this would not have been looked for.

The next parable is, "The kingdom of heaven is like unto leaven, which a woman took, and hid in three measures of meal, till the whole was leavened." Whatever this parable may mean, it implies the spread of some principle throughout a certain body until its influence becomes universal. Does this, then, mean good or evil? Many would reply that "the kingdom of heaven" could not be compared to anything evil. On this I have already remarked; but observe that the similitude has respect to the *whole* parable: the parity is not connected with one word or thing, but with the *whole* similitude. So, in the last parable, the kingdom of heaven is likened to a *net*, not *in itself*, but in certain circumstances and connections. There will be a day when Christ shall gather out of His kingdom all things that offend, and then "the kingdom of heaven" shall be only comparable to what is good. Thus it is from the parable itself, and its connection, that we must judge as to whether this is a similitude of good or evil.

The notion of universality in its aspects seems to exclude the idea of good being here intended: those who thus interpret apply the parable either to the spread of the gospel—the diffusion of Christianity—or else to the results wrought by the regenerating influence of grace on the individual Christian. The first of these interpretations would be in entire opposition not only to the testimony of the apostles in their Epistles, as to the spread of evil in the latter days of this dispensation, but also to that of the parable of the tares of the field; the interpretation of that parable shows that evil will *continue*, and the prophecies in the Epistles show that it will *spread* and *increase*. As to the second interpretation, it is manifest that these parables do not refer to individuals separately; but even if they did, it is not true that certain principles of grace introduced ever do or can so transform a man as to change the carnal mind and the flesh into something good and holy. The carnal mind remains as really in the holiest believer as in the most abandoned sinner; it continues to be "enmity against God, for it is not subject unto the law of God, neither indeed can be": in the case of the believer, new principles of life and action are introduced, spiritual powers are bestowed for *keeping under* the flesh, but the flesh remains up to death or the resurrection-state. To apply this parable, then, to regeneration is wholly opposed to the nature of the gospel, and to the remedy which it proposes for fallen man.

It is thus impossible to understand this parable as teaching the diffusion of good, without contradicting the whole analogy, as well as the direct statements of revealed truth.

But what is *leaven*? It is the incipient corruption of the mass of kneaded flour, in which that fermentation commences to work, a small portion of which, if put into wetted flour, will produce incipient corruption of exactly the same kind, and so leaven the whole lump.*

---

* In this country, where *yeast* is so commonly used for making bread, what *leaven* really is, its nature and effects, are often but little understood: hence it is often not known to be incipient corruption spreading through the mass of dough, rendering the whole *sour* and, if not baked presently, also corrupt.

And thus leaven is always spoken of in the Old Testament: it invariably means, when used there as a symbol, that which is corrupt and productive of corruption. The disciples knew the Old Testament far too well to suppose that they were now to take this term in a good sense, unless they were expressly taught so to do. But is the New Testament use of the term "leaven" different? In Matt. xvi. 6 (and the parallel place, Mark viii. 15, and in Luke xii. 1) the Lord warns against "the *leaven* of the Pharisees and of the Sadducees". The disciples imagined that He referred to bread, until He showed them that He meant the doctrine—the evil doctrine of the Pharisees and Sadducees: in Luke xii. 1 He says, "the leaven of the Pharisees, which is hypocrisy"—certainly not a good thing. Twice in the Epistles of Paul do we read, "a little leaven leaveneth the whole lump"; in the one case it refers to practice, and in the other to doctrine. In 1 Cor. v Paul speaks of the necessity of putting away, from fellowship in the Church, the notorious sinner whom the Corinthians were inclined to uphold. "Your glorying is not good. Know ye not that a little leaven leaveneth the whole lump? Purge out, therefore, the old leaven, that ye may be a new lump, as ye are unleavened. For even Christ our Passover is sacrificed for us: therefore let us keep the feast, not with old leaven, neither with the leaven of malice and wickedness, but with the unleavened bread of sincerity and truth." The toleration of moral evil was *leaven* introduced, and this would leaven the whole lump with its corrupted and corrupting nature. In Gal. v, after

---

The common notion that was attached to *leaven* is shown in the following sentence of Plutarch (as cited by Wetstein): ἡ δὲ ζύμη καὶ γέγονεν ἐκ φθορᾶς αὐτή, καὶ φθείρει τὸ φύραμα μιγνυμένη. "Now leaven is both generated itself from corruption, and it corrupts the mass with which it is mingled." This sentiment of a heathen might check the thoughts of many Christians in their interpretations of leaven.

the apostle had said "Christ is become of no effect unto you, whosoever of you are justified by the law: ye are fallen from grace", he adds (verse 9), "a little leaven leaveneth the whole lump": the introduction of anything, however little, as relating to a believer's acceptance, besides faith in the finished work of Christ, is then a doctrinal leaven—a leaven which has worked, as we know, extensively and grievously.

These are, then, all the occurrences of leaven* in the New Testament, besides it being mentioned in the parable itself; and in all there is one consistent meaning connected with the symbol—the same idea of corruption as is found in the Old Testament. It would be, indeed, strange if our Lord had, in the parable, introduced a meaning the exact opposite of every idea connected with

* A phraseology connected with *leaven* is current in the mouths of many Christians: they talk of a *leaven of holiness*, *of righteousness*, the *good influence* of a *leaven* that has been spread, etc. This mode of speech was probably borrowed from this parable, but it also leads to a *traditional* interpretation of the parable itself. It is strange that the *habitual* use of a term should be taken from *one passage*, in which it is *supposed* that the term means the direct opposite of what it signifies everywhere else. We should never hear of "a leaven of holiness", etc., if the symbolic language of Scripture receive its *Scripture* interpretation; this is a test as to the correct use of Scripture language, or the contrary. Put, instead of "leaven", *corruption* or *defilement*, and then it will be seen how strange such expressions must be to those habituated to the general use of Scripture language.

In Dante, the following lines occur:—
       "Di voi pastor s'accorse il Vangelista,
        Quando colei, che siede sovra l'acque,
        Puttaneggiar co' regi a lui fu vista:
       Quella che con *le sette teste* nacque,
        E dalle *diece corna* ebbe argomento,
        Fin che virtute al suo marito piacque."
                             *Inf.* xix. 106–111.

Some of the Italians suppose this to be "La Santa Chiesa armata de' *sette sacramenti* e de' *dieci comandamenti divini*", an interpretation which sounds passing strange to the ears of any who know the Scripture use of these terms. But is this really more strange than the popular use of "leaven"? I might find a parallel in a verse which speaks of "the *ever-blessed* leaven", as if the terms could be compatible: "ever-blessed" might as well be joined to "hypocrisy", "false doctrine", "immoral practice", "malice", or "wickedness"; for these are *inspired* definitions of what leaven means.

the term, and had used what not only symbolises corruption, but *is* corruption, as expressive of something good.

Thus, not only the universality expressed in the parable, but also the corrupt and corrupting thing, leaven, would lead us to see the similitude as one of evil. Do we not see that 2 Tim. iii, etc., show us how Christendom will be leavened with evil? And do we not *now* see this to a great degree? Let an intelligent Buddhist or Mahometan come into Christendom, and he will see the mass of the nations holding fast *corrupted doctrine*, and presenting this corruption of truth (in Scripture language *leaven*) to the attention of external nations.

Thus do the three parables, spoken *to the multitudes* show us what Christendom would be in its darker characteristics, as *truth* would testify against its doctrinal and moral condition.

But this was not all: the Lord gave instruction *to His disciples* in the three following parables, in which we see the inner truth of a real Church, known to Christ, and known to faith, despite of all the external change.

The "treasure hid in a field" shows us what Christ did for His people: they were in the world, and because they were given into His hand to redeem, He bought the whole for their sake. Let this be individualised as is often done, and then the notion is introduced of all being given up for the sake of Christ or of the gospel, in fact to *procure* salvation—a doctrine utterly opposed to Christian faith; it is the leaven which was at work amongst the Galatians.

The parable of the one pearl of great price has often been treated as though this were something which *we* must obtain—a mode of interpretation similar to that applied to the preceding parable, and equally contradictory to the freeness of the gospel. Just as the former parable spoke of the Church as looked at by Christ, as that which was precious in His sight when buried in the world, so here it is presented under the heavenly symbol of "one pearl of great price"; this shows us the character which the elect Church will fully sustain in the glory and which it ought to aim at now.*

The last parable brings out the issue of all in the present dispensation—that when the net is drawn to shore, and the bad fishes are cast aside, the good shall be gathered into vessels.

These three similitudes are parallel in an inverse order to the former three; the last answers to the tares of the field; the "one pearl", which has nothing about it but its own individuality, stands in contrast to the "grain of mustard-seed", which grows into earthly greatness; and the treasure hid in the field, which had to be taken out of the place where it was unseen, contrasts with the leaven, also hidden, but which corrupts to its own corrupted nature the mass in which it is placed.

Thus clear is it that Scripture does warn us most fully how corruption would come into the Church, and this fact is presented to us wholly independent of any supposed applications of the predictions concerning *the* antichrist to the papal system. As the apostle mentions *many* antichrists, we may in that sense speak of the *Papal* antichrist, or of any other, whenever we see a sys-

---

\* Toplady saw plainly that *Christ* was here the purchaser:
"Deathless principle, arise!
Soar, thou native of the skies!
*Pearl of price, by Jesus bought,*
To His glorious likeness wrought;
Go, to shine before His throne,
Deck His mediatorial crown;
Go, His triumphs to adorn:
Made for God, to God return."

He *individualises* the idea, however, which in the parable belongs to *all* the redeemed as *one pearl* unitedly.

tem or thing especially opposed to Christ and His Gospel; in doing this we must not, however, forget the *crisis* of evil, concerning which we are warned, and the true characteristics of *the* antichrist.

We must expect, in accordance with Matt. xiii, that, through all this our dispensation, tares will grow up with the wheat, so that there can be no universal blessing till Christ has come again; and also we learn from Daniel, from the Apocalypse, and from 2 Thess. ii, that an earthly potentate will arise to supreme power over the Roman earth who will so fully carry out the antichristian idea of "denying the Father and the Son" that he will succeed by persecution, and by delusive power, in causing the name and profession of Christianity to be cast off by all except the true spiritual worshippers who are willing to suffer for their Master's sake. This interference in holy things will not give this "man of sin" an exclusively spiritual character: his temporal sovereignty will be supreme, but (like Nebuchadnezzar) he will extend it to divine worship as well.

*Outside* his dominion corrupt and mingled Christianity will continue (although many there may be influenced by his delusive claims); and thus the parable of the tares and the wheat (nominal and true professors) will still be applicable, as we know from our Lord's words that somewhere it must, up to his coming again.

It is in Popery that corrupt Christianity has shown itself in its most *systematised* form: the lapsed Churches of the East may hold no more truth, and may be quite as much tainted with idolatry and superstition, but still they do not present the united and consolidated form of potent and influential evil which Rome exhibits.

Nominal Protestants may often have cared but little for

the gospel of Christ, and in the practices of Rome they may often have had some share; but in these things they have acted *contrary* to their principles, whereas Rome, in the same things, has acted *in accordance with* hers.

Thus persecution is a stain from which few bodies of real or nominal Christians are *wholly* free; the mistake, that we ought to root out the tares, has been repeatedly made: but when Protestants have persecuted, it has been an inconsistency, a contravention of principle, ever to be condemned and lamented; while Romish persecution is carried out *on principle,* and in full accordance with that Church which still condemns as heretics those who teach *"that it is contrary to the mind of the Spirit to burn heretics".**

* This stands in the "Instructions to Theological Candidates," still published by authority at Rome. Let the Papal Church *formally renounce and condemn* the *doctrine* of persecution, and let her leave off the *practice*, and then, but not till then, may the accusation on that ground cease: she would own, however, if she did this, tht she was fallible in principle and in acts.

If Protestant States do *now* persecute, they show how inconsistent they are: it may, however, be asked whether there is any *body* maintaining the true gospel of Christ which teaches and upholds persecution, and whether any such acts, in nominally Protestant countries, are not carried on in spite of those who are really actuated by Christian principle.

Persecution is a thing which Protestants have been able to cast aside when they learned its evil: they neither are, nor ever professed to be, infallible. There was a time when nonconformists at home suffered imprisonment and persecution from the same government which compelled the nonconformists in New England to leave off the practice of putting other nonconformists to death. These inconsistencies are owned and confessed as sin, and they are not to be charged on Protestants, to whose principles they are opposed, by those who still maintain the principle of persecution, and carry out the practice wherever their hands are not restrained.

The continued practice of Romish persecution is shown in the exile of Count Piero Guicciardini and others, from Florence, *simply for reading the fifteenth chapter of St. John's Gospel together.*

While this page is in the compositor's hands (June 8, 1852), the Romish authorities have sentenced Francesco Madiai, and Rosa, his wife (already imprisoned, on suspicion, in separate cells, for ten months), to *solitary confinement, with hard labour*, the one for *four years and a half,* the other for *three years and a half,* for the possession of the word of God in Italian, and for their confession of the name of Christ! [To this note, written in 1852, all that need be added is a reference to the Spanish persecutions from 1860 to 1863. May God grant liberty of worship in Spain as He has in Tuscany!]

If nominal Protestants fall into any Romish doctrine, such as non-recognition of our acceptance, solely on account of the merits of Christ through faith, or if they adopt any Romish practice, such as devotions to saints, or the superstitious use of crosses, pictures, or images, then Protestantism is set aside and a spurious Popery, which insidiously borrows a name and a garb not its own, is introduced instead. In statements of *doctrine* many have often almost or quite coincided with Rome; but, in our day, this *syncretism* or double-dealing has extended itself to the practice of *idolatry*— that idolatry which we cast aside three hundred years ago. It is no excuse for these idolatries that they are done in *secret*, and that their symbols are worn in secret. "*Cursed be the man that maketh an image an abomination unto the Lord, and putteth it in a secret place.*"

"To the law and to the testimony": through the mercy of God we have the Scriptures; and in this we stand in contrast to Rome, who forbids their circulation in languages known to the people, and persecutes those who read them. In *this*, Rome shows her departure from the faith, and how, having shut out the light, she has left the door open for every Satanic delusion, even for that rejection of God and of Christ which is yet before us.\*

It behoves us to uphold the *authority* of holy Scripture,

\* Of late some who profess to be Protestant teachers have set forth very Romeward doctrines on the subject of the Imputation of Christ's righteousness to us, and His vicarious life for us. The true doctrine of the word of God is that our Lord, who was very and eternal God, became very man, taking our flesh and blood, but without sin: that in life He obeyed perfectly for us, that in death He perfectly bore the curse for us: that all His obedience in life or death was *meritorious* and for us; that every suffering, whether in life or death, was *penal* and for us. Many know how grievously these truths have been set aside, and how Christ's obedience to the law of God for us has been denied. All who oppose these truths are dangerously false teachers, and as such must be shunned. (See *Christ the End of the Law for Righteousness. Five Letters to the Editor of the 'Record' on recent Denials of our Lord's Vicarious Life*, by S. P. Tregelles, LL.D. Price 6d.)

for this is a safeguard, and if we have loose views on this point we lay ourselves open to the attacks of Rome on the one hand and of Rationalistic infidelity on the other. If we add our own thoughts to Scripture, then we do just what Rome does with her traditions and her assumptions of Church authority.

If we cast a veil of uncertainty over holy Scripture, then do we open the door to Romish claims, as if Scripture required to be interpreted by some other tribunal, or else we cast aside all confidence in Scripture as being an objective revelation from God, and are left to the guidance of our own thoughts.

Maintaining holy Scripture in all its fullness, we may, by God's blessing, meet the fundamentally false doctrines of Rome, and thus sustain the integrity of Scripture (which is impaired whenever its statements are *softened*, so as to apply them to Romanism) by pointing out how Romish and Romanising doctrines are fully met by the plain teaching of the word of God, that it is in virtue of the merits of Christ *alone*, applied to the soul *through* faith, that we are justified and accepted from first to last, our salvation being *wholly* of God's grace.

[It has been thought that 2 Thess. ii could only be met by an application to Papal claims, especially through comparison with the terms used by Pope Nicholas V in writing to the Greek Emperor. But however blasphemous the terms adopted were, *Imperial* Rome had gone much further, even as the antichrist will again. "The State, which was always the real object of a Roman's devotion, had found a personal embodiment: and the people were willing to concede to the Emperor the divine titles which he claimed.—*Introduction to the Study of the Gospels*, by B. F. Westcott, M.A., p. 81. He adds in a note: "The climax was reached by Domitian, whose edicts ran: *Dominus et Deus noster sic fieri jubet* (*Suet. Domit.*, c. 13)."]

# CONCLUDING REMARKS

IN order rightly to learn the things written for our instruction in the Scripture, it is needful for Christians to mark with attention and with Spirit-taught intelligence *what the Scripture itself says*. Very many of the difficulties which are connected with the contents of the word of God arise wholly from the thoughts which have been added to what it says, and hence there has been a supposed obscurity about the truths there taught.

The reader of these Remarks on Daniel will, I trust, see that everything *essential* for the understanding of this portion of Scripture is to be found within the limits of the word of God itself; and the more we can confidently lay hold of this as a principle with regard even to one book of Scripture, the more will it lead us on in applying it to the word of God as a whole.

These "Remarks" arose, indeed, out of an endeavour to use this portion of prophetic Scripture simply as seeing what it might teach. To this end I had read the prophetic portions of Daniel with Christians at various places and times, and these readings, and the inquiries and statements of difficulties which arose out of them, had, I believe, their use in bringing before several minds the definite clearness with which Scripture teaches. Subsequently I was often requested to *print* the substance of these Readings on Daniel, and when I was about to go through the book again with others, as an aid to me in *writing*, a Christian friend had the kindness to take full and accurate notes of the readings. Thus,

I had placed before me memoranda of what had passed at the time, including the difficulties which had occurred to particular minds, and the inquiries to which the portions of Scripture led on.

With the notes so taken before me, the "Remarks" were drawn up: in doing this I did not confine myself to what had been thus taken down, but I rather used the notes as an efficient aid in bringing before me points which needed attention, in order to meet the minds of different readers. Thus, in using the notes, I reconsidered the whole of the prophecies in Daniel, and this was my occasional occupation during a considerable period, and in various countries: part was prepared for publication while in England, and part in Rome—that city to which prophecy leads us as the centre of the dominion of the Fourth Monarchy foretold in Daniel, and in which the New Testament history ends. I mention these particulars that the reader may know the origin of these "Remarks", and how they were drawn up in their present form, and that the subjects of which I have treated (even when apparently digressions) are *real points* which arose from inquiries, etc., in readings on Daniel; and also I give this information, that all who find my "Remarks" to be of any assistance to them in understanding this book may know that they are materially indebted to that Christian friend* whose notes aided me so efficiently—I might, indeed, say essentially—and to whom I wish thus to acknowledge my obligation.

Close and *scriptural* study of prophecy will be found

---

* Miss Dorothy Trevelyan Haydon, to whom reference is here made, has, during the preparation of the fifth edition of this book, fallen asleep in Jesus, June 28, 1863.—1 Thess. iv. 14. Her name may fitly find a place here as a memorial of a Christian friendship and regard of more than twenty-eight years' continuance.

a powerful safeguard against mere speculation as to the future; for thus the Christian student will be in some measure instructed as to the mind of God relative to coming events: in studying the prophetic word, it is of essential importance that the outlines should be truly and definitely known, for this alone can prevent mistakes being made as to the application of specific predictions. Thus it is needful to see that no promise of universal or widespread blessing *can* be fulfilled prior to the coming of Christ in clouds of glory, and that nothing which speaks of the people of Christ as suffering persecution or rejection can be after that time. So, also, if the saints are described as "reigning", it must be after the coming and judgment of Christ, for until then power and authority are not given to them: if the nations of Israel are spoken of as scattered and cast off—wrapped in blindness and unbelief—it must be previous to that event.

Thus we must learn in prophecy how to distinguish the characteristic marks of different periods, else we shall seek for the fulfilment of promises to be effected through the preaching of the gospel and similar means, which never can be thus accomplished. This only can tend to disappointment, and to a feeling of painful uncertainty as to the force of Scripture promises, in which, indeed, there can never be anything really doubtful; for every promise of God is as secure as He is unchangeable, and is confirmed in Christ His Son. Those predictions which relate to "the Jews, the Gentiles, and the Church of God" must not be confounded with one another, otherwise we shall not discern the very bearing of the lessons which Scripture would thus teach us.

The book of Daniel has an especial value in leading the minds of Christian students to clear and well-defined thoughts as to *Gentile* prophecy, and thus it is a key to many other parts of Scripture. We must not look in these visions for *details* connected with the glory of Christ when He shall have taken His kingdom, nor yet for the particulars which belong to Israel's final forgiveness and restoration: on the contrary, here we have everything of the outline of the prophetic history of those ruling over the earth, up to the time when Christ takes His Kingdom and when Israel is restored. The prophets testified before hand the sufferings of Christ and the glories that should follow: but while this is their general scope, we find different but harmonising features of truth presented in different books; so that *here* we have before us more of what is introductory to the glory than of the glories themselves; though just as plainly as it is here predicted that "Messiah shall be cut off", so are we also instructed as to "one like unto the Son of Man" receiving a kingdom, and of "the stone", which shall fall in judgment upon the whole fabric of Gentile power, becoming a great mountain, and filling the whole earth.

Let the scope of prophecy be attended to, and let the application of prophecy be learned from the Scripture itself; then we shall be kept from those speculations which have so painfully hindered many from avowedly using prophecy at all; although all Christians, who believe that they may apply a single warning or promise of Scripture, do this *in some measure*. The prophetic word is a light shining in a dark place; but if the speculations of men intervene, all on which the shadows fall is involved in obscurity.

Whatever is learned from Scripture can never weaken or set aside one of those foundation truths on which the hopes of the believer are set for time and for eternity. Prophecy may display new details of truth, it may give new and fuller views of the glories of Christ, it may teach the Christian his true place in the prospect of this world's judgment, but it can never shake one point of those truths which are the basis of Christian profession. I wish to speak distinctly of this, because I know that when any new truth is learned there are some minds that wish to find *new* truths on every possible point; and thus they incline to doubt or deny even the fundamental verities which had been previously learned.

There are points of Christian truth which ought to be so known from the word of God as to be felt to be beyond question or discussion. I do not speak merely of those points which relate to the being of God, the Trinity, the true Godhead, proper manhood (real though sinless), and atonement of Christ, but of such also as relate to the application of these truths to us. Thus we ought to hold firmly fast what the Scripture teaches as to our condition by nature as *lost* sinners, the reality of God's wrath against men as sinners, and the need of *his* being reconciled to them, and the absolute truth of the sacrifice of *propitiation* rendered by Christ, and the imputation of his righteousness to those who believe. If any of these points are touched by those who profess to aim at advance in divine truth or "progress",* then we need not wonder if questions should be raised as to the

* "It has been said by some of late that there never can be any progress in real truth, unless we get rid of the absurd doctrine of imputation. No doubt it is a doctrine peculiarly adverse to the schemes of those who wish to make men happy apart from Christ. Men say, Where is it taught in Scripture? We might rather ask, Where is it *not* taught? Every page that alludes to the altar sending up the sweet-smelling savour of its offerings teaches it. Would the Scripture, which cannot lie, teach me that that ascends for me which does not ascend for me? and if it ascends for me its excellency is attributed to me; and that is imputation."—*Thoughts on Parts of Leviticus*, by B. W. Newton, p. 14.

reality of the Church's connection with the priesthood and mediation of Christ, or its standing in covenant relations. "Justification through faith", the turning point of all Christian truth in its application to our souls, might just as well be called in question.

Scriptural study of prophecy leads to no such truth-rejecting results. In fact we might be sure that *Scripture* never could lead to doubt or denial of its own fundamental doctrines. Any supposed conclusions in opposition to *such* truths might well lead the mind to pause, and then to rest assured that free speculation *about* the truth of God had been substituted for learning *from* his word.

The belief of evangelical Protestants on fundamental truths is clear and defined: such points may be regarded as settled, and settled for ever. We have no occasion to discuss over again (as though none had inquired into the teaching of Scripture) points on which orthodox Christians have been agreed for ages, and which have been stated in scriptural Confessions of Faith, such for instance as the doctrinal Articles of the Church of England, the Heidelberg Catechism, the Old Scottish, and the Westminster Confessions.

I know that some deprecate all *reference* to "Creeds, Confessions of Faith, and Articles of Religion" (applying to them designations such as I will not here repeat), as if any such reference were an acknowledgment that they possess an *authority*, or as though "opinions of men were maintained instead of the truth of God". I do not speak of such documents as possessing *authority*, for that belongs to holy Scripture alone, and its authoritative teaching is learned from its direct statements, or else by necessary deductions therefrom. But I do refer to orthodox confessions of Christian doctrine as showing the record of what holy servants of Christ, in past ages, have believed. The Scripture is the alone standard of appeal; but in learning from Scripture I do not desire to forget that the Church of God is one body dwelt in by one Spirit, and that the communion of saints is a truth; so that I would gladly know what holy and intelligent Christians now living have learned from the word of God, not as deferring to their *authority*, but as being willing to be shown what the Scripture teaches. And just as I value the teaching of the living, so do I prize the instruction given by the dead; and thus I am glad to learn from Athanasius or Augustine, from Anselm or Bernard, from Luther, Tyndale, or Calvin, or (in later days) from Ussher, Owen, Bunyan, Pearson, or Romaine —even as I would if I had lived in the days of any of these. Granted, that in many things I differ from all or any of these: am I, therefore, to be blind to the truths which they held and taught? Ought I not to be thankful for the instruction *from Scripture,* and resting on *Scripture authority* alone, which I may receive through any of Christ's servants in past ages? And thus I have been accustomed to refer, in common with orthodox Christians in general, to the confessions of faith of evangelical Protestants as embodying those foundation truths of Christianity which cannot be regarded as points at all debatable. They rest on the sure warrant of holy Scripture, to which they direct as the source of all their authority.

I know that it has been said, "The moment you *define*, you limit: human definitions are not DIVINE INFINITUDES." The force of this argument rests entirely in its *form* and seeming point; but is it soberly meant that we are to have no definite thoughts at all about divine truth? A definition does set up a *limit*: the only thing of which we have to be careful is that the definitions are such as Scripture teaches, and that the limitations are such as exclude error. The early Church had especially to combat false doctrine relative to the Trinity and the person of Christ the Lord; and thus in defining that the Son of God was Himself "very God", "of the substance of the Father, begotten before the worlds", it set a *limit* against the unscriptural speculations of those who denied His Godhead. So, too, as to His manhood: in defining that He was "man of the substance of his mother born in the world", a *limit* was marked out against those who denied the verity of His humanity both in body and soul. The authority of all such limitations is always the Scripture on which they are based; such, for instance (in the points to which I have referred), as the distinct teaching that Christ is "God over all, blessed for ever", that "He took part of the same" "flesh and blood" as his "brethren", although "without sin". And so, too, at the Reformation, the definition "that we are justified freely for Christ's sake through faith" was at once a limit against the endeavours to introduce self-righteousness.

This, then, is the use which I would make of orthodox confessions of faith; I value them as showing what points of Christian verity have been distinctly apprehended, and I would learn from them even as I would learn from a letter, or from the spoken words of a living Christian whom I knew and honoured.

"But (it is said) why not keep to Scripture words simply?" Those who thus object are not themselves accustomed so to restrict themselves; but the real reason is that error commonly seeks to shelter itself behind Scripture terms *used in new senses*, and thus it is needful *occasionally* so to state a definition of doctrine as shall meet this mode of evading the force of Scripture. It has been truly said that "definitions which were unknown before error was introduced have become needful from that time and onward"; they become, in fact, safeguards for the maintenance of Scripture truth.

It is of the deepest importance to see that there are foundation truths which can never be admitted to be *at all* debatable ground. Such truths should be thoroughly learned from Scripture; and so far from their being invalidated by their being contained in "creeds and confessions of faith", this fact only shows how general a thing has been their place in the apprehensions of Christians.

The apostle tells us to be ready to give an account of the hope that is in us: a mere stringing together of Scripture expressions will not suffice for this: it behoves us, therefore, to be able to give an *intelligent* statement of what the Scripture teaches as the ground of Christian confidence.* And thus the confession of our faith, even though in our own words, or in those of Christians who have gone before us, is our AMEN to what the Holy Ghost has taught in the Scripture. How can any such *Amen* be responded if foundation truths are at all involved in uncertainty?

It has, indeed, been asked whether an *adherence* to the theological opinions which have been commonly received is consistent with the *development* of truth. On this it may be observed that there is no *development* of Christian truth, but the revelation was given perfect and complete

* And so, if Christians are not to express Scripture doctrines in their own words, they cannot uphold God's ordinances of teaching and preaching. A mere string of texts will often edify but little, even though they may be well chosen; whereas the same texts, *properly explained*, might be found to be most valuable and profitable teaching. This is not *departing* from Scripture, but *using* Scripture, and that for the very purposes for which God gave it forth (2 Tim. iii. 17).

to the apostles of Christ, and it is written complete in the New Testament. Thus, if the doctrines stated by Christians in any past age are scriptural, then let them be adhered to as they stated them; not indeed using them as lords over our faith, but as students of Scripture, by whose experience we may be aided, if we believe in the *Communion of Saints* as a fact. It has indeed been said that "very likely such points as the nature and true character of divine inspiration have not been understood by the good and holy men who have preceded us". And this has been defended by the assertion that they were *less qualified* for thought or discernment than the moderns, as "we have the advantage of knowing all that they thought and knew on the subject".\* If then we have the *advantage* of being able to refute all that Christians of former ages knew and held as foundation truths, then, indeed, there would be a "development"—but whether of the truth of God or of the lie of Satan is the real and momentous question.

But can there be no *progress* in divine truth? Is not *prophecy* a case in point? Surely there may be progress; but this is not to be attained by turning our backs on all that the babe in Christ should know of the ground of our acceptance before God, and of the authority of His holy word, but by knowing all foundation truths as *unquestionable*, and then holding all that may afterwards be learned in harmonious connection with them.

\* It might be well asked, whether those who can thus think and write, do really know what holy men, whose consciences were exercised about the truth of God, did *think* and *know* on fundamental doctrines. Intellectual acuteness is a very different thing from the spiritual intelligence granted to the prayerful and humble Christian. It is a vain thing for any to seek to exalt themselves by speaking in language of scorn and disparagement of the holy men who have gone before us. Granted that they may have been ignorant of many things; if *we* know them at all, we know them from the word; and must we not say that they did use well and for God's glory what they had learned (whether much or little) from the same word?

If we rightly learn a new truth, it will never lead us to undervalue those previously known. And thus with regard to prophecy; we may learn the second advent of Christ to be foretold as needful before any time of millennial blessing can arrive: we may apprehend something of glories which shall then come to pass; but even if these things are *new* to us, or to other Christians who have firmly held the foundation doctrines of evangelical belief, why should we undervalue truths previously learned? or why should we engage in a vain search for *new truths* as to what the grounds of our acceptance are—what the relations in which the Church stands to God the Father, and to the Son, as redeemed by Him, and what its connection with His atonement, priesthood, and mediation, and with the new covenant sealed with His blood?

# APPENDIX

### SAMUEL PRIDEAUX TREGELLES, LL.D.
### HIS LIFE AND LETTERS

MANY well qualified students do not hesitate to claim that Dr. Samuel Prideaux Tregelles was in fact the greatest Biblical scholar of the nineteenth century. He was born at Wodehouse Place, Falmouth, on 30th January, 1813. His father, Samuel Tregelles, was a merchant and related to the Foxes; his mother was Dorothy Prideaux, of Kingsbridge. His early training among the Tregelles, Prideaux and Foxe families was in the Society of Friends; he did not, however, become one himself. In the early days of the Brethren movement he was in some matters associated, but did not identify himself with them. In the later years of his life he worshipped with Presbyterians,* but it may be said of him that he was one of those who are best described as "Christians unattached".

From his early childhood he was remarkable for a retentive memory. At the age of twelve he entered Falmouth Classical School, where he remained for three

---

*That Tregelles became a Presbyterian after his dissociation from the Plymouth meeting of Brethren is also stated by E. C. Marchant in his article on Tregelles in the *Dictionary of National Biography*. F. H. A. Scrivener, however, says that "his last years were more happily spent as a humble lay member of the Church of England, a fact he very earnestly begged me to keep in mind"; and adds in a footnote: "He gave the same assurance to A. Earle, D.D., Bishop of Marlborough, assigning as his reason the results of the study to the Greek New Testament" (*Plain Introduction to the Criticism of the N.T.*, 4th edition, 1894, vol. 2, p. 241). This conflict of evidence suggests that Mr. Fromow is fairly near the mark in using the epithet "unattached"!—F. F. BRUCE, D.D.

years. The headmaster of the Classical School, which he attended in 1825-28, wanted him to proceed to a University, but his upbringing among the Society of Friends made this impossible, for in those days the Universities were forbidden to such. It is surprising to find that Tregelles, who had shown a definite inclination to academic study, was employed for six years, from 1828 to 1834, at the Neath Abbey Iron Works in Wales. Possibly his practical-minded father distrusted youthful enthusiasm and thought it well for him to learn something of the hard reality of life.

*The Western Morning News* as recently as January 17th, 1957, said: "Largely self-taught, personally modest and gentle-natured, Tregelles must rank as the most learned man ever associated with Plymouth; which was remarkable in the last century for producing several noted scholars in Divinity and Biblical literature, notably the celebrated deaf workhouse lad, John Kitto; Dr. R. F. Weymouth, best known for his *New Testament in Modern Speech*; and more recently, the erudite Dr. Rendle Harris. A portrait of him painted about 1870, by the local artist Francis Lane, was presented by his friends and admirers to the Plymouth Institution, and another by the same artist was given to the Royal Cornwall Polytechnic." No. 6, Portland Square, was his home during 1846-75, and a bronze tablet recording the fact was placed on the house.

As a young man, Tregelles was drifting from Christian teaching. Christendom's misapplication of the Scriptures of the Prophets and the Psalms utterly failed to satisfy his keen sense of proportion. His intelligence recoiled against the glosses, traditions, explanations and interpretations of the spiritualizing schools and would have driven him to the verge of infidelity. But it pleased the

Lord to draw his attention to prophetic truth through a tract on that subject which changed his whole outlook on religion and life; indeed, God used it as a means which wrought the vital change of his regeneration. What a student he became! What a scholar! What books and translations of the ancient languages and Bible manuscripts! Henceforth his cousin B. W. Newton became his helper spiritually, and in his publications, financially.

After conversion, the iron works could not hold him; he was led forward into the plan of his life work. His ambition was not less than that of an authenticated Greek Text of the New Testament.

He returned to Falmouth, where he spent two years as a private tutor. At the age of twenty-five (1838) he announced his proposals:

(1) For the formation of a text of the Scriptures on the authority of ancient copies, without allowing "the received text" any prescriptive right.

(2) To give to the ancient versions a determining voice as to the insertion or non-insertion of clauses, letting the order of the words rest wholly upon the MSS.

(3) To give the authorities to the text clearly and accurately, so that the reader might at once see what rests upon ancient evidence.

In order that he might himself collate the ancient Uncial MSS. (i.e. the earliest written in capitals) he went abroad in October 1845. He spent five months in Rome studying, under great difficulty, the famous Vatican Codex. He was not allowed to transcribe any part, but it is said that he made an occasional note on his finger-nails.

At other great libraries he received every facility—at the Augustinian Monastery in Rome, at Florence, Modena, Venice, Munich, Basle, Paris, and many other places. The great work of the Greek New Testament was not completed until 1872, when he was an old man, stricken in health. His work, however, remains still in publication—one of the great classics.

By 1850 his writings had become known all over the world, and his ripe scholarship was acknowledged in Europe and America. At the age of thirty-seven the University of St. Andrews conferred on him the honorary degree of LL.D. Many works came from his pen. For the students he prepared *Heads of Hebrew Grammar,* and *Hebrew Reading Lessons.* He wrote many works dealing with the prophetic books of the Bible. C. H. Spurgeon said of him: "Tregelles is deservedly regarded as a great authority upon prophetical subjects." Many of these books are still in circulation and some are still obtainable; notably his *Remarks on the Prophetic Visions in the Book of Daniel*; his *The Revelation: A New Translation*; his *The Historic Evidence of the Authorship and Transmission of the Books of the New Testament*; and *The Hope of Christ's Second Coming: How is it taught in Scripture? and why?* His health prevented him from serving on the Revised Version Committee; he had been invited as a matter of course, but his refusal was inevitable. Had he thus have served, it is probable that he would have pleaded for a more faithful revision of those passages which Mr. Newton felt called upon to dispute in his book *Remarks on the Revised Version.*

In 1862, on Lord Palmerston's recommendation, he was granted a Civil List Pension of £100 and in Mr. Gladstone's administration this was supplemented in 1870 by a further £100. His portrait in oil, by Lane, was placed in the Polytechnic Hall, in Falmouth. He died in Plymouth, on 24th April, 1875, and was buried in Plymouth Cemetery. J. Brooking Rowe in a memoir said of him that "he was able to shed a light upon any topic that might be introduced; it was dangerous to ask him a question; doing so was like reaching to take a book and having the whole shelf-full precipitated upon your head". In theology he devoutly upheld the Reformed Faith in all its Free Grace implications, and in prophetic teaching he was a premillennialist of simple futurist convictions.

The *Dictionary of National Biography* gives a copious review of his life-story of literary and linguistic accomplishments (Vol 57 (1899), pp. 170 f.).

Articles by Dr. Tregelles are to be found in: *Cassell's Dictionary, Smith's Dictionary of the Bible, Kitto's Journal of Sacred Literature*.

# INDEX

Aben Ezra on Dan. xii. 2, 165
Abomination of desolation, 106, 146, 182.
Actium, battle of, 53
Advent of Christ, Second, 22, 23, 29
Alexander's Empire included in the Roman Empire, 82
Abrose, words of, used, 183
Ancient of Days, judgment of, 38, 39, 41
Antichrist, doom of adherents, 186
  in Daniel xi, 179
  Jewish notion of, 180
  meaning of the word, 194
  rise of the kings of north and south, 141, 152
Antichrist's idolatry, 151
Anti-Scriptural year-day system, 126
Apostasy, 145
Arles, British bishops, 56
Armillus, 180
Artaxerxes, decree of, 100
Association in empire, 57, 62
Augsburg Confession, 190
Augustus, 57
Autocracy, 17

Babylon, king of, Isa. xiv, 153, 154
Babylonian empire, 12
Bambino of Ara Celi, 197
Beast, dreadful and terrible, 36
Beasts, the four, 32
Belshazzar's blasphemy, 30
Birks on the year-day theory, 119
Blasphemy of the horn, 37
  persecuting power, 82
Blayney's alterations in our English Bible, 76
Boniface III "Universal Bishop", 70
  VIII, 72
Britain relinquished by Rome, 62
  Roman, 56
  Roman law in, 74

Brute (Walter) inventor of the year-day theory, 112
Budding of the fig tree, 1

Calling of God, 47
Cassander, kingdom of, 79
Chaldee portions of Scripture, 7
Charlemagne, age of, 70
  crowned emperor, 65
Chittim (Cyprus), 143
Chronology, Ussher's 122
Church builded on Christ "the stone", 22
  defined, 47
  on earth till the end, 110
Claudia, 56
Clay and iron, 19
Clouds of heaven, 38
Coblentz, division of the empire at, 66
Comparison of chapter xi with vii and viii, 83
Conder, Josiah, 69, 112
Confessions, 95
  of faith, 222
Constantine, 59
Contrasts in Daniel vii, 50
Corrupt Christianity, 44
Covenant, holy, indignation against, 144
  with Antichrist, 105
Cunningham (Dr.) quoted, 193

Dacia of Trajan: of Aurelian, 56
Daily sacrifice, 87
Daniel a witness against the year-day theory, 125
  confession for his people, 94
Dante quoted, 208
Danube a Roman boundary, 56
Darius's decree, 29
Days understood literally by the early Church, 112
Deliverance of Daniel's people, 157
Demoniacal power real, 200, 202

## INDEX

Demons, worship of, 197
Desolation, transgression of, 90
Destruction of Antichrist, 153
Dispensation, characteristics of, 49
Divisions of the book of Daniel, 7
  of heptads, 90, 106
  of the Roman empire, 41, 58
  under Diocletian, 57
  under Valentinian, 58
  under Arcadius and Honorius, 61
Domitian, blasphemy of, 214
Dragon gives power to the beast, 86

East and West, division into, 59
  not to be excluded from tenfold division, 70
Edom, Moab and Ammon, 152
Edward III, Imperial Vicar, 66
Egypt invaded, 143
  kings of, 136
  third invasion of, 152
Elect, all rejectors of Popery not, 185
Elliott for the year-day system, 120
  quoted by Conder, 113
Emperor excommunicates the Pope, 71
Evil, full at the Lord's coming, 87
  worst form of, 46
Exposition of the year-day theory, 127

Faith, departure from, 196
Fallacy and falsehood of the year-day theory, 125
Flight from Jerusalem, 151
Foundation truths never shaken, 294
Four parts of Alexander's empire, 80
Fourth kingdom of Daniel vii, 14, 17
France, empire in, 68

Gabriel sent forth, 97
Gentiles brought into the Church, 6
German empire, 68
Grecia, king of, 78

Grecian empire, 14
Greece becomes a monarchy, 34

Heptads, Seventy, 93
Hiddekel, scene of Daniel's last vision, 129
Hills of Rome, 53
Historic transmission, 249
History not revelation, 14
Holy, Most, 100
Holy Place, abomination in, 108
Horn, last, not the Papacy, 69
  of blasphemy, future, 41, 42
  the great, broken, 79
Horns (Ten) of the fourth beast, 36
Host of heaven cast down, 87

Identity of horns in chapters vii and vii, 83
Idolatry of Rome, 213, 197
Imputed righteousness a necessary doctrine of Christianity, 219
Indignation, time of, 78, 80
Innocent III, Pope, 71
Interpretation of Daniel xi, 171
Interval in prophecy, 80, 134
  in the seventy weeks, 110
Ipsus, battle of, 62, 79
Israel, signs and wonders in, 49
Israel's conversion, 138

Jeremiah's prophecy, 93
Jerome on Daniel xi, 173
Jerusalem under Gentile rule, 33
Jewish commentators on Dan. xii. 2, 164
Joachim (Abbot), 124
Justification the turning-point of popery, 192
Justinian's reign and the Papacy, 69

King assuming divine honours, 150
  of Babylon, blasphemy of, 89
  persecuting, 81
  rise of one after the ten, 37
Kingdom of heaven, 204
  of the Son of Man, 38, 40
  taken by the saints, 45
Kingdoms, four 32
Knowledge of God, 149
Krummacher (Dr.), 194

# INDEX

Language of Daniel, 7
Latter days, prophecy of, 127
  time of Daniel's last vision, 130
  time of Alexander's kingdom, 133
Leaven, parable of, 205
Legions stationed in Britain, 59
Leo III, Pope, 70
Leopard with wings and four heads, 34
Life everlasting, 167
Lion with eagle's wings, 34
Lists of the kingdoms, 48, 49
Luther quoted, 73
Lysimachus, kingdom of, 79

Maccabees in Daniel xi, 182
Man of sin, 150
Maskilim, 149, 160
Media and Persia, kings of, 76
Mediterranean sea, 32, 34
Medo-Persian empire, 12, 13, 14
Messiah the Prince, 103
Metals in the image, 14
Michael the Archangel, 156
Miracles of Rome, 199, 200, 197
  Satanic, 202
Modes of teaching Scripture, 8
Mustard seed, parable of, 204

Names, variation of, 132
Naples in the Eastern Empire, 66
Nebuchadnezzar's dominion, 12
Net, parable of, 210
Newton, B. W., on Daniel xi, 167, 171
Nobility, European, 63
North, kings of, 136

Obedience, duty of, 1
Odoacer, 64
Olives, Mount of, 145
Otho becomes emperor, 65

Palaeologus (Andreas) transfers the empire, 67
Papacy, last horn not the, 42, 68
Parables, instruction by, 8
  of Matthew xiii, 204
Patience of hope, 163
Pearl, parable of, 210

People, evil power derived from, 18
  of the saints, 47, 49
Persecution, 212
Persia and Media, king of, 77
Persian empire, 13
  kings of Daniel xi, 132
Philomena (St.), 197
Plutarch on leaven, 207
Popery and prophecy, 186
Popes independent sovereigns, 73
Prideaux (Dean), 181
Prince that shall come, 103
Progress, 219
Prophecy, exactitude of its fulfilment, 28
Prophetic day or year, 112
  interpretation and corrupt Christianity, 184
Protestantism not to be negative, 193
Ptolemy, kingdom of, 79
Pudens, Linus and Claudia, 55

Ravenna, 59
Remnant saved, 158
Remnants, two, 156
Resurrection, first, 159
  Jews on, 156
Rhine a Roman boundary, 56
Roman character impressed, 63
Romanism, concrete evil of, 195
  disguised, 213
Rome becomes a monarchy, 34
  republican, 53

Sacrifice, daily, 87
St. Peter's not the temple of God, 188
Saints allowed to suffer, 48
  take the kingdom, 47
  warred against, 38, 41
Sanctuary cast down, 87
Saxon rule, rise of, 65
Scripture proof for the year-day theory, 115, 161
  sufficiency of, 10
Second kingdom, 13, 35, 78
Seleucus, kingdom of, 79
Septenary reckoning, 97
Seven-hilled Rome, 52

# INDEX

Seven "times" of Nebuchadnezzar's years, 125
  years covenant with the prince, 105
Seventy heptads, 92
Shushan, scene of vision, in Daniel viii, 76
Son of man receives the kingdom, 39, 40
Sower, parable of, 204
Spirit, how given, 92
Stars as a symbol, 87
Stone, a designation of Christ, 21
  in connection with Israel, Gentiles and Church, 23
Study of prophecy, 216
Summary of chapter viii, 91
Synchronism of horns in chapters vii and viii, 83
Syria in Daniel xi, 139

Tares of the field, 204
Tenfold division of the Roman earth, 35
Ten-horned beast, 41
Ten horns of the fourth beast, 36, 37
  kingdoms, lists of, 69
  kings to be of Roman earth, 62
Testimony in Jerusalem ends, 150
Third kingdom, 14, 36, 78
Time and times, and dividing time, 42, 106, 162

Times of Nebuchadnezzar and year-day, 125
Toplady quoted, 210
Trajan's empire, extent, 56
Transgression of desolation, 89
Transgressors come to the full, 85
Treasure hid, parable of, 209
Tribulation unequalled, 131, 157
Tribuneship and the plebeians, 54
Truth, God works by, 114
  not novelty, 122
Twelve hundred and sixty days, 45, 106
Twentieth of Artaxerxes, 101, 102
Two horns of the ram, 76
Two thousand three hundred days, 88

Understanding ones, 148
Ussher's chronology, 100, 101

Vigilius heretical pope, 69
"Vile person", 140, 141
Vision, Daniel's last, 128
  of Nebuchadnezzar, 10
  of the four beats, 32

Week of Daniel, the last, 103

Xerxes invades Greece, 132

Year-day theory, 111
  a false addition to Scripture, 124, 126

www.ingramcontent.com/pod-product-compliance
Lightning Source LLC
Chambersburg PA
CBHW050349230426
43663CB00010B/2053